NEW YORK

in a

DOZEN DISHES

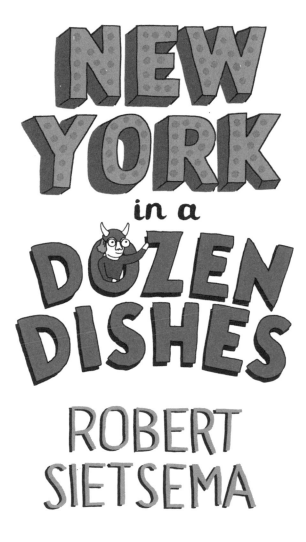

NEW YORK
in a
DOZEN DISHES

ROBERT SIETSEMA

ILLUSTRATIONS BY
JAMES GULLIVER HANCOCK

HOUGHTON MIFFLIN HARCOURT
BOSTON NEW YORK 2015

For information about permission to reproduce selections from this book,
write to Permissions, Houghton Mifflin Harcourt Publishing Company,
215 Park Avenue South, New York, New York 10003.

www.hmhco.com

Library of Congress Cataloging-in-Publication Data is available upon request

ISBN 978-0-544-45431-6 (hardcover); 978-0-544-45363-0 (ebook)

Illustrations by James Gulliver Hancock
Book design by Alex Camlin

Printed in the United States of America

DOC 10 9 8 7 6 5 4 3 2 1

CONTENTS

INTRODUCTION

I've noticed that people who move to the city from elsewhere often make the most avid New Yorkers. That was certainly the case with me. I arrived in the late '70s having washed out of a graduate program in Wisconsin and made a beeline for the East Village, where I found a neighborhood teetering on the verge of dissolution from drugs and decay, but with wildly cheap rents. Within one week the city's worst blackout occurred, which found residents of Stuyvesant Town across the street lowering buckets from their windows to get drinking water. A few days later, an illegal curbside welding operation saw a car burst into flames that shot up past my third-floor tenement apartment, causing me to leap out of my kitchen bathtub and run naked to the window. Becoming a New Yorker seemed a baptism by fire.

I didn't have much money, and I soon discovered that tasty and interesting food was one of the cheapest delights the city had to offer. Zeroing in on the fare of recent immigrants, I purchased a bagful of subway tokens and was soon traveling the five boroughs in search of unreconstructed ethnic eats. I joined a rock band and soon had companions on my treks of urban exploration, which found us feasting en masse on Peruvian beef-heart kebabs, delicious Indian vegetarian pancakes called *dosas*, tamales furtively sold by Mexican women from shopping carts behind the Port Authority, and hand-pulled Korean noodles stumbled upon on one of Flushing's most obscure streets.

In 1989 I began to publish my findings in a quarterly journal called *Down the Hatch*, surreptitiously photocopied on colorful paper at one of the offices I worked at as a temporary secretary by day. It was the forerunner of the modern food blog. It wasn't long before the *Village Voice* came calling, and in 1993 I was installed as its resident restaurant critic, a job that was to last 20 years. Other freelance gigs followed in profusion, from *Gourmet*, the *New York Times*, *Lucky Peach*, and a dozen other publications, including *Eater New York*, where I am currently a full-time New York restaurant critic.

A city can be defined by its superlative dishes, the ones that induce pride among the citizenry and excitement among visitors and speak eloquently of its history and current condition. This book presents a dozen dishes (actually 13, a baker's dozen) that framed my appreciation of New York food over the years. Some of these, such as pizza and fried chicken, are well-known, though their full stories have yet to be told. Others, like guinea pig and veal brains, will never be popular enough to become lunchtime favorites, but nonetheless contribute to a full appreciation of what makes this the most interesting and diverse place to eat in the world. More than anything else, this book recounts my culinary journey through New York City over three decades, and I'm grateful to you for undertaking it with me.

PIZZA

When I was growing up in the '50s, my parents displayed an almost religious belief in convenience foods. Chicken stew with noodles, chili con carne, and mac and cheese invariably came in jars, cans, and boxes, respectively. Seafood originated as crumb-coated frozen fish sticks waiting to be popped in the oven, or in salmon-filled tins destined to be tossed into casseroles with cream of mushroom soup and baked till the timer dinged. It wasn't that my parents were lazy, it was just that they believed processed foods were put on this earth by scientists intent on making our lives easier.

We were certainly not gourmands, and neither was anyone we knew in Northbrook, Illinois (a small village north of Chicago), and later in Golden Valley, Minnesota (a suburb of Minneapolis)—but we craved our salty packaged foods. A meal in a restaurant was such a rare experience that before I reached college I could count the times I'd eaten out on the fingers of one hand. "If you have a kitchen stocked with groceries," my mother would intone, about to use a rare expletive, "why the hell would you ever want to eat out?" So restaurants remained a mystery to me until I left home.

Of the foods my mom would prepare, no packaged product excited me and my younger twin brothers, Bill and Dave, more than boxed pizza. I can't even remember the brand name, but it must have been Chef Boyardee. The box was tall and red, and like the Russian nesting dolls everyone displayed on their mantelpieces, it contained packages within packages. A green cardboard cylinder was filled with dry, crumbly "Parmesan" cheese, more salt than dairy product, and a squat can contained tomato paste. Envelopes were bursting with flour and yeast—mix the yeast with a little warm water, and foamy alchemy happened. The task of making the pie was delegated to us kids, and 15 minutes after starting the project, after a few testosterone-induced tussles, a pizza would be in the oven. Sometimes pepperoni was involved—slices shaken from a can.

When the pizza came out of the oven, the crust had the texture of cardboard and tasted slightly of baking soda, the tomato sauce was too sweet by a mile, and the dried cheese had resolved itself into little swatches that floated atop the sauce like rubber rafts on a red lake. We loved it. Pizza day was party day. As the years flew by and franchise pizzerias appeared, I had the rare chance to relish the pies at Shakey's and, later, Pizza Hut but I never imagined my obsession with pizza would eventually take me not only all over the five boroughs of New York City in a decades-long odyssey but also to Boston, Hoboken, Tunisia, Argentina, and Naples itself to ferret out pizza's deepest secrets.

THE FIRST AMERICAN PIE

Pizza as we know it—family sized, generously topped, sturdy enough to eat by hand—was invented in lower Manhattan. In 1895, Gennaro Lombardi arrived in New York City on the good ship *Kronprinz Friedrich Wilhelm* from Naples, Italy. Most of his extended family were already in New York working as tailors, and several had set up shop in the Lower East Side, then in full swing as an Italian immigrant community. But Lombardi decided to become a grocer, and established his neat little *bottega* at 53½ Spring Street—with cans of tomato sauce stacked in perfect pyramids in the display window and bunches of bananas on a cart trundled out front, according to a historic photograph. The picture shows Lombardi on the right adopting a somewhat reticent pose, and on the left a shorter Anthony Pero glaring at the camera, with a carefully waxed handlebar moustache and brilliantined hair shooting up in waves. He was clearly a ladies' man. Both wear long, impeccably white aprons tightly cinched at the waist. A sign in the window advertises pizza.

The photo is dated 1905, the year Lombardi was granted an official permit to operate a restaurant, but I'm pretty sure it was taken earlier, since the place is clearly still some sort of grocery store/pizzeria hybrid. Nicknamed "Totonno," Pero had arrived in New York from Naples in 1903. Sometime soon thereafter he strolled into Lombardi's shop and offered to make pizzas. Whether he had been a baker in the old country is not recorded, nor is exactly where he came from, since immigrants from Calabria and Apulia also would have sailed out of Naples. "Pero" is a name of Greek origin derived from *petrus*, meaning "rock," which suggests he originally came from one of the southerly Italian regions, where Greeks had migrated one thousand years earlier.

Since Lombardi's store was a grocery in 1903 without a commercial oven, I'm assuming Pero made those pizzas somewhere else and transported them to the store, at least initially. There were literally dozens of Italian bakeries—most equipped with coal-fired ovens used to make bread in various Old World shapes and sizes—dotting the Lower East Side at the time. In fact, there was one just a few doors down at 32 Spring Street. To get an idea of what kind of early pizzas were being created at these bakeries, the kind of pizza Pero first intended to make, we must travel west, leaving the pair for a moment standing in front of Lombardi's store.

Across the Hudson River from Manhattan in Hoboken, New Jersey, you'll find a pair of bakeries that specialize in focaccia—Marie's Bakery and Dom's Bakery Grand. Their focaccias, which can be purchased hot out of the oven, are turban-shaped round loaves, not as flat as pizza and with a crumb more like bread, typically coated with tomato sauce and sometimes onions, but never cheese. In this they resemble the original Naples pizza pies, but puffier and doughier. Both bakeries—it's a miracle they're still in business—are descended from a single immigrant, Leopoldo Policastro, who grew up in the town of Saviano, near Naples.

Located in now out-of-the-way neighborhoods far from the main shopping strip of Washington Street, both bakeries deploy coal-burning brick ovens to make their breads, which also include baguette-style Italian loaves (which date to the 1920s, when a craze for French bread caused Italian American bakeries to develop their own version), and round loaves more typical of traditional Italian breads of the kind sometimes called Policastro loaves in Brooklyn (though whether because of Leopoldo Policastro is an open question), but the focaccia has been around since at least the last decade of the 19th century.

The oven in Dom's Bakery (named for Dom Castellitto, who took over the bakery in 1975) was constructed around 1880, making it about the same vintage as the coal ovens on the Lower East Side. Did Pero make something like this focaccia for Lombardi's store? It's a good possibility, since this kind of bread, with its moist topping, can keep for days when well wrapped, which would be an asset to a grocery store without its own oven. It seems unlikely to me he would have been initially making actual thin-crust pizzas, which wouldn't have made sense in a grocery or even at any of the local bakeries. Thin-crust pizza needs to be eaten hot and doesn't taste fresh for more than a few hours. Nobody wants a limp and stale pie.

While this theory suggests our thin-crust pizza initially supplanted the local bakery focaccia, a trip to Boston's old North End might imply a different sort of precursor for American pizza. Home to an Italian (mainly Sicilian) community that arose a century ago, this neighborhood isolated from the rest of the city still harbors several Sicilian markets and bakeries. When I first visited 30 years ago—my future wife, Gretchen Van Dyk, had recently moved to Boston—I was amazed to find that many North End bakeries also functioned as pizzerias. Every hour or so, like clockwork, a thick square pie would emerge from the oven and be laid on the marble counter. The pizza had tomato sauce and cheese distributed irregularly over the top, and as it sat there flinging off fragrant odors, neighborhood types would drift in to buy a slice or two, still hot. What a simple and wonderful way to enjoy pizza, I thought; the thick square slices with their rigid crusts facilitated walking and eating.

In 2012 I revisited Boston to see if these pies were still being made at the remaining Sicilian bakeries. Gorging myself all along the way, I visited Boschetto's, Bova's, and Parziale's, all within a block or two of each other. The bakery pizzas, prominently displayed with a half dozen other types of bread, were as good as ever, whether eaten warm or at room temperature. And they could easily be nibbled while walking the crooked streets of this old neighborhood, stepping nimbly around groups of tourists looking for Paul Revere's church.

Could Pero's bakery pies, the ones he offered to make for Lombardi, have been the thick, square sort seen in Boston's North End? Brooklyn was a destination for Sicilian immigrants as early as 1900, as evidenced—for example—by the Sicilian restaurant Ferdinando's Focacceria in Red Hook, which opened in 1904 (a *focacceria*, confusingly, does not refer to focaccia bread, but to a Sicilian shop specializing in sandwiches of spleen and ricotta, and also ones made with chickpea fritters called *panelle*). But the Italian immigrants from that period who settled in lower Manhattan tended to be from Naples, and later, Apulia and Calabria, not Sicily.

By the way, if you want to try Sicilian-style pizza in New York City, made in a real bakery instead of in a pizzeria, take the N train up to the last stop (Ditmars Boulevard) in Astoria, where Rose and Joe's Italian Bakery makes the sorts of pies you find in Boston's North End.

WE RETURN TO SPRING STREET

Back at Lombardi's grocery, how was the business doing after Pero arrived? Maybe, as the commercial relationship between Pero and the store progressed, Pero started improving the focaccia in several key regards, or maybe one day Lombardi said to him, "Let's install a real oven and start making Naples pizzas, like we had in the old country, to be eaten right away instead of taken home and eaten cold." Well, something suggests that the product being peddled—whether out-and-out focaccia, or some pizza precursor—must have been exceedingly popular and maybe even caused something of a sensation. Otherwise, how to explain Lombardi's decision two years later to abandon the grocery store and open the first American pizza parlor? Maybe Pero started putting mozzarella cheese on top, since the cheese (made with cow milk instead of water buffalo milk as it was back in Italy) was so available at neighborhood *latticinis* and so inexpensive. Maybe the breads he delivered early every morning after baking stints in the wee hours started to resemble pizzas more than focaccias.

Indeed, the addition of cheese may be the key to the creation of American pizza. It had never been used on pies in Naples until 1889, when Margherita of Savoy, the queen consort of Italy, visited the port city. What has come to be called the margherita pie, the first to have mozzarella on top (originally from water buffalo milk), was invented to celebrate her visit, reputedly attended by raucous processions through the streets. Had Lombardi and Pero been in on the festivities as children and become powerfully convinced of the connubial rightness of pizza and cheese?

Perhaps the other groceries in Lombardi's store—the tins of sardines, the dried pastas imported from Campania, the raisins, the oil-cured Gaeta olives, and the salted capers and codfish—started gathering dust as Pero's pizza became more popular, and the idea at last struck Lombardi that they should bag the store and start a Naples-style pizzeria on the premises. One way or another, Lombardi installed an oven in his original storefront at 53½ Spring Street between Lafayette and Mulberry. The original oven was faced in white ceramic tiles, with "1905 Lombardi" emblazoned in two rows in black tiles across the front. This may have grated on Pero, who was probably the brains behind the operation, as the future of New York pizza would eventually prove. It's hard to discern the dimensions of the city's first pizzeria, since the original storefront was much altered over the succeeding decades, but it was certainly deep and narrow, with the oven in the back.

In 1984, an economic downturn and streets that were considered unsafe due to the crack epidemic closed the original Lombardi's. Ten years later, under a new partnership that included Gennaro "Jerry" Lombardi, the grandson of the founder, the pizzeria reopened at 32 Spring Street, at the corner of Mott Street, where a coal oven was already in place from an earlier bakery. (These coal ovens, exempt from later city regulations, are quite a rarity these days.) This oven was refaced with the original white tiles and now constitutes something of a facsimile of America's original pizza oven.

In 2004, the storefront next door was annexed, making the modern Lombardi's mazelike, including a glassed-in rooftop area. To get to this space, you have to traipse down crooked hallways painted red, through a cluttered kitchen, and up a narrow stairway, past myriad tables with checked tablecloths, the walls coated with awards, reviews, and bric-a-brac. Indeed, the Lombardi's of today is one of the Lower East Side's biggest tourist traps, and one is well advised to visit late in the evening or at midafternoon to secure a table.

Yes, the Lombardi's of 1905 was the country's first full-blown pizzeria, with a spare menu that probably consisted of a few fundamental pies in a single large-circumference size, which were apparently folded into fours and wrapped in brown paper when delivered to the table. Pero and Lombardi's genius lay in taking what had been fundamentally a pita bread slicked with tomato sauce fit for a single diner back in Naples and transforming it into a communal experience, large enough for a family and scattered with ingredients that represented the wealth and opulence of the New World. They turned the pie into a party.

And, oh what a crust these newly invented pizzas had! The coal-burning oven Lombardi built burned hotter than anything

Naples had, 900 degrees versus 700 degrees Fahrenheit for the average wood-burning beehive ovens of Italy. This meant that pies cooked in an amazing three to five minutes, as they still do in New York's small collection of ancient pizzerias with coal-burning ovens; that the crust had to be thin, so that it baked evenly without remaining raw in the middle; and that American pies had spots of char here and there rather than the mere stipples found on the puffy and anemic-looking pies of Naples, which made the American pies more beautiful and more flavorsome.

Thin as they were, these beautiful crusts could support only a modest amount of ingredients, lest the totality burn on the outside while remaining raw in the middle in the perdition-like heat of the coal oven. (Later, pies descended from the original Lombardi's style, because they were baked at a lower temperature in gas ovens, could support a larger mass of toppings.) The giant cans of tomato sauce from the old country that had been a feature of the grocery window were now applied to these pizza crusts. For the Calabrians in the customer base, pepper flakes might be sprinkled on top; for the Apulians, maybe crumbled Italian sausage. Everyone likes their pizza customized in different ways.

Gradually the roster of potential pizza toppings must have grown to include pitted and canned black olives, anchovies imported from the Sorrento Peninsula, slivers of onion and finely chopped garlic, ricotta cheese, and pepperoni—a long hard salami colored with paprika unknown back in Italy. My guess is that pepperoni was inspired by the chorizo that Lower East Side Italian cooks borrowed from their Spanish or Portuguese neighbors, who were a major presence nearby in the southern part of Greenwich Village during much of the 20th century.

In the Unites States, the form of pizza invented by Lombardi and Pero was christened "Neapolitan pizza," in deference to where the pizza had originated, though in far less substantial form. When I first arrived in New York in 1977, every neighborhood pizza parlor served two kinds of pie: thin-crusted round Neapolitan pies, and square thick-crusted Sicilian pies. The term *Neapolitan* has since become confused: it now refers to pizzas that seek to approximate the original Naples pies—smaller, floppier, from wood-burning ovens. So I would propose that the larger, family-style pie invented by Lombardi and Pero now be called simply New York pizza.

Indeed, it was the New York pizzas and not those of Naples that so seized the world's imagination, mainly after World War II when, as we shall see, New York pizzas became more widespread in the city and, eventually, all over the country. In fact, this type of pizza was re-created in idiosyncratic form all over Europe, North Africa, South America, Asia, and even back in Italy. But here in New York, a century later, real Naples-style pies would eventually seek their revenge . . .

PERO DEPARTS, STAGE LEFT

Maybe the seeds of their dissolution can already be seen in the expressions of the two men in the old photo. The egotistical Lombardi couldn't have been easy to work for, and Pero undoubtedly had an ego of his own. Because in 1924, Antonio Pero packed up his *pala* (the wooden paddle, or "peel," used to pull pizza from the oven) and struck out to start his own pizzeria. He chose a back street in Coney Island, Brooklyn, a ribbon of beach that had hosted a grand resort in the late 19th century. By 1924 it had become a thronged Italian immigrant ghetto, an ethnic presence that would soon spread to the nearby neighborhoods of Bensonhurst and Dyker Heights, and eventually Bay Ridge.

He called the place Totonno Pizzeria Napolitana, giving a shout-out to his Italian compatriots back home. Though he'd been in America 21 years, the name suggests he still had a longing for the old country. Indeed, he may have chosen Coney Island for its strangely compelling resemblance to the Bay of Naples, from which the Ischia and Sorrento Peninsulas extend on either side like embracing arms, just as the Rockaways and Sandy Hook do for Coney Island, both hovering on the horizon as the sun glints off shimmering blue waters.

The line of descendants that still operate Totonno's has been unbroken, and I'm guessing the pizza tastes about the same, since the raw materials and methods of manufacture have remained consistent over the years: thin-but-cushiony pies, artfully charred in spots from the coal oven, mozzarella so fresh it squeaks, and a plain sauce that manages to taste piquantly of tomatoes grown on sunny hillsides. I'm willing to go out on a limb here and say this is the world's best pizza, better than any other in New York, at least, where the fiercest competition lies.

Right on Neptune Avenue, a few blocks from the beach, in a hardscrabble neighborhood of Russian auto body shops, sneaker stores, and small Latin bodegas, Pero's small pizzeria improbably still stands. The front is fake brick and the structure is one-story frame. The interior holds six or so tables and a couple of wooden booths. Presiding over the scene is Louise Ciminieri, Pero's granddaughter, whom everyone calls "Cookie." She's a gruff old gal and has little patience with newbies who enter the sainted facility and want to be coddled into ordering a pie. Flaunting its purity, the place sells pizzas in two sizes, with toppings that are limited to Italian sausage, mushrooms, pepperoni, peppers and onions, anchovies, onions, garlic, and extra cheese. No salads. No desserts. No calzones.

I went in there recently with Peter Meehan, editor of *Lucky Peach*, who had his sleeping daughter, Hazel, with him. Showing her heart of gold, Cookie rushed over to help with the stroller and to make sure the toddler was comfortable, offering little bits of motherly advice along the way. A spare but harried woman in a white waitress outfit, her gray hair pushed back from her face, she is at once waitress and current head of the world's greatest pizzeria, and she displays an appropriate amount of gravitas.

She's quick to point out that she believes her grandfather is entirely responsible for the invention of American pizza. In an interview with Peter Genovese of the New Jersey *Star-Ledger*, she points to that photo of Lombardi and Pero in front of the shop and notes of Lombardi's shiny and expensive shoes, with an almost Sherlock Holmesian tone of analysis, "This is not a pizza maker." Then she puts her finger on Pero's flour-dusted footwear. "This is a pizza maker. My grandfather was born in Naples. He worked for Lombardi's making pizza. His pizza. My grandfather created pizza in this country."

The continued existence of Totonno's in its original state is something of a miracle. In 2009, the coal oven caught the wood underneath it on fire, and the place was so damaged that it didn't reopen for months. Bad luck struck again late in 2012, when Hurricane Sandy sent a wall of water rushing through the premises, closing the place a second time. I toured the area two weeks later by bicycle, and Totonno's looked like a soggy wreck, the place shut up tight and water seeping from under the metal gate. It didn't reopen till late March 2013. Several rechecks later, I can assure you that the pizza is as good as ever. Even better.

OTHER LOMBARDI LEGATEES

Whether he personally had a hand in the development of the pizza or only adopted a supervisory role, Lombardi had a penchant for hiring talented bakers, and he stands at the head of a dynasty of coal-oven pizzerias. These places, including Lombardi's and Totonno's, are not only New York treasures but national ones. And since coal ovens are now frowned upon by the city and indeed the federal government, and coal is more difficult and expensive to acquire, and frankly very messy, this small collection of ur-pizzerias cannot be replaced.

In 1929, *pizzaiolo* John Sasso left Lombardi's to found John's Pizzeria in an Italian neighborhood that ran along Bleecker Street in Greenwich Village. Few evocations of the old neighborhood still stand (the wonderful Faicco's Pork Store is another vestige). John's is now a ramshackle pairing of two side-by-side storefronts, each with a coal oven all its own. The booths and tables are all ancient wood, carved with so many names and initials that the exposed surfaces look like mountain land-scapes seen from outer space. Covering one wall, a crude mural of Capri's Blue Grotto with a tiny boat floating in the lagoon is so badly limned and so smoke blackened, it can barely be made out.

The menu, as at Totonno's and Lombardi's, is exceedingly spare, though at John's you can also get salads, a baked pasta or two (beloved by southern Italians), and a giant calzone made with the same dough as the pizzas. The pizzas are almost as wonderful as Totonno's, with a crust slightly thinner and slightly more charred, and a tomato sauce that tends to be splattered on rather than evenly spread. The cheese, too, is every bit as good as Totonno's. Only the connoisseur of coal-oven pizza would be able to discern the differences.

In 1933, Lombardi suffered the departure of another key pizza maker. Soon after he married his wife, Carmella, Pasquale "Patsy" Lancieri set out for East Harlem's thriving Italian community and established Patsy's Pizzeria in a narrow storefront still extant, so dominated by its giant coal oven that there's barely room to stand and eat your pizza. Lancieri's output differed from the other coal-oven pies by having a more highly pureed tomato sauce that, I swear, has not a single ingredient added to it, making the sauce one of the most magnificently bland in the business. The mozzarella is plain and fresh tasting, making the pies served here austere in the extreme, and all the better for it. And the crust is even thinner than John's, but not as crisp.

Another distinction is that Patsy's sells slices in addition to the whole pies that are the exclusive output of its coal-oven competitors. This places the East Harlem haunt at the head of a slice movement that came to dominate the New York pizza scene from the '50s to the present. Over the years, many celebrities visited Patsy's, including Frank Sinatra and Francis Ford Coppola, and a couple of modern dining rooms have been added. But for that old-time flavor, you can't beat strolling into the original storefront—on the far north end of the collected complex—and getting just a slice with nothing extra on it. Only then does the monumental contribution of the original coal-oven pizzerias become entirely apparent.

NEIGHBORHOOD PIZZA IS BORN

When I quit grad school and moved from Madison, Wisconsin, to the East Village in 1977, I knew nothing of the ancient coal-oven pizzas of New York City. Inhabiting a crumbling, "old law" tenement apartment that dated to 1895, I found a city in turmoil, with arson fires burning nightly in the East Village in a manner more commonly associated with the South Bronx. A number of buildings in my immediate vicinity were already abandoned; years later the plowed lots became community gardens.

Many buildings were occupied by squatters, including one to the south on 13th Street that generated power via a windmill on the roof, which could be seen lazily turning from my own roof on 14th Street, where my friends and I began staging yearly rock concerts each Fourth of July. Next door to and behind my own building were a pair of lots where burned buildings had already been torn down, and the heaps of random earth made nice places to hold outdoor barbecues in an amphitheater-like setting. Friends would bring acoustic guitars and we'd cook hot dogs on sticks and host bonfire hootenannies. We became urban rustics.

Heroin had the neighborhood in a stranglehold, but one of the bright spots in the landscape was the assortment of neighborhood pizzerias that seemed to sprout on every corner. They were simple affairs: stacked Bari gas pizza ovens, a Formica counter or two, a cash register, and maybe a map of Apulia or Sicily, telegraphing the pizzaiolo's geographic point of origin.

Sometimes the pizza was great, sometimes just mediocre. And, unlike the coal-oven places, or Shakey's or Pizza Hut, these pizzas were divided into eight slices that could be purchased individually. In those days, and well into the '90s, there were virtually no franchise restaurants anywhere in the East

Village, except for a lonely McDonald's on First Avenue and Sixth Street that always seemed in trouble with the Board of Health. We didn't patronize it anyway, because we'd figured out that real New Yorkers—whom we were desperate to emulate—ate only one lunch: two slices and a Coke. For an extra 25 cents you could have pepperoni on your slice, or, for the real connoisseur, crumbled or sliced Italian sausage.

We learned to modify our slices from a caddy of condiments that twirled on the counter: salt, black pepper, dried oregano, red pepper flakes, and screw-top jars of dehydrated garlic so rancid you didn't have to even shake any out to smell how awful it was. The more generous places provided dried cheese as well. The oregano was considered something of a signature herb in Italian American cooking, maybe suggesting the remote Greek heritage of many southern Italians.

These neighborhood slice joints, of which the East Village had probably 20 at the time (almost half still remain), packed a lot of variability into a single commodity. Some pizzerias made their own dough, some had it delivered by truck. Some used tomato sauce, some deployed crushed tomatoes. Some made their crusts relatively thin, while others wadded the dough in the circumferential hump of crust (called by aficionados "the bone"), or made the crust thicker in the middle the better to fill you up with dough.

Some pizzerias herbed up the sauce and, if the proprietors were Sicilian, added sugar. The cheese was often of mediocre quality. I later learned from Jonathan Kwitny's *Vicious Circles* (1981) that this cheese was controlled by the mob, using a distribution system that had originated with Al Capone, who owned dairy farms in Fond du Lac, Wisconsin. And the "No Slices" sign on the awning of John's of Bleecker Street was a signal that this historic pizzeria was mob protected and should not be firebombed if they refused to buy the mob cheese. Take a look at the awning when you go there. It still says "No Slices."

But somehow mediocre cheese, slightly doctored tomato sauce, and crusts of varying quality melded to form a perfect totality that excited fierce opinions among me and my new boho friends. My favorite pizza parlor was Stromboli's, which still stands at the corner of First Avenue and Saint Marks Place. Before renovation a few years ago added an incongruous outdoor dining area, as if pizza were something one might linger over, it, too, had been one of those narrow storefronts that turned out pizza pies as the main attraction. But in the style of those dedicated pizza joints, and using some of the same raw materials, it also offered meatball heroes and the eponymous strombolis, open-ended rolls of dough containing the same sorts of toppings you might get on a pizza—but we stuck with the pies.

In addition to offering an excellent slice, Stromboli's had endeared itself to me and my friends by being one of the only eating establishments that stayed open till 2:00 a.m. every morning, sometimes even later on weekends. In the late '70s, most East Village restaurants catered to a breakfast and lunch trade only; few did business past 6:00 p.m., and almost none were open after midnight. Stromboli's used lots of sugar in their tomato sauce, and that suited me just fine as I staggered home from rock shows at CBGB or Max's Kansas City. In those situations, you craved that sugar charge to speed you on your way home.

As my corpus of activities in the city expanded, I learned that nearly every neighborhood had a slew of pizza parlors much like the Bed-Stuy place in Spike Lee's *Do the Right Thing*. (A movie about a New York pizza parlor!) My friends and I were impressed. But how did these plebeian parlors come to be, and how did pizza become not only the late-night recourse of night owls like me but also the New York workingman's lunchtime sandwich, hamburger, and hot dog, all rolled into one?

TURNING ON THE GAS

The gas-fired pizza oven was invented sometime in the late 1940s, as the nation was just getting over the worst world war it had seen. To make pizzas, you previously had to have a coal-burning oven that burned so hot you were in some danger. As far as I can tell, in America wood ovens were rarely used in restaurants and not yet for pizzas. But suddenly the gas pizza oven allowed you to bake pies at the more moderate temperature of 500 degrees or so. These ovens had very little headroom (they could cook a pie but not a cake) and arrived stacked in multiples so you could keep several ovens on at different temperatures.

The pizza maker could rotate pizzas between ovens, initially cooking a pizza very hot, then transferring it to a cooler oven, or develop other idiosyncratic ways of cooking pies depending on thickness of crust or density of toppings. A particular oven in the stack could also be dedicated to reheating slices, and even making baked pastas. Of course, this multiple-oven versatility was of a very narrow sort, so outfitting pizza parlors with such ovens tended to cause them to remain forever pizza parlors—conferring a sort of permanency to these neighborhood cheap-dining institutions.

The gas-oven pie was quite a different beast than its coal-oven older brother. Pizzas cooked longer at a lower temperature developed a crisper crust and did not as easily become charred. Thus, the smoky flavor of the coal-oven pie was somewhat lacking as was the char, but it was easier to hoist a slice and eat it while walking. (Especially if you used what came to be known as the "New York fold"—grasping the slice by the bone and folding it in upon itself along a line that stretched from the middle of the bone to the pointy end.) The gas-oven product wasn't better, just different.

Many of the gas-fired ovens bore the name Bari, which was a restaurant-equipment jobber on Bowery named for the capital of Apulia, the heel of the Italian boot. Whether Bari actually invented the gas pizza oven or simply popularized it, I've been unable to discern. But these ovens revolutionized the pizza industry, so that returning servicemen and just-arriving immigrants from Italy found the pizza business an attractive one, and many corner pizzerias around the five boroughs thus date to the 1950s or 1960s. You can tell by the shabby decor, the frayed plaid curtains, the straggly plants, the torn linoleum on the floor, all signs of the gradual, decades-old maturing of these institutions. The most famous of these still extant, of course, is Di Fara Pizza on Avenue J in Midwood, Brooklyn. There, in 1964, a young immigrant named Dom DeMarco from Provincia di Caserta, near Naples, got into the neighborhood pizza business for the second time. (He'd previously opened another pizzeria, Piccola Venezia, in 1959 in Sunset Park, Brooklyn.)

The story of how he became the city's patron saint of pizza is an interesting one. DeMarco made pizza in obscurity for decades until he was "discovered" by Jim Leff, the founder of the food-obsessed cyber bulletin board Chowhound, in 1997. It was Leff's habit to highlight just a few places visited in his five-borough wanderings and then post relentlessly to promote the hell out of them. In Di Fara Pizza he found a perfect object of his attentions—an old guy working in anonymity in colorful surroundings. Of the premises, Leff said in his *Eclectic Gourmet Guide to Greater New York City* (1998):

> *This early 1960s-style Brooklyn neighborhood pizza parlor has seen better days . . . You eat at long, industrial, junior high art-project type tables beneath faded posters showing Italy as it looked two generations ago; scratchy Italian opera blasts from the kitchen. Sit here a few minutes and you'll be drawn back in time.*

Clearly, DeMarco's faded institution, in a neighborhood quickly being colonized by Orthodox Jews who couldn't eat the pizza anyway due to the ingredients' lack of kosher certification, was a matter of romantic inspiration for Leff. Thanks to his efforts, it became famous among foodies who followed Chowhound, food writers, and eventually the wider pizza-eating public. It was one of the first instances of a food establishment's popularity nearly reaching mass hysteria, causing long lines to form in this lonely neighborhood hard by the Q train tracks in the center of Brooklyn.

(This phenomenon of people becoming excited about food way out of proportion to its actual worth has continued to grow over the ensuing two decades, culminating in long lines forming in front of seemingly random food establishments. The most exaggerated example was certainly the Cronut hysteria, whereby lines wound around the block in front of a bakery on Spring Street on a daily basis for a hybrid croissant/donut. Could the taste of a single pastry merit a three-hour wait? The excitement surrounding Di Fara Pizza was every bit as nutty in its day.)

I'd visited the pizzeria in the mid-'90s with Leff and thought the pizza very good for its type—that is, a neighborhood pie cooked in a gas oven by an Italian immigrant who put extra effort into his pizzas. But by that time I could name a dozen or so parlors across Brooklyn that were every bit as good. In the ensuing decade, other food writers did much to further popularize the place, and I eventually listed it among the 100 best Italian restaurants in the city in a 2004 *Village Voice* cover story, which featured a memorable picture of DeMarco, wrapped in his white apron, his glasses slightly askew, standing by his prep counter. In the interim he'd risen to the occasion, multiplied the number of cheeses used on his normal slice, grown more pots of fresh herbs that he actually used on the pies, and had become the pizza prodigy that Leff partly made him out to be. In celebrating DeMarco, we were celebrating an entire class of toiling neighborhood *pizzaioli*.

A QUICK TRIP TO NAPLES

In 1996 La Pizza Fresca opened on East 20th Street in the Flatiron District, the first place in town to actively try to reproduce the original pizza of Naples, flying in the face of nearly a century of our own pizza history. And it pretty much succeeded at re-creating the small, floppy, one-person pies, using fine-textured Italian flour, Italian olive oil, and other imported ingredients. Damp and thin in the center, doughy and puffy along the circumference, they arrived uncut and had to be eaten with a knife and fork. Cynics might say that the appearance of these pies corresponded with a desire on the part of restaurateurs to sell an only slightly glamorized version of pizza at a higher price, but they really were something of a revelation in a town already crazy for pizza.

In a strange move, La Pizza Fresca arranged to have their pies certified as "genuine" by the Associazione Verace Pizza Napoletana (AVPN), a modern alliance of pizza makers from Naples who parachuted into town (well, maybe not literally) to examine and judge the pies that sought their approval. By implication, since they were only certifying a small number of pizzas as genuine, the other pizzas in town were fakes. In doing so the AVPN was showing more than a little pique at the worldwide popularity of New York–style pizza, trying to seize the high ground and grab the pizza crown back from New York City.

In the ensuing decade, the city saw a half dozen more of these places flogging the small foreign pies, including, most notably, Motorino in Williamsburg, Brooklyn, and Una Pizza Napoletana on East 12th Street in Manhattan. These establishments received intemperate praise from critics and foodies who had presumably never eaten pizza in Naples. So it was that I decided to make a pilgrimage to Naples as perhaps the first of the city's food critics to visit specifically for the purpose of checking out the pizzas. I went with Gretchen and our teenage daughter, Tracy, and we found Naples and the Sorrento Peninsula very different from the central Italy we had been visiting for years.

We stayed in Sorrento, a Renaissance-era city of faded glory that had a century earlier been an important stop on the Grand Tour taken by generations of English gentry and Romantic poets. We quickly learned that the highways connecting Naples and Sorrento were often dirt tracks so poorly marked, so filled with crazy turns through narrow village streets, that you were as likely to end up in Amalfi as in Naples. So we got in the habit of taking the train to Pompeii and Naples. In Pompeii, I learned that the residents had been obsessed with fast food, and one of the dining establishments even served a semblance of pizza—basically just a flatbread with salt and sometimes fish sauce on top—and had some characteristics of a pizza parlor, a narrow warren with no seating where the oven was the main feature. All of this implied that Naples pizza may have originated in ancient Rome rather than with the pitas of Saracen invaders, as I'd originally thought.

Once in Naples, we felt right at home. Garbage blew through the streets, filthy wash hung from lines between apartment buildings, and women leaned on pillows in the windows of those buildings, surveying the scene. African men hung out on street corners offering to park your car, and most Italians would allow them to do it. I later figured out that you weren't paying these guys to actually park your car, but rather to drive it around in circles until you returned to reclaim it. In short, Naples looked a lot like Brooklyn.

We'd primed ourselves with the larger and more luxurious pies of Sorrento and approached the Naples pizzerias, specifically L'Antica Pizzeria da Michele and the Pizzeria Trianon da Ciro, with great reverence and respect. They turned out to be tiny places, the first founded 35 years before Lombardi's, the second 18 years after. Both served pies a little less than a foot in diameter that were floppy and soppy and surprisingly delicious in their overweening blandness. Da Michele only sold two types of pie, a margherita and a marinara. Interestingly, the latter, in addition to finely sieved tomatoes, had a good charge of crushed garlic and plenty of oregano, making it seem almost Greek and explaining the presence of that herb in traditional New York pizzerias. (Why not sage or rosemary, I'd wondered, other herbs readily available for free throughout the Italian countryside?)

I later wrote in the *Village Voice*, "Delivered uncut, the pies must be eaten with silverware, and it's comical to see an Italian boho clad in jeans and torn sweatshirt hop off a Vespa, run into a pizzeria, then daintily scarf her pie with a knife and fork." In New York we gobble slices with our hands. New York had nothing to worry about, pie-wise. I later returned to New York and gave my photos to Adam Kuban of the then-independent blog

Slice. He put them up and they caused a sensation.

Having experienced the plain pies of Naples firsthand, I returned better equipped to appraise the Naples-style pies of New York. Naples-style pizzerias—which came to include about two dozen, including Keste, Long Island import (and Motorino descendant) Pizzetteria Brunetti, and Donatella Arpaia's Donatella (since closed)—had certainly managed to get the crust almost right: soft like a glove, a bit puffy, and, though dotted with char, still anemic looking. But where they fell down was the toppings. While those of Naples were stately and austere, New York Naples pies were often slathered with diverse ingredients (including that execrable substance, artificial truffle oil) intended to lure customers and justify prices that sometimes ran to $20 or more for a small, personal-size pizza, including off-the-wall pies that would never have been seen in Naples. Ultimately they were not the true pies of Naples, just another New York invention. These establishments also cut their pies into slices—which is generally not done in Naples—and sometimes added appetizers, pastas, and pricey wine lists to their sprawling menus, though the slurp of choice in Naples pizzerias is that great Italian beverage, Coca-Cola.

Really, I wouldn't have minded what these upstarts had done with their sides, their effete wine lists, and their toppings—it was their claim to be entirely authentic, and the willingness of a Naples association to verify it, that annoyed me. Nevertheless, as part of the city's ever-expanding pizza landscape, retro-Neapolitan pizzas represent a formidable and desirable addition. Long may they wave!

PIZZA AROUND THE WORLD

Since starting my food zine *Down the Hatch* in 1989, and during my 20-year tenure at the *Village Voice*, I have made a point of sampling pizzas wherever I travel. If I happened to be in Brooklyn or the Bronx, say, and working on an unrelated story, I'd still stop at random pizza parlors and sample the plain slice, just to keep track of what direction neighborhood crusts, cheese, and sauces were headed, and also to locate the very best slices around town. Sometimes appetite permitted only a nibble of the bone and nip of the soft tip of the slice. Sometimes, the slice was so good, I'd wolf the whole thing down hungry or not. In that way I gradually compiled a collection of the great, unsung neighborhood pizza parlors of the city.

Traveling in other states and overseas, I'd do pretty much the same thing. On Avenue Habib Bourguiba in Tunis, the capital of Tunisia, a long thoroughfare that extends from the new city to the old and leads directly into the souks, I chanced upon a handful of snack shops that specialized in soul-fortifying Sicilian-style slices but topped with tuna and a runny egg. The tuna makes some sense if you realize that a main industry of Tunisia had long been tuna canning. The runny egg also makes sense, since Tunisians are prone to put a runny egg in or on nearly everything, including their signature pastry, the brik—a phyllo affair with the egg inside. Take one bite and the yolk squirts onto your shirt. At least with the pizza, you can see the yolk jiggling and behave accordingly.

Further north in central Italy, my wife, daughter, and I would stay in the Umbrian town of Panicale, where a rudimentary form of pizza was sold in the town's bakeries in big sheets. No tomato sauce, but the top would often be thickly covered with cauliflower, zucchini, or, when in season, zucchini flowers, which we considered wonderful. A more American-style pizza parlor lurked in nearby Cortona just off the flagstone-paved main square, perhaps functioning as a sop to all the Americans who visited after *Under the Tuscan Sun* was published, with the medieval walled village as the main character.

Pittsburgh proved to have a wealth of wonderful pizzas when I visited around 2003 on behalf of *Gourmet*. One I remember in particular was like a broad shallow bowl filled with white cheese that burbled out when you cut into the crust. There was also a pizzeria west of the Ohio River in a working-class neighborhood where thick, round pizza was cut horizontally, and the top and bottom half of the wedges stuffed with meat and cheese to make cold sandwiches. In San Francisco I encountered a pizzeria that claimed to make perfect New York pies in the Mission and almost succeeded. Near Mountain View, where Tracy worked as an electrical engineer at Google, a pair of former Brooklynites made what they called New York pizza, but it wasn't quite right. The crust just didn't taste the same.

The most impressive pizzas I encountered outside of New York or Naples were in Buenos Aires, in 2012. The first thing I noticed as I hit the streets were pizza parlors everywhere: from little neighborhood joints using a round crust with a biscuit-like texture and a very limited choice of toppings to historic Sicilian pizzerias serving thick square pies. The pizza that really blew me away was found at Banchero, a place founded in 1932 in the hardscrabble La Boca neighborhood on the southern end of the old city, where the crumbling gray buildings and decrepit condition of the streets and wharves reminded me of Havana.

The founder of the magnificent Banchero pizzeria—a favorite of tourists warned not to tarry after dark and Argentine school groups that arrive on buses, their uniforms neatly pressed—was Agustín Banchero, a native of Genoa who emigrated to South America with a wave of his countrymen in the previous century, creating the bedrock of Buenos Aires culinary culture. The round, New York–style Neapolitan slice is superb, a little thicker than ours, with the cheese—more like provolone than mozzarella—on the bottom and fresh tomatoes on top. The tomatoes are dressed with a parsley and chopped garlic condiment reminiscent of chimichurri. This is a slice I dream about, totally unavailable in New York, where the closest analog is the "upside-down" Sicilian slice found at pizzerias in Staten Island such as Brother's on Port Richmond Avenue, and in Fort Greene, Brooklyn, at Pipitone's, where the cheese is snuggled right next to the crust to keep it crisp, and the tomato sauce poured on top, with a sprinkling of raw garlic.

But the most unusual output of Banchero is the fugazetta, a sort of stuffed pizza made with a bowl-shaped crust heaped with things like artichokes, black olives, ham, and red peppers. The most basic form is really just a round boat filled with onions, a real poor man's meal. Buenos Aires's neighborhood pizzerias tend to substitute a cheesy béchamel for simple grated cheese, probably for reasons of economy. Buenos Aires is not a wealthy city. As another oddity, pizzerias in working-class neighborhoods often have a cospecialty of empanadas, a Spanish import in Argentina.

NEW YORK PIZZA INTO THE NEW MILLENNIUM

The vast smorgasbord that is the city's current pizza scene has added varieties at a bewildering rate, some novel, some only infinitesimally different from preexisting types. In the former category is the pizza cone, a crust rolled into a shape something like an ice cream cone, with the sauce, cheese, and other toppings poured inside. One place opposite the Empire State Building on Fifth Avenue, K! Pizzacone, introduced it as a new form of fast food, then promptly went out of business. So it's not true that New Yorkers will stand for *any* kind of pizza.

Also on the lower end of the pizza scale, economically, was the arrival of dollar pizza, whereby plain cheese slices were sold for a dollar at a spiraling number of storefronts in Manhattan, and eventually Brooklyn. The first spot to do this opened in about 2007 and caused a stir. Some of this pizza wasn't too bad, but usually with crusts—frequently prerolled and stockpiled—that were often doughy and incompetently cooked. Still, the 2 Bros. chain, with key locations on Saint Marks Place, Sixth Avenue in Greenwich Village, and behind the Port Authority, did a pretty good pie. Unfortunately, while a hit with the cheap-dining public, these places have contributed to the decline of the traditional neighborhood pizza parlor, which had been charging an average of $2.50 for their plain cheese slices.

On the upper end, we saw the advent of what might be termed hipster pizza. Leading this phenomenon were such Brooklyn restaurants as Roberta's and Franny's, both of which

ostentatiously used wood-burning ovens to make smallish pizzas influenced by Naples style but pointedly different. In the
early days, Roberta's—which occupied an isolated and walled
encampment in an industrial part of Bushwick—had a gonzo
style of pizza making that put unusual ingredients like sunny-
side-up eggs and guanciale on top of their pies, and sometimes
burned the fuck out of them, as if the oven was out of control.
Franny's offered more austere small pies, perfectly formed.

Early on, both emphasized locally sourced ingredients and
an artisanal approach that went beyond simple pizzas: Franny's
was soon making charcuterie in the basement, some of which
made it onto the pies, while Roberta's had a rooftop garden
where pizza ingredients were grown and a radio station built
out of a shipping container that webcast shows often dealing
with food sustainability and culinary politics. With no seeming limit to its ambitions, Roberta's eventually added an expensive wine list and a small, ultra-expensive boutique restaurant as
part of its sprawling complex, and eventually ceased to be a hipster hang as its prices rose and it became jammed with strollers
in the afternoons and filled with wealthy Wall Streeters in the
evenings, out on a slumming lark.

Of course, calling New York pizza better than any other pizza
in the world depends on your criteria. You can go to any pizzeria in Naples and find just about the same output, and these are
indeed delicious in their plainness. But I say a delicious plainness is inferior to the perfection our own pizzaioli have achieved
by relentless tinkering. With making the tomato sauce more
piquant, or omitting it entirely, with adding more varied toppings, or simply larger quantities. With doing just plain weird
things like creating mind-bogglingly large slices at Koronet
near the Columbia University campus, or putting ziti on a
pie at Gourmet Brick Oven 33 in Murray Hill—an irrational
pizza/pasta hybrid that never would have flown in the old country. By treating pizza as a blank slate, the city has explored every
corner of the possible pizza universe, and our pizza is better as
a result.

So what is New York pizza at this point? Its diffuse development, especially as the general public's interest in food has ramped up over the last two decades, has left pizza stronger than ever as the snack and cheap meal of choice, but it has also left pizza with something of an identity crisis. Throw a rock in any direction in the five boroughs and you're likely to hit a pizza of some sort. But this has done nothing to tarnish the reputation of pizza as the city's greatest and most ubiquitous foodstuff—in fact, the phenomenon has buffed pizza's reputation to a high gloss. We are clearly living in the golden age of pizza, and New York remains its epicenter. The question is no longer simply, "Would you like a slice of pizza?" but "What kind of pizza would you like?"

A BAKER'S DOZEN OF PIZZAS YOU MUST NOT MISS

Some sell slices, some sell only whole pies.

1. TOTONNO'S PIZZERIA NAPOLITANA
1524 NEPTUNE AVENUE, BROOKLYN, 718-372-8606

Quite simply the world's best pizza. Go for the basic cheese pie and add an extra ingredient (my fave: Italian sausage), but don't go overboard on the toppings.

2. JOHN'S OF BLEECKER STREET
278 BLEECKER STREET, MANHATTAN, 212-243-1680

Another of the early coal-oven places, with a pair of well-worn dining rooms. The pizzas are more thin-crusted than Totonno's, and you can get draft beer and even a salad (!). A historic Greenwich Village hang.

3. KESTÉ
271 BLEECKER STREET, MANHATTAN, 212-243-1500

Directly across the street from John's, and to many, constituting a sort of insult to our venerable coal-oven pies, Kesté specializes in the Naples revival style of pies that has sprung up in the last two decades. Small, expensive pies, but worth it.

4. DENINO'S PIZZERIA & TAVERN
524 PORT RICHMOND AVENUE, STATEN ISLAND, 718-442-9401

This classic Sicilian Staten Island bar with a pizzeria in back once catered to mariners, serving the flat crisp pies that are characteristic of one of the myriad types of Staten Island pizza. Go for the clam pie or the MOR (meatball, onion, and ricotta).

5. STROMBOLI PIZZA
83 SAINT MARKS PLACE, MANHATTAN, 212-673-3691

The notorious late-night East Village slice joint, serving rockers like the Beastie Boys for decades.

6. KRISPY PIZZA

7112 13TH AVENUE, BROOKLYN, 718-745-9618; 11 HOLDEN BOULEVARD,
STATEN ISLAND, 718-983-5900; 33 HUDSON STREET, JERSEY CITY,
NEW JERSEY, 201-685-7313; OTHER LOCATIONS

*Classic pizzeria of the long-Italian Dyker Heights neighborhood (with
other locations as well) and pioneer of the "nonna," or "grandma," slice,
taking a contemporary New York–style slice and substituting fresh
mozzarella for store bought, creating a sort of pizza back-construction,
as linguists might say.*

7. FRANNY'S

348 FLATBUSH AVENUE, BROOKLYN, 718-230-0221

*Wood-oven pizzas, small and kid-glove soft, in a boho bistro setting with
lots of vegetable apps and house-cured charcuterie like lardo and pancetta.*

8. PIPITONE'S PIZZA

100 DEKALB AVENUE, BROOKLYN, 718-858-4376

*Fort Greene mainstay beloved of generations of Brooklyn Tech students;
get the "upside-down" Sicilian slice, then take a stroll through
Fort Greene Park.*

9. LA VILLA PIZZERIA

261 FIFTH AVENUE, BROOKLYN, 718-499-9888; 6610 AVENUE U,
BROOKLYN, 718-251-8030; 8207 153RD AVENUE, QUEENS, 718-641-8259

*This Park Slope spot (with other locations as well) evolved from pizza
parlors in far-off Marine Park, Brooklyn, serving a wide variety of pies
in a setting that befits a shopping mall. The Abruzzi-style stuffed
pizza—with top and bottom crusts—is the delectable oddity to get.*

10. 2 BROS.

542 NINTH AVENUE, MANHATTAN, 212-695-2642; OTHER LOCATIONS

*For pizza at its rock-bottom proletarian cheapest, doing just what the
slice joint was originally intended to do, try this place or one of its myriad
branches around Manhattan.*

11. ROSE & JOE'S ITALIAN BAKERY

2240 31ST STREET, QUEENS, 718-721-9422

In Astoria, a short train ride from Manhattan, one of the few places in the five boroughs to get square sheet, bakery-style pizza, and is it ever good!

12. L & B SPUMONI GARDENS

2725 86TH STREET, BROOKLYN, 718-449-1230

Founded in 1939 in the sinister-sounding Gravesend section of Brooklyn, the pizzeria at the left of this three-building compound, thronged in summer, peddles Sicilian square-slice pies (called "sheets") that are left slightly raw in the middle—an acquired taste.

13. GRANDAISY BAKERY

250 WEST BROADWAY, MANHATTAN, 212-334-9435;
176 WEST 72ND STREET, MANHATTAN, 212-334-9435

This split-off from Sullivan Street Bakery produces admirable single-topping square pies like the bakery pizzas of central Italy. Scented with fresh rosemary, the potato pie can't be beat! And the zucchini and mushroom pies are pretty unforgettable, too.

NEW YORK–STYLE CHEESE PIZZA
MAKES TWO 12-INCH PIES

Look, unless you have a deck oven, you're never going to achieve what your local pizzeria is doing. That being said, you can achieve pretty decent results quite simply. Get a pizza stone or a bunch of unglazed ceramic tiles from Home Depot, crank your oven, and keep the toppings simple. You can also get a ball of dough from your local pizzeria to make things even easier.

1 (28-ounce) can whole plum tomatoes
1 garlic clove
1 teaspoon dried oregano
2 teaspoons dried basil
$\frac{1}{2}$ teaspoon red pepper flakes
Large pinch sugar
2 teaspoons kosher salt
2 tablespoons olive oil
1 ball of pizza dough (about 1 pound)
Flour for dusting
1 pound grated mozzarella cheese

1. Place a pizza stone or tiles in the center of the oven and set the temperature to 500°F. The oven should heat up for an hour to let the stone get hot.

2. In a food processor or blender, combine the tomatoes with their liquid, garlic, oregano, basil, red pepper flakes, sugar, salt, and olive oil. Pulse until smooth.

3. The dimensions of your pizza stone or tiles will determine the size of pizza you can make; a ball of dough from your local pizzeria will make approximately two 12-inch pies. Lightly flour a work surface. Divide the dough ball into 2 even pieces. Press out the first wad of dough into a circle, then gently stretch it by draping it over your knuckles or fingers, working your way around the circumference of the dough and stretching with both fists as you spin it. Stretch the dough to a uniform ½-inch thickness.

4. Transfer the dough to a pizza peel dusted with flour. (If you do not have a pizza peel, an overturned cookie sheet dusted with flour will do the trick.) Working quickly, spread about ½ cup of the sauce over the surface of the crust, leaving a ½-inch border. Sprinkle half the cheese over the sauce. Shake the peel to make sure the pizza is not stuck and will slide off. Slide the pizza onto the pizza stone and bake for 8 minutes. Rotate the pizza with tongs for even cooking, and bake for 4 to 6 more minutes, until the crust is nicely browned and puffy. Remove the pizza from the oven and cut into slices. Serve immediately. Use the other wad of dough to make a second pie. You will have sauce left over.

EGG FOO YONG

The doorbell rings. You look through the peephole in your apartment door and, done up in helmet and slicker, it's the Chinese delivery guy dripping wet, just arrived on his motorized bicycle in the rain. The transaction is rapid: He hands you a white plastic bag, you fork over eight dollars plus a generous tip due to the weather, and he runs back down the stairway. You set the bag on the table and unload it, hands trembling in anticipation. Inside—if you're lucky and your carry-out place is obsessed with details—there will be one squat plastic receptacle and two bone-white trapezoidal paper cartons, the tops sealed with interlocking flaps and crowned with an aluminum wire handle. (No one has yet figured out what the handle is for. Are you supposed to pick up the carton and parade it around your apartment like a purse?)

The plastic receptacle brims with brown gravy, like the kind you might expect to find on a Salisbury steak. The first paper carton contains white rice, still fluffy. In the second are three patties the size and shape of hamburgers, tightly wedged so you have to turn the carton upside down and shake it to get them out. Welcome to your splendid dinner: egg foo yong!

Many places give you only two cartons, so that the patties swim in gravy and get completely soggy somewhere between the restaurant and your place of residence. I've chosen the carry-out Golden Woks in Greenwich Village, not for its proximity to my tenement apartment, but because the place deploys the three-container system. I arrange my dinner on the paper plate also provided, the rice in a giant mound, the patties atop, with the entire pint of gravy cascading over the top, like flood-waters choked with alluvial dirt—but great-tasting dirt! Poking at the mass with chopsticks is useless. Violating the most basic principle of Chinese dining, egg foo yong demands to be attacked with a fork.

The patties are delicious, crisp and brown and dotted with small shrimp, and the salty gravy screams "Umami!"—livening up and enriching the repast immeasurably. The rice soaks up all the extra gravy. This is fast-food nirvana, and it arrives, as most Chinese meals do, so hot that you have to blow on it before you dig in. Time was, this excellent dish enjoyed enormous popu-larity in takeout containers across the city, but its popularity has declined precipitously in recent decades.

THE ANATOMY OF EGG FOO YONG

The dish is a curious one, but it perfectly represents Chinese-American cuisine as developed by Chinese restaurants all around the country over the course of more than a century. Currently in total disrepute among foodies due to their pref-erence for purer and more authentic regional Chinese cuisines, the sainted canon of Chinese-American food includes familiar dishes that may have originated in China but were aggressively adapted for American tastes: egg rolls, chop suey, fried rice, pepper steak, sweet-and-sour pork, chow mein, fried wontons, sesame chicken, orange chicken, stir-fries such as beef with broccoli (a vegetable virtually unknown in Asia), and, most recently, General Tso's chicken. The last was invented in the '70s in midtown Manhattan at either Peng's Restaurant or Shun Lee Palace, depending on whom you believe. Unfortunately, Chinese-American cuisine ceased to evolve after the 1970s due to a number of factors, and though the iconic dishes remain supremely delectable, it's now moribund.

The standard recipe for egg foo yong involves pouring beaten eggs—into which soy sauce, salt, sometimes sugar, finely ground white pepper, and (if you're lucky) MSG, have been added—into a wok seething with cooking oil, making a loud hissing sound and sending up towers of steam. Next, some combination of bean sprouts, cabbage, and bamboo shoots gets tossed into the middle of the egg mixture as the cook keeps the blossoming patty confined to a disk in the center of the wok by pressing it inward with a spatula. Minced ham, shrimp, chicken, beef, or pork is then added to the vegetable-and-egg mélange, and voilà! A perfect egg foo yong patty is deftly flipped from the wok; two more are made in quick succession, since three is the universal serving.

If we were to categorize egg foo yong generically we'd have to call it an omelet. But while a French omelet is cooked in clarified butter at relatively moderate temperatures, the Chinese version uses much hotter vegetable oil to caramelize the exterior of the beaten eggs and create a crispness alien to soft and squishy Western omelets. The sprouts provide a bouncy matrix and attenuate the most expensive ingredient—eggs. By today's way of thinking, they also ramp up the "healthiness" factor. The gravy is clearly inspired by English or German gravy—nothing else in the world could be so dense and brown, verging on the texture of pudding—though sometimes a bit of fish sauce is added to make it taste more Chinese. While the rice and its cooking method are entirely Chinese, the totality of the dish is perfect East–West fusion: a French omelet with Teutonic gravy cooked in a Chinese wok with that most quintessential of Asian ingredients, bean sprouts.

The name *egg foo yong* itself (sometimes transliterated *egg fu yung*, *egg foo yung*, or *egg foo young*) straddles two languages: *egg* is good grunty Anglo-Saxon English (probably originally Old Norse), while *foo yong* is Cantonese for hibiscus, referring, perhaps with ironic humor, to the flowerlike appearance of the patty as it crinkles and puffs in the wok, like a flat bud turning into a 3-D flower. On the other hand, in the Cantonese dialect of Guangdong, a southeastern coastal region where many of our early Chinese immigrants came from, *foo yong* also means "egg white," so we may have a pun at work here, with the meaning boiling down to something like "flower of egg."

According to a chapter on Chinese-American food in the Time Life book *American Cooking: The Melting Pot* (1971):

> *At its best, with the crispness and stringiness of celery dispersed through a rich gravy and the whole ladled steaming over a bed of white rice, [chop suey] can be a roundly satisfying one-course meal. The same can be said for egg foo young, shrimp chow mein, fried rice—each has its Oriental antecedent, yet each underwent a sea change during the long Pacific crossing into something that, if not precisely exotic, is somewhat more Chinese than American.*

Thus egg foo yong, along with its gravy and rice, was intentionally packaged as a one-course meal aimed at American diners accustomed to the same proportions of protein, grease, and starch in what they considered their normal diet. It became a cognate of the all-in main courses being plated across the United States, much like the bland meat-and-potatoes Anglo-German-Irish-Polish food I grew up eating.

When I lived in Minnesota in the early '60s, Chinese food was not unknown to my family. On a few occasions, we carried out fried rice and meat-vegetable stir-fries in the iconic white containers. We loved the exotic taste, squirting on the plastic sleeves of soy sauce in an attempt to make the salty food even saltier. But our main exposure to Chinese fare came through the battling supermarket potentates La Choy and Chun King. Via their boxed and canned meals, these brands familiarized us for the first time with such ingredients as fried noodles, bean sprouts, water chestnuts, and bamboo shoots, incorporated into chop suey, chow mein, and *subgum*—a catchall term we endlessly pondered. Was it related to chewing gum? Or something inferior, as the prefix implied? (The meaning in Cantonese is "numerous and varied.") As I eventually realized, Chun King and La Choy represented a processed and canned version of the cuisine developed by legions of Chinese immigrant restaurateurs, totally lacking in the inventiveness and freshness that made Chinese-American food great. But the seed had been sown by these supermarket products for cravings that were to become more intense as my life proceeded.

Some articles on the subject maintain that egg foo yong first became popular in the 1930s, as Chinese restaurants catering to middle-American tastes first spread throughout the country. But it certainly seems much older than that. Apparently, egg foo yong possessed just the perfect combination of the familiar and the unfamiliar to appeal to Americans accustomed to bland, overcooked meat, lots of starch, and vegetables from cans. Seasonings aside, what could be more American than beaten eggs cooked quickly and served hot out of the pan? Chinese-American food can also be said to have whetted American appetites for other seemingly exotic cuisines—and, later, for the regional cuisines of China itself—brought here by immigrants late in the 20th century.

Around the same time that Chinese food was becoming a staple of the American diet in the first half of the 20th century, glimpses of Arab and Mexican cuisines were providing similar culinary diversions. But even when I lived in Dallas in the late 1960s, any kind of foreign food was still hard to come by, mainly limited to a string of strip-mall chain restaurants slinging Tex-Mex platters swimming in canned chili gravy and cheese, and a single Japanese joint wowing Dallasites with beef teppanyaki, delivered with a floor show of flying knives and somersaulting shrimp by chefs wearing red toques that sat like mushrooms on their heads. Chinese food was part of this exotic mix, though rarely eaten in the restaurant it came from—much more often delivered by automobile. Miraculously, it arrived still piping hot. There was something thermodynamically magical about those white carry-out containers . . .

A THUMBNAIL HISTORY OF CHINESE FOOD IN AMERICA

Chinese immigrants arrived on America's west coast in two waves in the 19th century. The first was motivated by greed.

Back in China, news of the gold rush had arrived soon after the first strike in 1848, and California quickly became known as the "Golden Land." Chinese prospectors began arriving in San Francisco midway through 1849, as fast as their boats could ferry them, bound for the gold fields east of Sacramento. They weren't the only ones: there were large contingents also arriving from Mexico, Chile, Oregon, and even France, beelining en masse for the region. The Chinese immigrants came mainly from the Pearl River Delta in Guangdong, where traveling around the world seeking economic opportunity had been a habit of the local population for centuries, as detailed by Lynn Pan in *Sons of the Yellow Emperor: A History of the Chinese Diaspora* (1990).

Chinese immigration to America at that time was blissfully unrestricted, and the newcomers set up a sort of base camp in San Francisco, where they found a small Chinese population already in residence. That neighborhood was the country's first Chinatown, and it persists today. Walk its hilly streets and you can still get a feeling of the rambunctiousness and bohemianism that were a feature of the neighborhood in the mid-19th century, when honky-tonks, whorehouses, and opium dens contributed to a Wild West version of Chinatown that radiated outward from Portsmouth Square like a spilled can of red paint. Within two years of the discovery of gold, the permanent population of San Francisco had zoomed from 1,000 to 15,000, and a significant proportion was Chinese.

The immigrants were nearly all male, and most soon set off for the gold fields. While the earliest arrivals found claims they could stake, and a few did indeed achieve wealth, those who reached the same destination in the early 1850s found that gold that had once been strewn in nuggets on the ground now had to be extracted by more labor-intensive methods, including the back-breaking work of mining and stream panning. What's more, they found newly passed restrictive laws that made becoming rich an even more remote possibility for the foreign born. In particular, taxes were levied against Chinese miners, and racism on the part of white miners toward yellow and brown ones soon burst out.

Not to be defeated by adversity, many unsuccessful Chinese gold seekers turned their attention to other professions, becoming launderers, carpenters, agricultural day laborers, and—most interesting to us—cooks and restaurant owners. San Francisco itself, and gold towns such as El Dorado, Placerville, and Diamond Spring soon had Chinese restaurants in addition to the usual complement of title companies, assay houses, dry goods stores, and saloons.

What kind of food were they making in these new Chinese restaurants? Well, most of the immigrants had not been cooks back home, so their evocation of food from far-off Canton was hit or miss, to say the least. While in the initial phases they were probably cooking for fellow Chinese, it probably didn't take too long for other gold seekers to realize a strange hot meal could be just as good as a familiar one, or perhaps even better.

The neophyte Chinese cooks had a restricted catalog of ingredients to work with, so making more than just a semblance of their native cuisine became doubly difficult. Actually, Cantonese food, subtly flavored and possessing a storehouse of ingredients considered by many to be bland, or at least bland in the way Cantonese cooks treated them, was probably easier to knock off than other Chinese regional cuisines. So it was lucky the first Chinese cooks in the New World came from Guangdong; if they'd been from Sichuan, say, or Yunnan, their home diet might have been much harder to evoke, not to mention retrofit to the typical American meat-and-potatoes fare of the time. Like two compatible signs of the zodiac, Cantonese and American food seemed perfectly aligned, and fusion was the order of the day.

THE FIRST CHINESE-AMERICAN DISH

The menus created by the immigrant Cantonese cooks certainly included chop suey—the earliest known Chinese-American dish. The name means simply "assorted pieces"; the stir-fry probably consisted of tidbits of meat and sometimes egg cooked in a skillet with sprouts, cabbage, water chestnuts, and onions bound together with cornstarch, some of the vegetable ingredients undoubtedly canned, with no soy or fish sauce, no rice wine vinegar, and no other powerful flavors. Utilizing a shifting assortment of raw materials, the dish could accommodate what was at hand.

Chop suey could be seen as a Chinese spin on the American dish known as "hash." However, University of California ethnobiologist E. N. Anderson has found an antecedent for chop suey in the agricultural Taishan district of Guangdong. The dish, known as *tsap seui*, constitutes an impressively wide-ranging vegetable mélange using shrunken and small unsold vegetables, just as the fishermen of Marseille used the unsaleable fish in the bottom of the boat to make their world-famous bouillabaisse. As with bouillabaisse, both tsap seui and chop suey arose spontaneously as a way of cooking with scraps and whatever else was cheaply at hand.

In terms of the availability of familiar foodstuffs in a new country, I've seen worse situations for Chinese cooks. During a 2003 visit to Havana's Chinatown—which probably arose in midtown Havana soon after indentured cane cutters arrived on the island in the mid-19th century—I found Chinese restaurants making do mainly with pork skin and rice, substituting matchsticks of cabbage for sprouts, swatches of spinach for bok choy, and Swiss Maggi for soy sauce. Such is the creativity of Chinese restaurateurs on difficult terrain.

This same Chinese menu dating from Cuba in the 19th century was transferred to Chelsea and the Upper West Side of New York by refugees fleeing the Cuban Revolution in the 1960s. Mainly mixed race themselves and speaking only Spanish, they set up Cuban-Chinese restaurants that offered both cuisines on competing (and usually facing) pages. Most are now gone, or a similar menu is being made by Chinese cooks who never were in Cuba. Where once the Chinese side of the menu sucked and the Cuban side shone, now you're better off ordering the Cantonese food and leaving the pernil and asopao alone.

I recently visited old-timer Wo Hop, an ancient restaurant on the southernmost block of Mott Street in Manhattan's Chinatown. Dating to the 1930s, it is one of the few Chinese-American joints left in the neighborhood, and one of the only places that still serves chop suey. I ordered the chicken version in the well-lit basement dining room as blue-coated waiters looked on, approvingly it seemed, as if this is what I was destined to eat. As antique as the long plate of vegetables and shredded chicken in white goo tasted, it was also oddly contemporary, focusing as it did on vegetables, in this case celery, bamboo shoots, sprouts, and water chestnuts, quickly cooked and not denatured of their fundamental character, along with skinless boneless chicken. No wonder this sort of Chinese food, now rebranded as health food, persists in the frozen food case, mainly in the diet section.

The longer the Chinese stayed in California during the 19th century, the more ingredients came to be imported from China, so that seasonings like oyster sauce, soy sauce, rice wine vinegar, and dried and canned meat and seafood became part of the Chinese cook's arsenal. But still, Chinese-American food continued to be a mash-up of Eastern and Western culinary practices and ingredients—it always had to appeal to non-Asian diners who were increasingly the largest part of its audience.

Many of the Chinese who transformed themselves from gold miners to agricultural workers settled around Fresno or in the lush Sacramento River valley, where they were responsible for constructing a network of canals and levies, making the region strongly resemble the Louisiana bayou country. It still does, as I discovered during a 2011 trip to the area exploring the foods of the gold rush. There amid the hummocks and swampland I stumbled on Locke, founded in 1912 as an entirely Chinese town, after the Chinese ghetto in the nearby town of Walnut Grove burned down.

A plaque in Locke commemorates the effort expended by Chinese men that made the surrounding area fit for agriculture: "Chinese laborers by the thousands formed the backbone of the early manual labor force. From 1860 to 1880, manual laborers—most of them Chinese—reclaimed approximately 88,000 acres of rich delta land."

The town—consisting of only a handful of streets girt round with a wall of reeds and cattails—boasts some amazing frame architecture that looks like the set of a Western movie, only with Chinese elements thrown in. A former men's dormitory has been restored at the north end of town to serve as a historical center, and there are a few curio shops and two Cantonese restaurants serving the familiar menu set up to attract the stray tourist who visits this relatively remote place. The town currently has only 15 permanent residents where once there had been 1,500, and lots of abandoned houses and stores. It makes a very picturesque and interesting day trip from San Francisco.

HUNTING FOR HANGTOWN

But I didn't go to the Sacramento area to admire Locke. I was tracking down a largely forgotten dish known as Hangtown fry, a possible precursor of egg foo yong or maybe just a related dish, basically an omelet made with oysters. The name fascinated me, of course, but I was more interested in how it came to be that gold miners in landlocked eastern California ended up eating oysters in an omelet.

Tracking down Hangtown wasn't much trouble. A gazetteer in the Sacramento Public Library told me that the name had been conferred in 1849 on a mountain mining village not too far east of the city, previously known as Dry Diggings. Hangtown had been chosen because of the numerous hangings that occurred there, presumably the work of rival mining gangs rather than proactive investigations on the part of lawmen. The name was quickly supplanted by the more sober Placerville by 1850. I was overjoyed. What it meant was that the time of origin of Hangtown fry could probably be limited to a single year, or at least a short succession of years in which the colorful name Hangtown was still in use.

As I drove the twisting main street of the town, which tacked back and forth between foothills, I could almost see gun battles and other hubbubs arising on either side, with plug-ugly miners in pork-pie hats getting drunk on rotgut paid for by the meager strikes they'd made. I could see honky-tonks with tin-kly piano music blaring, and small shacks spewing smoke where food was cooked by Chinese men still sporting skullcaps, black pajamas, and pigtails.

On the eastern edge of town, I found a diner that still served Hangtown fry. It wasn't a tourist sort of place, being patronized mainly by local business people, farmers, truckers, and drifters. Chuck's Restaurant, there since 1964, occupied a concrete-block structure with a peaked gray roof, picture windows, a shaft of rusticated random stone plastered right in the middle of the façade, and a Jetsons-esque sign hoisted far above the establishment on a pole.

Chuck's advertised itself on the menu as a "Chinese and American restaurant" and mainly offered burgers and breakfasts, with a scattering of Chinese-American dishes. The Hangtown fry was featured not among the Chinese dishes, but among breakfasts. My heart fluttered waiting for it to arrive. A ravaged couple a few tables over seemed to be twitching in the throes of crack withdrawal.

The thing came sided with fried potatoes and had two strips of bacon perched awkwardly on top. It was constructed like an omelet, with the eggs constituting a sort of outer sleeve to a filling that was mainly diced green peppers, onions, and tomatoes. But then the first oyster, glistening black as a snail, tumbled out. A light bulb must have gone on over my head as I realized the oyster was canned. I'd already resolved that this was fundamentally a Chinese dish that had been back-constructed as more of a diner omelet, but one whose antecedent, maybe already looking like egg foo yong, had been invented by Chinese cooks in 1850 or soon thereafter.

Was it canned oysters, then, that the Chinese cooks originally used in this dish? Oysters were apparently canned on the California coast as early as the late 1840s and transported by wagon throughout the Western part of the United States. But there's also the possibility that the oysters used by Chinese cooks in the original Hangtown fry were dried ones. Either way, it was a revelation to me in 2011 that canned oysters were still a popular product in the diners of this dilapidated mining town, and they were still being used to make an omelet probably invented by Chinese cooks.

In New York, I'd eaten oyster omelets in Fujianese and Taiwanese restaurants. They are quite different from everything else on the menus, where food is more often decimated into little morsels fit for chopsticks. Like egg foo yong and Hangtown fry, these East Asian omelets seemed to have been invented for the fork. The normal supposition is that these oyster omelets inspired Hangtown fry and maybe egg foo yong. But what if the truth is the other way around: perhaps Hangtown fry or egg foo yong traveled back to China in the mid-1800s along with disappointed miners returning to their homeland. The idea of American dishes inspiring ones back in China 150 years ago is intriguing. Certainly, such a thing happens all the time in the modern era. Just look at the preponderance of pastry-wrapped hot dogs in Hong Kong bakeries, both in New York City and in China.

In fact, in 2013, the first Chinese-American restaurant opened in Shanghai, serving egg rolls, fried rice, tofu chop suey, shrimp toast, and, yes, General Tso's chicken, as reported by the *Canadian Globe and Mail*. According to owner Fung Lam, "There's 23 million people in this city, at least 1,000 pizzerias, every variation of burger that you could think of, a hot dog shop in front of bars—and you're telling me there's not one American Chinese food restaurant? . . . Dude, why don't we just do that?"

Just as the oyster omelet may have gone back to China, egg foo yong persevered further into the heartland of America borne by a second wave of Chinese immigrants, also mainly from Guangdong. As I write this, Chuck's is sadly closed. It was the last place in Placerville that served the Hangtown fry.

THE GOLDEN SPIKE

The first wave of Chinese immigration lasted from 1849 until 1858, corresponding to the gold rush, and it boosted California's population by an estimated 100,000. The second wave of Chinese immigration was motivated not by gold but by the declining economy of southeastern China at the time and the Taiping Rebellion, a massive civil war that engulfed much of southern China.

From 1864 till 1869, the First Transcontinental Railroad was constructed over mountains and through deserts from Oakland to Omaha, a distance of roughly 1,900 miles. Many of the workers were indentured servants from China, paid $30 per month minus their food and lodging, such as it was. The Chinese worked alongside a few African-Americans hired under similar dismal circumstances (remember, the American Civil War was ongoing at the start of this period), and most of the supervisors and technical advisers were reportedly Irish. A document from 1865 shows 3,000 Chinese and 1,700 white workers were employed by the Central Pacific Railroad, which was building the part of the route that originated in Oakland, but was eventually extended westward to San Francisco.

Though some of the Chinese rail workers (who were generally referred to as "Celestials") were undoubtedly former gold miners, the vast majority were recruited directly from China and supervised by other Chinese who had been in America longer and spoke some English. According to the PBS special *Transcontinental Railroad* (2003), Chinese workers were organized into gangs of 30 or 40, and each gang had its own cook. The cooks sourced dried foods from San Francisco and Sacramento, purchased fresh vegetables where they could, and kept live chickens and pigs in the camps, as the Chinese railway workers gradually worked their way eastward, digging and blasting, building tunnels and trestles, and generally doing back-breaking work with little complaint.

The mess tents of these labor camps were undoubtedly crucibles for the invention of early Chinese-American dishes; they certainly established a pattern of making meals out of less expensive ingredients sourced in America, and simpler preparation techniques suited not to the grandiose banquets that were the apex of cooking back in southern China, but to immigrant laborers squatting in the dirt, relishing food that reminded them of home, however faintly. The Chinese drank tea, boiled in the morning and then consumed all day long, which kept them from getting dysentery, while the Irish ate only boiled meat and potatoes and drank whiskey. Resentments between the groups quickly began to smolder.

The new Chinese-Americans who worked on the railroad have been ably represented in books and in cinema. My own favorite evocation of the era came from the television series *Bonanza* (1959 to 1973). The time period depicted was 1861 to 1867. The Cartwright family, who lived on a thousand-square-mile ranch in Nevada, had a Chinese cook named Hop Sing, who wore a black silk jacket and kept his long hair in a pigtail. In the TV show, discussions of important events among the father and his three sons took place around the dinner table, and my brothers and I would crowd around the black-and-white TV, straining to see what the family was eating. One day in the early 1960s, we had a discussion about what food a Chinese guy would cook for a family of friendly gunslingers. "It must have been chop suey and egg foo yong," my brothers and I concluded. We were probably right.

Despite all the false tropes of the TV Western, the series turned out to be fairly accurate in terms of the position of Chinese-Americans in the post–Civil War era: they indeed were moving eastward, and they carried their newly synthesized food with them, eventually landing in every town across the land, and from there into our own culinary hearts.

But as far as Chinese immigration goes, it was halted by a series of four acts passed by Congress starting in 1882. Few Chinese, men or women, would be arriving for 80 more years, and even then under severe restrictions, which included obtaining certificates from the Chinese government attesting that they were not laborers, a hurdle that proved exceedingly hard to overcome. The measures were rescinded by the Magnuson Act of 1943, but it would be decades before Chinese immigration recovered and returned to pre-1882 levels.

CHINESE-AMERICAN CUISINE IN NEW YORK

When was the heyday of Chinese-American food in New York? Though there were two Chinese restaurants in Manhattan's Chinatown as early as 1884, as reported by Andrew Coe in *Chop Suey: A Cultural History of Chinese Food in the United States* (2009), using exotic vegetables that had been grown in Westchester by Chinese farmers, it took many decades for the food to spread to random residential neighborhoods across the city. The embargo on Chinese immigration and anti-Chinese racism certainly provided deterrents to the more rapid spread of Chinese restaurants, but once outsiders had a taste of the salty and enthrallingly greasy Chinese-American fare, they were hooked.

Early in the 20th century, Chinese food had begun to slip its bounds in Chinatown and appear in commercial Manhattan neighborhoods where there were theaters, bars, and other sorts of tumultuous nightlife. Times Square was a place where one could get a plate of chop suey, chow mein, or egg foo yong, and so was the Bowery, a nightlife area in the blocks north and east of the four streets of Chinatown proper. There was indeed something raffish about eating Chinese food, the perfect complement to an evening of clubbing or theater going. Coe reports that there were 14 Chinese restaurants along Broadway north of Times Square in 1924, and many also served as dance halls—an entire entertainment package in one spot. The predominant music was big band jazz.

But it wasn't until after World War II that Chinese restaurants began to appear outside commercial neighborhoods in all five boroughs as the quintessential carry-out food for a new generation. Certainly, women who'd joined the workforce while the men were away at war continued to work as the men returned home, and Chinese takeout became a key part of making the family with two working parents a success. Many men returned with a new appreciation for foreign food, and Asian food in particular after stints in the Pacific theater of war, and suddenly the Chinese seemed like allies rather than aliens. Chinese restaurateurs had honed their skills at providing just the kind of food needed at the moment, somewhat exotic but also fairly nonchallenging.

Jews in Brooklyn were one group that particularly relished Chinese food. Not only because it tended not to mix dairy and meat, somewhat paralleling their own traditional diet, but because it provided a respite from the traditional foods of immigrant parents. By the 1950s, Chinese restaurants were common in Flatbush, and Barbra Streisand worked in one when she attended Erasmus Hall High School. Of Chinese restaurants in Brooklyn in the 1960s, Peter Cherches writes enthusiastically in his blog, *Word of Mouth*: "The restaurant we mostly patronized was Joy Fong, on Avenue J, a now-defunct place that retains an almost holy status in the memories of Brooklyn Jews of a certain age. I wouldn't be surprised if people visit the site of the former restaurant and wail against the wall."

By the 1960s, there were even kosher restaurants that served Chinese food, sometimes as part of a larger menu that also included Eastern European and even Sephardic Jewish specialties, too. In all five boroughs, the 1950s through the 1970s represented the high-water mark of Chinese-American food, an era when you could get egg foo yong in nearly every neighborhood, in every one of the city's boroughs. Sadly, that ubiquity is no longer the case.

CHINESE-AMERICAN FOOD TODAY

When a cuisine stops creating new dishes out of both internal needs and outside influences, it has effectively died and become a museum piece. Such is the case with Chinese-American food, whose canon of dishes has essentially stopped growing. While the handful of Chinese-American restaurants in the city's five Chinatowns and elsewhere in New York have expanded their menus, it has been exclusively with dishes from Chinese regional cuisines, or by adding faddish Thai and Japanese dishes. Chinese restaurants making bad sushi are part of this movement. But these dishes have not expanded the actual Cantonese-American menu in any way, shape, or form.

Chinese-American restaurants are, in many ways, the victims of their own success. They ushered in an era in which Americans became interested, even obsessed, with immigrant cuisines. The new internationalism represented by relaxed immigration laws in the '60s and '70s meant that the immigrant population of the U.S. not only increased but diversified as well. When I wrote the first edition of my guidebook *Good and Cheap Ethnic Eats in New York City* (1994), I was able to uncover restaurants representing 33 ethnic cuisines in the metropolis; by the 2004 edition of the book (titled *The Food Lover's Guide to the Best Ethnic Eating in New York City*), I'd counted 145. Why go to a too-familiar Chinese-American restaurant when there are so many other cuisines to explore?

Chinese-American restaurateurs themselves seemed ready to abandon the canon. In the early '90s, a Chinese couple relocated from Mexico City to New York and brought with them a tortilla-making machine. While they might have traditionally opened a chop suey parlor serving typical Chinese-American fare, they started instead the Fresco Tortilla Grill chain with a single store at 36 Lexington Avenue, which featured mainly stewed meats cooked in a quasi-Mexican style, served in Tex-Mex fashion on freshly made flour tortillas with lots of guacamole. The empire expanded, imitators sprang up, and now the city has an estimated 200 such establishments, competing in the same neighborhoods and in the identical price range with traditional Chinese restaurants.

Meanwhile, during the same period, Chinese-American restaurateurs were adapting to a changing dining climate by filling Latin American niches. Specifically, their establishments began serving french fries and fried chicken to a predominantly Puerto Rican and Dominican customer base. Cooked in woks, the heavily crusted bird was quite good, and these restaurants were soon underselling African-American–, Puerto Rican–, and Dominican-owned dining establishments, and even franchise restaurants like KFC that produced nearly the same commodity. Other Chinese restaurant owners broke camp and started serving more popular (and higher priced) Thai and Vietnamese fare, since both their ingredients and equipment could be adapted to do so, and they found they could charge a few dollars more per dish for this food in most city neighborhoods.

But what might have been the death blow to Chinese-American food was the appearance of all sorts of regional Chinese fare, prepared by a newer wave of immigrants from Xi'an, Sichuan, Hunan, Yunnan, Tianjin, Taiwan, Qingdao, Dongbei, Shanghai, Hong Kong, and Beijing itself, who re-created dishes of their home regions. Often these were demonstrably spicier, more nuanced, and generally more culinarily exciting than the fare of the old Chinese neighborhood restaurants. These new, increasingly popular regional cuisines also depended on a vaster palette of imported Chinese ingredients newly available at the hulking Hong Kong–style supermarkets starting to dot the landscape of the five boroughs—many not even in the city's traditional Chinatowns. It all started with the first Sichuan restaurants in the city in the '70s, mainly on the Upper West Side.

But is Chinese-American food dead? Well, it's harder to find, and slightly more expensive, and you may have to wade through a morass of sushi and Thai dishes to find the real stuff. But it's still worth seeking out as one of the pillars of New York vernacular dining throughout the 20th century, worth experiencing, not only as an antique cuisine, but for its inherent deliciousness. And I recommend that you begin with a white carton of shrimp egg foo yong.

SIX PLACES TO GET EGG FOO YONG

1. GOLDEN WOKS

159 CHRISTOPHER STREET, MANHATTAN, 212-463-8182

This is one of the few classic Chinese–American restaurants left in Greenwich Village and my go-to spot for egg foo yong. For an extra thrill, sit in the tiny dining room with a view of the kitchen, in which two or three cooks gyrate before their flaming woks.

2. GENTING PALACE

RESORTS WORLD CASINO, 110-00 ROCKAWAY BOULEVARD, QUEENS, 718-215-2828

In the opulent casino attached to the hardscrabble Aqueduct Racetrack in Ozone Park lurks a spectacular Chinese restaurant. It's upscale, for sure, with amazing dim sum, but still venerates the Chinese–American classics. The egg foo yong comes in a rather effete demi-glace, but it's still acres of fried brown goodness.

3. KING YUM

181-08 UNION TURNPIKE, QUEENS, 718-380-1918

This Fresh Meadows old-timer serves up good versions of Chinese–American classics, with a crazy Polynesian flair appropriate to its 1953 founding date. Expect little umbrellas in the mixed drinks.

4. WO HOP

17 MOTT STREET, MANHATTAN, 212-962-8617

Opened in 1938, this may be Chinatown's oldest continuously operating Chinese–American restaurant, and not even serving General Tso's chicken. Most dishes are made without soy sauce (too radical a flavor?), and you can tell the diners are really into this extremely old-fashioned cuisine.

5. HOP KEE

21 MOTT STREET, MANHATTAN, 212-964-8365

Of about the same vintage as Wo Hop; aficionados argue continuously over which place is better. Both serve outstanding egg foo yong. The arcade

*across the street used to house the famous Dancing Chicken, now long
banished by animal welfare activists.*

6. KING FOOD CHEN

489 AMSTERDAM AVENUE, MANHATTAN, 212-787-1888

*This Upper West Side mainstay is one of the few typical Chinese carry-outs
left in a neighborhood where most places of this sort have been transformed
into more upscale culinary uses. I once proclaimed their egg foo yong the
best in the city.*

EGG FOO YONG

SERVES 4 TO 6

*As Cantonese carry-outs have disappeared,
this historic Chinese-American recipe has
become something of an endangered culinary
species—someday, you may have no choice
but to make it yourself.*

FOR THE SAUCE AND GARNISH:

2 cups chicken stock

2 teaspoons sugar

3 tablespoons soy sauce

2 tablespoons dry sherry

1 tablespoon oyster sauce

2 tablespoons cornstarch, mixed with 2 tablespoons
   of the stock to form a slurry

1 garlic clove, smashed

$\frac{1}{2}$-inch piece fresh ginger, peeled and thinly sliced

4 scallions, thinly sliced, for garnish

FOR THE OMELETS:

6 eggs
2 tablespoons cornstarch
3 tablespoons soy sauce
1 tablespoon rice wine vinegar
1 teaspoon dry sherry
1 teaspoon sesame oil
1 teaspoon kosher salt
1 carrot, shredded
6 ounces shrimp, peeled, deveined, and finely chopped
$\frac{3}{4}$ cup water chestnuts, drained, finely chopped,
  and squeezed dry
$\frac{1}{3}$ cup bean sprouts
1 cup sliced scallions
$\frac{1}{3}$ cup vegetable oil

1. First make the sauce. In a small saucepan, combine the stock, sugar, soy sauce, sherry, and oyster sauce and bring to a boil. Whisk in the cornstarch slurry, garlic, and ginger. Bring the sauce back to a simmer and cook until it thickens. At this point, strain the sauce through a fine-mesh sieve, return it to the pot, and keep warm.

2. Make the omelets. In a medium bowl, whisk the eggs and cornstarch together until homogenous. Add in all of the remaining ingredients except the vegetable oil, and mix well to combine. Heat half of the oil in a large sauté pan over medium-high heat.

3. When the oil is hot, use a ladle or measuring cup to pour ⅓-cup amounts of the mixture into the pan. Fry the omelets in batches, flipping once, until they are puffed and brown, 1½ to 2 minutes for each side. Transfer to paper towels to drain. Keep cooking in batches until all of the mixture is used up, replenishing the oil in the pan halfway through. Serve the omelets over rice with the sauce poured on top and thinly sliced scallions sprinkled over everything.

CLAM CHOWDER

A bowlful of red, a bowlful of white
It all depends on your appetite.

So Billy Joel might have sung in his 1977 hit "Scenes from an Italian Restaurant" had he been crooning about chowder and not cheap wine. Except if we happened to be in an Italian restaurant like the one he describes, there probably wouldn't be a choice of chowders. You'd have to settle for red—a phenomenon which will be explained shortly.

I didn't taste chowder until long after I'd reached my 20th birthday, on a trip to Boston to visit my future wife, Gretchen, before we moved together to New York City. Chowder was unknown to me growing up in the Midwest and later in central Texas. It was never on a menu, never served on the University of Texas lunch line, never offered or even mentioned by the Houstonians or New Orleanians with whom I became acquainted at college. Chowders are a form of regional cuisine mainly limited to the northern portion of America's Atlantic Seaboard. And the creamy variety, known as New England clam chowder, is a signature of what is sometimes called Yankee cuisine.

It must have been 1976. Gretchen was living in Brookline, a gritty suburb of Boston that sounded suspiciously like *Brooklyn*. In the morning we'd wake up and go to a bakery that sold all sorts of Viennese and Eastern European breads and pastries, where the counter gal sported poofed-up hair dyed blonde and displayed a forearm revealing a concentration camp tattoo. Yes, the neighborhood was exceedingly Jewish and still contained Holocaust survivors. This shook me up, though I'd grown up in the Jewish and Protestant suburbs of Minneapolis. In those days, no one mentioned religion; it was considered a very private affair.

One day at lunch, we headed downtown to Faneuil Hall, a structure that had been a marketplace and meeting hall since 1742, housed in an impressive four-story brick building with a peaked roof and white tower on top. The Midwest simply didn't have buildings of that antiquity. But our destination wasn't the Freedom Trail, or the market itself—one of the world's worst tourist traps—but a restaurant implanted in the side of the market that dated to 1827. Gretchen had not only heard about Durgin-Park, where lines to get in ran around the building and across the cobblestones of the square, but had learned how Boston natives circumvented the long wait. I was impressed at her restaurant-investigating prowess.

Following her friend's instructions, we entered a barroom around the corner, ordered a beer, and then carried it with us up a back stairway to the restaurant, where we were seated immediately. The place was wood-clad and cavernous, and steam proceeded in a cloud from the bustling kitchen. The air was moist and briny. Soon, a gruff waitress approached in a starched white uniform, only slightly stained here and there. She threw down a menu that was byzantine in its length and complexity.

This was before the days of Google and Yelp, so we were out to sea as far as what to order. I remember musing over the menu, the highlights of which included potted beef, Indian pudding, fishcakes, chicken livers sautéed with bacon, baked Boston scrod (which the menu spelled "schrod"), a corned beef sandwich, chicken pot pie, something called "poor man's roast beef," Ipswich clam roll, shrimp cocktail, oysters and clams in a bewildering array of presentations both raw and not, roast prime rib, and corned beef and cabbage (a dish I later discovered was invented in the United States, courtesy of Hasia Diner's

1991 *Hungering for America: Italian, Irish, and Jewish Foodways in the Age of Migration*).

We feasted that day, exposed to Yankee cooking for the first time and realizing it was as spice poor as the food we'd grown up with in the Midwest, the flavors owing mainly to onions, butter, and the salty taste of the ocean. Even then we instinctively picked out the things we sensed were locally sourced. We had a big plank of broiled scrod basted in butter, promising we'd tell our pals back in the Midwest, "We got scrod in Boston," emulating our waitress's thick Massachusetts accent. We also marveled at the Indian pudding—the first Native American dish either of us had knowingly tried, a soft brown mass tasting of cornmeal and blackstrap molasses. It wasn't pure Native American, of course, but a mash-up of Indian and English cuisines.

We were frankly frightened of the raw oysters, audible all around us as the shucked bivalves and ice rattled on great aluminum trays held aloft as they were carried across the room. We didn't learn to love them until years later. One section of the menu, though, particularly caught our eyes. The list of chowders was short, but prominently positioned: a choice of clam or fish. No geographic designation, like New England or Manhattan, just clam or fish. We ordered a bowl of fish chowder, since we were as uncertain of the clams—never having tried them—as we were of the oysters.

When it arrived, the thick soup (or was it a stew?) sloshed at the sides of the shallow bowl. Indistinguishable under their cozy blanket of cream, tiny nuggets of potato and scrod bobbed lethargically. But one taste engendered a permanent addiction. First, the cream coats your tongue; next the fish (scrod, I later learned, is simply a diminutive cod) gently caresses your taste buds; and third, the bacon emerges as a strong concluding note. Then the flavors meld together magnificently as the soup splashes around in your mouth, so mellow you don't want to swallow. Fish chowder is an essay in mellowness—all sunshine, beaches, and rolling waves.

Years later, sitting at the undulant counter of the Oyster Bar in Grand Central Terminal, I learned to love white chowder all over again, in this case made with clams rather than scrod. Clam chowder takes the same recipe, introduces a darker and more bitter note, and provides a nice chew at the conclusion. Fish chowder is for the gastronomically timid; clam chowder is for the more adventuresome.

THE ORIGIN OF NEW ENGLAND CLAM CHOWDER

The category of soups called *chowders* is one of startling specificity. The word comes down to us from the French *chaudière*, which means a kettle or cauldron, or the contents thereof, just as we might say something cooked in a casserole is a casserole. A *Webster's New Collegiate Dictionary* my parents gave me as a child, now falling apart and extensively taped, goes further: "a thick soup or stew of seafood . . . usually made with milk, salt pork or bacon, onions and other vegetables (as potatoes)," offering not only a definition of the dish, but what amounts to a complete recipe. *Webster's* goes on to add a secondary definition, somewhat elliptically: "a soup resembling chowder." I guess the best example of that would be corn chowder, which contains no seafood.

In probing its origins, I first turned to the landmark Time Life *Foods of the World* series, published between the late '60s and early '70s. Out of its 27 volumes, 26 gather dust on my shelves. In one way, the web has made them obsolete, and especially these days I find the books riddled with mistakes middle-class white Americans might make when examining the foods of other ethnicities. But still, given the time they were written, the volumes are surprisingly authoritative and supremely lively, with astonishing pictures. (The one I'm missing: *American Cooking: The Great West.*)

Written by Jonathan Norton Leonard, with consultancy by James Beard, *American Cooking: New England* offers one of the most comprehensive views of the cuisine sometimes known as Yankee and sometimes as Down East, though the latter is usually used more narrowly to describe the cooking of Maine, New Hampshire, and Vermont. In it, Leonard traces the development of white chowders to the arrival of cows in the New World: "Fish chowder is another plain, lightly seasoned way of cooking fish. It is popular from Connecticut to Newfoundland and probably dates from the time when the first cows in the colonies provided the milk that is its essential ingredient."

He goes on to describe several variations on white chowder, recounting how his mother cut the potatoes in little wedges so the sharp side of the wedge disintegrated to provide thickening, and how some savvy cooks poach a whole fish so the skin and bones provide extra flavor, though he notes of this method, with maybe just a hint of the paranoia common in the '60s, "The eyes do no harm, but even when boiled they have a reproachful look." He also suggests, in his pre-fat-phobic age, that strips of salt pork be fried along with the onions that go into the chowder and then served alongside as finger food. The guy is simply brilliant, and other hints that might be utilized by today's chefs lurk within the pages of this volume.

So, "cow arrives, chowder appears"—was the story that simple? Probably not. The immediate origin also might be a Breton stew known as *chaudrée*—a word also inspired, like chowder, by the same cooking pot mentioned above—which was adopted by the English in the early 18th century, and from thence transported to New England. To further contradict the Time Life theory, the original fish chowder on these shores was apparently thickened with crackers and not milk, so cows were not necessary to its first concoction. A recipe in *American Cookery* by Amelia Simmons (1796) offers a chowder thickened with a dozen crackers that had previously been soaked in saltwater. If nothing else, the cracker-thickened version, which may have started out as a shipboard staple, also explains the lingering presence of crackers alongside modern bowls of chowder—the thickener became so associated with the soup that crackers made the transition from ingredient to accompaniment.

Richard J. Hooker, in his authoritative work *Food and Drink in America* (1981), maintains that Breton fishermen carried the dish to Newfoundland and coastal upper New England sometime in the 18th century, which suggests why the soup remains geographically localized: you needed bland fish to poach in soup, and that kind of fish—cod especially—was for centuries the stock-in-trade of the New England fishing industry. In other words, fish chowder as we know it is unthinkable with strongly flavored fish such as mackerel, salmon, or even the bluefish native to New York waters that is still caught today in fleets that sail from Sheepshead Bay, Brooklyn.

More surprisingly, Hooker highlights unusual chowder variations seen through the years. By 1801, chowder was appearing more frequently in cookbooks, with flavorings that sometimes included apple cider, lemon, curry powder, and ketchup. The latter is featured historically in the related class of Yankee seafood soups called, somewhat quizzically, pan roasts. At the Grand Central Oyster Bar, these roasts are soups consisting primarily of half-and-half and seafood, served from a special metal steaming contraption right at the oyster counter itself, operated with a hand lever. Using fresh oysters but no potatoes, the result is pink and insanely fresh tasting, but falls short of being actual chowder. Chowders benefit from steeping a while, while pan roasts—which can feature other kinds of delicate seafood than oysters, such as shrimp and lobster—must be eaten immediately.

So fish and clam chowders, whether thickened with crackers, potatoes, milk, or cream, seasoned with onions and bacon or fatback, and served with crackers or without, became one of my favorite dishes. Even more so for the American history they represent, the legacy of sea travel and association with the northeastern part of the United States, which, I never suspected as I sipped that first bowl of chowder at Durgin-Park, was to be my permanent home, though I would remain a midwesterner and Texas expat forever.

BOWLFUL OF RED

Hooker is clearly hyped on white clam chowder and makes no mention of red. Indeed, many writers speak of white, adopting a sentimental and sometimes even jingoistic tone about its historic origins. Hooker's only foray into pinkness finds him pointing out in a side note that chowders from the Mid-Atlantic states sometimes, like oyster pan roasts, contain ketchup as a flavoring. Yet, when I arrived in Manhattan in 1977, something called Manhattan clam chowder was a prominent feature of the menus still in place in many of the old-guard restaurants.

It is nearly impossible to imagine what the restaurant scene in Manhattan was like 40 years ago if you have only experienced the city in more recent decades. In my own East Village neighborhood, few places were open past six o'clock. Most cafés then catered to breakfast and lunch eaters who worked in the neighborhood. Ukrainian and Polish restaurants dominated the scene, with an undercurrent of old Italian places (of which John's of East 12th Street and Veniero's still remain), mainly red-sauced restaurants arrayed along First and Second Avenues, rumored to be owned by one of the city's six organized crime families. There were also a few Puerto Rican cafés in what came to be known as Alphabet City.

A typical restaurant meal would be at a Polish lunch counter, where potatoes, goulash, sauerkraut, and pierogis were ladled from vertical steam tables that looked like chests of metal drawers. An entire meal, sometimes including soup, would set you back three or four dollars. And, as I mention in a separate chapter, there were pizza parlors dispensing slices and subs.

Also dotted all over the city were antediluvian Irish bars with names like Blarney Stone, Blarney Castle, McGovern's, and McAnn's, which had fragrant steam tables containing corned beef and beef stew, baked ham, and other meat-driven meals to be downed at lunch with a lager or two. Then there were the upscale French and Italian restaurants, and a slew of mid- to upscale spots serving a plain menu of what was considered

American food. Most of these places have been swept away by what I've called the Age of Foodism, a time when the search for novelty and invention in our meals rendered most of our previous restaurant diet null and void. Ask yourself: When was the last time I ordered a liverwurst sandwich? A plain omelet? A bowl of Manhattan clam chowder?

I mention the last one because, in 1979, it was a staple of New York City restaurants. Looking through the book *Manhattan Menus* (1978)—which was basically a restaurant guide that presented quasi-facsimile menus along with further information and a graphic or two, with most restaurants probably having paid to be included—I find about a sixth of the restaurants serving either "American" or "Continental" cuisine. The latter term, now long out of use, still cracks me up. To everyone dining out, it must have been obvious which continent they were referring to: Europe. Now there would be no such consensus.

I find a soup listed merely as "clam chowder" at the Blue Mill Tavern, a Portuguese place on Commerce Street in the West Village; and the same nomenclature at Daly's Dandelion, a hamburger joint on the east side that served it only on Fridays, in a nod to the Catholic practice of eschewing meat on that day; at Gage and Tollner, a landmark downtown Brooklyn restaurant whose demise in 2004 was one of the city's great culinary tragedies, where the seafood-potage-heavy menu also featured soft clam soup, clam broth, fish chowder, soft clam bisque, lobster bisque, clam bisque, oyster bisque, and shrimp bisque; at the King's Wharf on Central Park South, where seafood and steaks constituted the entire bill of fare; and at the Lucchese House of Seafood in Staten Island.

Why do I surmise it was Manhattan and not New England clam chowder if the listings contained no designation? I distinctly remember eating it with some frequency in the '80s throughout the city, and it was invariably the red variety. When you encountered New England chowder, it was in a Yankee-type seafood spot, like the Grand Central Oyster Bar or Durgin-Park: nearly every city on the upper East Coast had at least one.

The only soups more popular than red clam chowder on Manhattan menus of the day were French onion soup (understandable, given the primacy of upscale French restaurants and their midpriced bistro counterparts; Italian restaurants were far less prevalent) and gazpacho, which enjoyed a burst of popularity that saw recipes reproduced in women's magazines around 1980, but pretty much disappeared by 2000. Now the modern tapas bar has brought it back.

These clam chowders were lively affairs of tomato paste, garlic, and minced clams that fairly danced with a cornucopia of diced vegetables. The flavors were a marching band of brightness, as opposed to the staid string quartet of New England clam chowder, which seemed to kowtow to Yankee sternness. Nevertheless, in my still-conservative tastes, I preferred New England–style and sought it out. While, as first a picture editor and later a secretary hired out by the day, my dining budget was limited, early on I realized that eating out was one of the greatest activities the city had to offer.

But where did Manhattan clam chowder come from, so diametrically opposite to the New England variety? By the late '80s, as I began to write about food and compare different cuisines, I realized there was something Italian about it, more specifically Sicilian and Genoese. It was so much like the tomato-laced cioppino of San Francisco (a meal-size soup of Genoese origin) and the Sicilian seafood stews (served with ship's biscuits rather than bread or rice) I was to encounter in the Bronx's Belmont neighborhood, often known simply as Arthur Avenue.

The Oxford Companion to American Food and Drink partially confirms that impression, noting that the first recipe for Manhattan clam chowder appeared in Virginia Elliott and Robert Jones's *Soups and Sauces* in 1934. (The same volume traces New England clam chowder to a 1751 recipe.) There were two great waves of Sicilian immigration to New York City, the first around 1900, the second 50 years later, and the 1934 date is consistent with dishes from that first migration finally making their way into the mainstream.

James Beard sides on the Italian origin of red clam chowder in *Beard on Food* (1974), while also partly reviling the red variety, going so far as to suggest that Manhattan clam chowder isn't really a chowder at all: "One of the most famous of the dishes considered to be all-American is clam chowder. . . . Then we have Manhattan clam chowder, considered by many to be a 'bastard' chowder. Certainly it must have had a Mediterranean base, because it includes tomatoes and is redolent of herbs that scream Italy or Greece, while the flavor, texture and quality are entirely different."

In the 1964 edition of *Joy of Cooking*, the Rombauers at least partly agree with Beard. They list a complete recipe for Manhattan clam chowder first, acknowledging its primacy in their circles and in their age, featuring diced tomatoes, green peppers, bay leaf, salt pork or bacon, canned tomatoes, and tomato ketchup. It sounds awful. Oddly, the recipe for New England clam chowder appears second and is written as a variation of the Manhattan recipe, simply indicating which ingredients are to be omitted. They preface the New England version by referring to the Manhattan recipe with words similar to James Beard's: "Most New Englanders consider the above recipe an illegitimate child." Pointedly, the mother and daughter were from Saint Louis, Missouri, and their mild contempt for New Englanders is palpable. Or am I reading too much into a tossed-off line?

Bastard or not, Manhattan clam chowder was firmly implanted in New York City by the 1980s. And it's still found, mainly in out-of-the-way places like the Georgia Diner on Queens Boulevard in Elmhurst; Corato Pizza in Ridgewood, Queens; the Lobster Smack in Greenwich Village (since closed); and the Red Lobster at Times Square. Still, something about it makes me think of Brooklyn, as if the dominant borough of Manhattan had fallen in love with the soup and swiped it. Manhattan has always afforded primacy to oysters where bivalves are concerned, as evidenced by the raw-oyster bars that were a prominent feature of 19th-century Manhattan dining, as described by Luc Sante in *Low Life* (1991). Brooklyn, by contrast, has had a raging love affair with the clam going back to the earliest days.

In the 1630s, when the first Dutch settlers started poking around in the swamps between Carroll Gardens and Park Slope in what is now Brooklyn with an eye toward turning it into agricultural land, they found Native Americans pulling clams from the Gowanee ("Leader") Creek. Eventually, it and the complex of waterways known by the English as Mill Creek would be dredged and consolidated into the Gowanus Canal, the new spelling reflecting the Dutch version of the name.

By the 19th century, the shores and beaches of Brooklyn were loaded with clam shacks and carts selling raw clams. It seems the borough's residents couldn't get enough of them. By the early 20th century, Sheepshead Bay was clam central, with perhaps a dozen clam shacks—many teetering on stilts—lining the waterway. One founded in 1907 gave rise to Lundy's, a seafood palace that lay claim to being the largest restaurant in the world, seating as many as 2,800 at one time. (By contrast, the largest restaurant in New York City today is Jing Fong on Elizabeth Street, seating 1,600.) Another clam shack on Sheepshead Bay, and the only one that remains from that era, is Randazzo's Clam Bar, where fried clams, raw clams, chowders, and rolls are still sold.

Indeed, the best place to get Manhattan clam chowder in the city is Randazzo's. Late into the night, the place presents a lively scene for the bivalve obsessed, and there's a bowl of red chowder on nearly every table, served with oyster crackers in little cellophane packets. Float the crackers for extra thickness and some crunch. But even Randazzo's is not immune to the white: It also serves New England clam chowder, and corn chowder, too. If you consider that a chowder.

SIX PLACES TO GET GREAT CLAM CHOWDER

1. GRAND CENTRAL OYSTER BAR

GRAND CENTRAL TERMINAL, 89 EAST 42ND STREET,
MANHATTAN, 212-490-6650

Get red or white by the bowl (why not try both?) while sitting at the iconic snaking lunch counter, or in the barroom, or even right at the oyster counter, where you can also see pan roasts being made to order.

2. PEARL OYSTER BAR

18 CORNELIA STREET, MANHATTAN, 212-691-8211

New England clam chowder only at this delightful Greenwich Village seafood café.

3. AQUAGRILL

210 SPRING STREET, MANHATTAN, 212-274-0505

Red only at this seafood spot known for its inventive dishes and pristinely fresh seafood.

4. RANDAZZO'S CLAM BAR

2017 EMMONS AVENUE, BROOKLYN, 718-615-0010

Enjoy waterfront views and see the sport fishing fleet come in at this ancient Sheepshead Bay institution, where red and white share equal status, but red is preferred by most diners.

5. LITTLENECK

288 THIRD AVENUE, BROOKLYN, 718-522-1921

Close by the Gowanus Canal, where Native Americans once dredged clams, this hipster spot somewhat ironically, given the possible Brooklyn origin of red clam chowder, only serves white.

6. UMBERTO'S CLAM HOUSE

132 MULBERRY STREET, MANHATTAN, 212-431-7545

Steeped in mob history, this Little Italy restaurant evenhandedly serves both red and white, though the red is preferred (by me, at least).

NEW ENGLAND CLAM CHOWDER
SERVES 4 TO 6

This mellow soup is the perfect winter warmer and the centerpiece of New England Yankee cuisine.

2 pounds cherrystone or littleneck clams (or 1 pound frozen chopped clams)

5 ounces bacon, cut into lardons

3 tablespoons butter

1 large white onion, chopped

$1\frac{1}{2}$ teaspoons freshly ground black pepper

2 bay leaves

2 stalks celery, chopped

1 cup bottled clam juice

$1\frac{1}{2}$ pounds russet potatoes, peeled and diced

4 cups milk

$\frac{1}{2}$ cup cream

Salt

1. If you are using fresh clams, rinse them in cold water. Heat 1 cup water in a medium saucepan over medium-high heat. Once it is boiling, add the fresh clams, cover tightly, and steam, shaking the pot occasionally. After 5 minutes, remove any clams that have opened and reserve. After 10 minutes, remove the remaining clams and discard any that have not opened.

2. Strain the cooking liquid through a fine-mesh sieve lined with cheesecloth and reserve. Pull the clams from their shells, roughly chop, and combine them with the cooking liquid. Refrigerate until ready to use (this step can be done a day ahead). If using frozen chopped clams, simply thaw them in the refrigerator overnight.

3. Rinse out the pot and set it over medium-low heat. Add the lardons and cook until they are crispy and golden on all sides, about 10 minutes, then remove with a slotted spoon and reserve. Add the butter, onion, black pepper, and bay leaves to the bacon fat. Raise the heat to medium and cook until the onion is soft, 5 to 8 minutes. Add the celery, clam juice, potatoes, and milk. Simmer until the potatoes are just tender.

4. In the sink, set a colander or strainer over a large pot. Carefully pour the soup into the colander, catching all of the solid bits and letting the liquid drain into the pot. Discard the bay leaves. Scoop out ½ cup of cooked potato and add it to a blender along with 1 cup of the liquid. Holding a kitchen towel over the lid to prevent the hot liquid from flying everywhere, blend the mixture until smooth. Return this to the pot and add the solids, the clams and their liquid, and the cream. Bring the soup to a bare simmer, check the seasoning, and add salt or more pepper if needed. Serve immediately.

MANHATTAN CLAM CHOWDER
SERVES 4 TO 6

Taming the bitterness of clams with the sweetness of tomatoes in a recipe that may have southern Italian origins.

2 pounds cherrystone or littleneck clams (or 1 pound frozen chopped clams)

¼ cup olive oil

1 large white onion, chopped

4 garlic cloves, minced

3 small carrots, chopped

Salt

2 stalks celery, chopped

1 medium green bell pepper, seeds and veins removed, chopped

1 leek, split, rinsed of any grit, and chopped

2 bay leaves

$\frac{1}{2}$ teaspoon freshly ground black pepper, plus more to taste

$1\frac{1}{2}$ teaspoons dried oregano

$\frac{1}{8}$ teaspoon celery seeds

$\frac{1}{2}$ teaspoon red pepper flakes

3 large Yukon gold potatoes, peeled and diced

3 cups bottled clam juice

1 (28-ounce) can whole plum tomatoes

A few sprigs of parsley

1. If you are using fresh clams, rinse them in cold water. Heat 1 cup water in a medium saucepan over medium-high heat. Once it is boiling, add the fresh clams, cover tightly, and steam, shaking the pot occasionally. After 5 minutes, remove any clams that have opened and reserve. After 10 minutes, remove the remaining clams and discard any that have not opened.

2. Strain the cooking liquid through a fine-mesh sieve lined with cheesecloth and reserve. Pull the clams from their shells, roughly chop, and combine them with the cooking liquid. Refrigerate until ready to use (this step can be done a day ahead). If using frozen chopped clams, simply thaw them in the refrigerator overnight.

3. Rinse out and dry the pot and set it over medium-high heat. Add the olive oil; when it starts to shimmer, add the onion, garlic, and carrots. Stir and season well with salt. After 5 minutes, add the celery, bell pepper, leek, bay leaves, black pepper, oregano, celery seeds, red pepper flakes, potatoes, and clam juice and bring to a simmer. Crush the tomatoes with your hands over the pot, adding them as you go, then add their liquid. Add 1 cup water. Simmer the mixture until the potatoes are just tender.

4. Add the reserved chopped clams and their liquid and return to a simmer. Chop the parsley and add to the soup. Taste and adjust the seasoning with more salt, if necessary. Fish out and discard the bay leaves and serve immediately.

THIEBOU DJENN

In 1979 my band, Mofungo, was playing a gig at the Mudd Club the evening before Gretchen and I were to leave for our first trip to West Africa, an exploratory trek that would include four countries. We had no particular reason for going there, except it seemed more interesting than visiting Europe, and Gretchen's brother, David Van Dyk, was holding down a remote U.S. Agency for International Development (USAID) outpost in the eastern bush lands of what was then known as Upper Volta (now Burkina Faso). An announcement from the stage of my impending departure—I was proud but a bit scared—was greeted with bemused silence. The gig went well; we got paid $500, split the money, and stopped at Stromboli's for a slice on the way home in the van. The next day my life would change forever.

We arrived in Dakar, Senegal, after a surprisingly short overnight flight from Kennedy Airport. It had taken only six hours, causing me to mentally redraw the world map I had in my head. How could Africa be the same distance from New York as Paris? For one thing, Senegal is on the continent's extreme western verge, but all the globes at the time, based on one Eurocentric projection or another, really did misconstrue the size and position of what was once known as the Dark Continent.

We were flying in December, and it had been frigid as we left Queens with our tiny rolling suitcases. But with the dawn arriving as we stepped off the plane that day in Africa, we were hit with a dry and hot Saharan wind that was like a hand slap across our faces. Instead of a motorized Jetway, we descended a trembling metal stairway pushed up to the plane, and we saw Senegalese men scurrying all around us dressed in sweaters and knit caps, even though the temperature was already 90 degrees Fahrenheit. It was their winter, and they were understandably feeling a bit chilly.

After a frenetic taxi ride across town, dodging donkeys, handcarts, and colorfully dressed pedestrians—the men in pajamas with intricate prints, the women sporting towering turbans on their heads—we arrived at the quays, where we were to hop on a ferry known for centuries as the *shaloop* (a corruption of *sloop*) to the island of Gorée. Known principally as a sacred site where hundreds of thousands of slaves were transshipped to the Americas, the island is like a jewel in a harbor that was teeming with tramp steamers and Russian fishing trawlers. Twenty minutes or so after we'd left the quay, the island began to loom over us as it got closer and closer, rising to a point at its far western end where we could barely make out the battlements of a ruined French fort situated on a rocky, scrub-covered promontory.

The island contained a patchwork of handsome tropical French houses dating to the 18th century, painted in pastel colors. Among the houses were irregularly shaped squares with palm trees, the occasional flickering gaslight, and kiosks selling baguettes and cigarettes, all of it recalling Senegal's colonial era. As the *shaloop* pulled up to the island's single dock, boys wearing only white cotton briefs jumped into the water to retrieve coins tossed by passengers on the boat.

We were to meet a friend of David's who lived on the island and worked as a higher-up Peace Corps official in Dakar. But first we sat on a low seawall by the small harbor, as I freaked out at the strangeness and uncertainty of our circumstances, and Gretchen comforted me. Until I get into the swing of things, I have always been a tetchy traveler. Behind us and to the east spread a French hotel dating to the 19th century, one of the few businesses on the island, now run by the Senegalese government. After a cursory exploration of the 40-acre island, we stood dazed outside the hotel's restaurant, contemplating the posted bill of fare. We were so famished that we felt we had to eat there, even though the prices were prohibitively expensive. Was all of West Africa going to be like this? I worried.

We went in and, after nervously rescanning the menu written entirely in French, finally ordered the cheapest thing, a bowl of soupe de poisson at five dollars—which back then seemed like a lot of dough for soup in a third-world country when a bowl of New England clam chowder cost $2.50 at Grand Central's Oyster Bar. We didn't have much money with us—how could our cash ever hold out against these prices? The soup, though, was fantastic—brick red, fishy, spicy as hell, and served in the French manner with slices of toasted baguette and a pot of pimento-laced rouille to be spread on the croutons and launched into the soup. We greedily drank a bottle of mineral water, too, afraid to drink the tap water that had been provided in a sweating pitcher. A ceiling fan lazily rotated overhead. The white tablecloth was stiff with starch and slightly yellow. The waiter was dressed in a short jacket.

Fortified, we went to look for David's pal, Harriet. There was no town hall, phone directory, or even a constable to ask her whereabouts. It was long before the age of the mobile phone, and any meeting of this sort required a leap of faith. I was lacking in that sort of faith. We had arranged to stay with Harriet for a couple of days, and the prospect of finding another place to room—or registering in the island's sole hotel—was daunting with our shallow budget.

Eventually, after traipsing around Gorée and even up the hill past yawning powder magazines, caves, and the island's only mosque, and inquiring of everyone we ran into on the dusty streets in our tentative French, we located Harriet in a small house on the north side of the island. On Gorée, everyone knew each other.

We found Harriet around four o'clock in a room swaddled in curtains, darkened against the afternoon heat. She was sitting on a low improvised bed with a pair of Senegalese guys of indeterminate age in sports clothes with close-cropped hair. They were very dark. She was very light, a woman in her 60s with wavy gray hair that fell almost to her shoulders. The room smelled of sex. She seemed surprised to see us, as if she hadn't taken it seriously when David had written to her from his remote outpost in Upper Volta that his sister and her boyfriend would be arriving from New York.

In Senegal and elsewhere in West Africa, no one seemed to take days of the week very seriously. As we traveled across the continent, we discovered that whether a given plane, train, or bush taxi actually left on the advertised day and hour was something left to chance. The train from Dakar to Bamako, Mali, was scheduled to leave once a week on Thursday, but it was just as likely to depart on the following Monday, in response to some problem or other, or due to a simple lack of personnel.

We stayed with Harriet for a few days, and she proved charming, though too busy to do much of a touristic nature with us. Accordingly, we explored the island and then the city of Dakar on our own. We attended a wrestling match at a neighborhood arena on the mainland—this being one of the few affordable forms of entertainment enjoyed by the African populace. We toured markets like Sandaga, filled with unfamiliar goods, where tailors pumping treadle sewing machines with their feet would make an entire suit of clothes for you in an hour or so at bargain prices. They'd use fabrics available in the same market, printed with jungle foliage, bold geometric patterns, or the faces of leaders long deposed from neighboring countries—that was the cheapest fabric that could be found. I had a complete suit made for myself, pursuant to careful tape measurements of all my limbs. It fit like a glove. Within two years, I'd grown too fat for it.

Many of the more attractive bolts of cloth used by the treadle tailors were batiks made by the Dutch wax process in Indonesia. The colonial world was still in complete operation in the winter of 1979 and 1980 in West Africa, despite decolonization. Most of the goods in the Sandaga Market were cheap and Chinese.

DINING IN DAKAR

We really had no idea what we'd be eating when we ventured to West Africa, despite already having a cursory knowledge of the diet in many other parts of the world, mainly as a result of eating in the five boroughs of New York City. The lack of an Internet back then made such research much more difficult. Even the tourist guides gave scant space to gastronomic matters apart from a slender list of restaurants one might find in Dakar. We grabbed food wherever we could find it. In the city we discovered a French restaurant run by nuns of a certain order, who'd probably been operating hostelries for travelers since medieval times; a couple of Vietnamese places helmed by refugees from the recent war (we later discovered Indochinese food had been popular in Dakar since at least 1960); colonial bars that could offer a decent steak frites, though the beer was extensively watered; and roadside pits—literal pits dug in the dusty pavement—where you could get spice-rubbed chickens at two dollars a pop. These chickens were exceedingly delicious, but to the American accustomed to sitting down to a balanced meal, eating only poultry with no accompaniments seemed strangely unsatisfying. Apart from a restaurant run for the benefit of new Peace Corps recruits as a sort of introduction to the cuisine they'd be enjoying in the outback, finding actual Senegalese fare in Dakar was not as easy as we'd hoped.

We ate well enough in the few days we were in Dakar. Sometimes we snacked in the market. Sometimes we breakfasted on baguettes from a bakery that had a kiosk on Gorée, but the bread always had weevils in it. "Mmmm, a little protein!" we exclaimed when we found one of the things amid the crumbs. That bread purveyor, along with the fancy French restaurant in the old hotel, represented the only visible spots on the island to eat, though the rail-thin women who lived on Gorée, part of the migrant Fulani, or Peul, tribe (said to have originated in Ethiopia), sometimes sold cheese or ham sandwiches or manioc fritters with a fiery dipping sauce from tables near the ferry's embarkation building. Some of the older ones still affected the dress of colorful aprons and small headscarves (oddly like those Tippi Hedren might wear in an Alfred Hitchcock movie) that were one of the legacies of Portuguese visits to Gorée some four centuries earlier.

But one day—unfortunately, it was the day before we were to leave for Upper Volta—we discovered a whole new set of dining opportunities right on the island.

POP-UPS, WEST AFRICAN-STYLE

We learned that eating out was not as unusual on Gorée as we'd first imagined. Women who were known as good cooks often ran little impromptu restaurants out of their kitchens. Their patrons were bachelors, commercial travelers, and visitors from the mainland who had no means of cooking for themselves. These places served a standard Senegalese menu, which had been in place since tribal times but included colonial influences, consisting of chicken or lamb peanut stews known as *mafes*; fish or chicken heaped with mustard-laced onion relish called *yassas* (the mustard constituted one instance of French influence on Senegalese cuisine); and assorted dishes featuring couscous or rice topped with grilled lamb chops, braised lamb shanks, or locally caught fish (which was invariably small and bony). Aside from cheb, that was pretty much the totality of the menu.

The cook and proprietor of this sort of establishment—in a second visit four years later we estimated there were 10 or so of these places on Gorée alone, with more in Dakar—would always be addressed as Madame plus her first name. You could identify these carry-outs at mealtimes by the line snaking out the door. On our first visit to one, the kitchen was on the ground floor of a narrow three-story house painted pale pink, approached through a shady garden behind a stone wall festooned with purple bougainvilleas and red hibiscus. The kitchen was situated a few steps down from the street. We went around sunset, and the line totaled about eight local guys, each of whom carried a battered pot or pan to put his supper in. No carry-out vessels were provided. Gretchen and I backtracked a few blocks to scrounge a square aluminum baking pan from Harriet's house, and then joined the line.

As we reached the head of the queue—which continued growing—Madame took our pan, put a huge quantity of red rice in the bottom, placed vegetables all around it, and then carefully arranged several pieces of fish with green stuffing leaking out on top. As a final gesture, she dropped a stewed Scotch bonnet pepper at the highest point in the mass of rice. It turned out to be the hottest thing we'd ever tasted.

CHEB DECONSTRUCTED

The dish known familiarly as *cheb*—more fully transliterated *thiebou djenn* in Wolof (the language of the country's dominant tribe) and pronounced "cheb-oo-jzen"—is considered the national dish of Senegal.

Cheb is made by first stuffing chunks of chopped-up whole fish with a bright-green paste of scallions, garlic, and cilantro. This paste is commonly made by pounding the ingredients with a giant pestle in a waist-high wooden mortar made out of a tree trunk. To make the version served on Gorée and in Dakar, fish were used that were caught by gaily painted pirogues—narrow, tapered surfboats with a shallow draft that typically couldn't go too far out into the ocean. By the time we visited, the most common fish these boats caught were tiny tuna and other small oily fish, very tasty but also possessing an insubstantial amount of flesh and too many bones. The Fulani and Wolof tribesmen who caught the fish, launching from beachside villages up and down the coast, blamed the Russian fishing fleets that operated just outside the territorial limits of the country for snagging all the larger fish.

The tiny tuna especially were also important in making another Senegalese dish, boulettes, in which the creatures are pounded, skin, bones, and guts included, along with onions and herbs in the same mortars. (We might think of them as standup food processors.) Balls made of the resulting coarse paste would be cooked in a frying pan with lots of fat. The result was something that tasted just like the meatballs served at IKEA, except as you ate them, you had to pick fish bones out of your teeth.

In preparing cheb, the stuffed fish would then be fried in a good quantity of bright-red palm oil until the skin browned. The stuffing seeped out to a degree and served to further flavor the oil. Next, the fish would be removed and a cornucopia of vegetables added. Dakar—located on a blunted peninsula at the westernmost point of Africa—had an ideal climate for growing vegetables, as we discovered when we drove around Senegal on a subsequent visit, with much more moisture than the rest of the sub-Sahara. Thus the city of Dakar was ringed with extensive private vegetable gardens and truck farms, and the produce made its way into most Senegalese cooking and especially cheb. Indeed, the Dakar area was a vegetable paradise, even by modern standards, with vegetables from all over the world taking root there in addition to indigenous ones like yams, manioc, collard greens, and okra.

In fact, the excellence of a given batch of cheb is most reliably judged by the number of vegetables represented. In plebeian versions intended for a quick, late lunch, three or four vegetables would be standard: slices of giant carrot, a wedge of cabbage, a hunk of eggplant, and a handful of okra pods. The most vegetables I ever counted, in a cheb served for dinner made in a private home by a cook who was clearly showing off, was 11. These included white and orange yams, chayote, rutabaga, yuca, parsnip, and taro. Imported from China and colorfully enameled with flowers and birds, the standard metal cheb serving platter can get mighty crowded!

These vegetables cook in the remaining palm oil with enough water added to cover them, and they pick up fishy and herby flavors as they cook. Next, the vegetables are set aside, waiting for the dish's final assembly, and tons of rice is added to the cooking liquid remaining in the pan—which is often a Chinese wok. As it boils, the grain absorbs all the flavors that went before it. The rice-cooking step provides further opportunities for stylin' the cheb. Some cooks add little pieces of sun-dried stockfish—a good way to use up the most miniature fish caught by the pirogues, ones that don't have much flesh and are preserved by drying in the sun. Other cooks add tamarind pods for tartness, or a little canned tomato paste for richness and color, as if such a ramping-up were needed.

Once assembled, with the rice layered on the bottom, the stuffed fish on top, and the vegetables strewn all around, the dish looks spectacular, gleaming with oily bright colors.

Where did cheb come from? Most food historians will tell you it was originally inspired by paella brought to Senegal by Portuguese mariners in the late 15th century. They'd been nosing around the Senegalese coast in between 1444 and 1447, but it took them a while to develop permanent settlements. The Portuguese established a cemetery and chapel on Gorée in 1450. Then, as now, death was a big deal for them, and being a mariner was a dangerous job, hence the cemetery was among the first things to be established in a new settlement.

Okay, you're likely to say, isn't paella more of a Spanish thing? Well, the Spaniards and Portuguese vied for dominance in the region during the latter half of the 15th century, and my guess is that there was a lot of swapping personnel between boats, since sailors who could withstand the sweltering climate and harsh conditions were in high demand. Don't forget that Christopher Columbus, a Genoese native, sailed on behalf of Spain. Besides, there are Portuguese dishes resembling paella, too, right? Well, Portuguese have rice dishes, such as arroz de bacalhau, but nothing of that complexity that I could find—in cookbooks, stateside restaurants, and even a culinary visit to Portugal in the mid-'90s.

Whether derived from it or not, cheb is better than paella. Stuffing a strong-flavored fish is an exceedingly good idea because it prevents the fishy flavors from dominating. The rice is unspeakably rich and red, oozing fat, the odor of funky stock-fish strong. And, once you've gotten over your fear of saturated fat, palm oil is one of the best-tasting lipids in the world. The dish has the pungency of salt-cod fritters and the subtlety of bouillabaisse. Cheb is a dish to be dug into with two fists. In the French manner, the vegetables are extensively cooked, the yams creamy, the okra relieved of its slime by breakage, the eggplant rendered into an agreeable mush.

I loved cheb then, and still do. I make it when friends come by if I want to show them how much trouble I'm willing to go to on their behalf. It takes at least half a day to make.

FURTHER INTO WEST AFRICA

Gretchen and I had many further adventures in West Africa on that trip, visiting Mali and Benin, which at the time had a Maoist government. The soldiers at the border waved us through without even checking our passports (visiting was technically not permitted by the American government), and we were able to enjoy a famous animal park, complete with hippos. Afterward, we drove all over Upper Volta in a Land Rover, admiring the striking red cliffs on the eastern frontier near the border with Niger. Since there were no hotels and only a few government guesthouses scattered here and there in the bush, we most often stayed in accommodations provided by tribal chiefs in the middle of nowhere. Their hospitality was nearly overwhelming, and each new place we stopped, we'd be surrounded by a ring of tribespeople eager to hear what was happening in the outside world. They had no newspapers or even radios, and depended on travelers for news.

In Upper Volta, Gretchen and I got married in a tribal ceremony, said to be the first of its kind in the history of West Africa, the first performed purely in a tribal fashion for visitors from elsewhere. Most westerners who chose to get married in West Africa did so by means of a pastor or missionary. Our presiding official was known as Madame Gandi, and her brother was the chief of the Gourmantché tribe, with 110,000 subjects. He wore a gold pillbox hat and flowing embroidered robes, and had the only telephone in town. After the ceremony, he held an audience for us in his round, cinder-block office, and was very gracious.

Our nuptials occasioned a three-day festival as the bride was paraded around the town of Fada N'Gourma, with a population of 10,000, making it the third largest municipality in the country. I was kept under guard in a mud-brick house by a guy playing the part of the bride's brother, a practice established to keep the groom from raping the bride, just one facet of a lengthy story line entailed by the wedding ceremony. The tale is too long to recount here, but there were men's dances and women's dances, with competing drum ensembles for each. Megaliter upon megaliter of the millet beer called *dolo* was consumed. A chicken was killed (and eaten) as a sacrifice to the natural gods. Two pigs were buried in clay and roasted. Much of neighborhood was fed, and musicians came from all over the country to take part.

THE APPEARANCE OF CHEB IN NEW YORK

My brother-in-law David had been working in Upper Volta, driving from village to village showing educational videos on behalf of USAID, when he orchestrated the tribal wedding for us. The next year he visited New York City. After wandering around Harlem one weekday afternoon, he came back to our East Village flat to report that he'd found cheb up in Harlem, and he gave us the address of a townhouse on West 114th Street.

That was a few years before nearby 116th Street became the axis of a thriving West African neighborhood still in existence, though today made more compact by the gentrification all around it. The West Africans (in this case mainly from Senegal, the Ivory Coast, Mali, and Guinea) who settled in that neighborhood proved to be less transient than the watch and handbag salesmen who came before them, more steadfast in their desire to put down roots. It has helped that many of the residents are devout Muslims of a particular branch of Sufism native to West Africa called the Mouride Brotherhood, which was founded in the 19th century. Their holy city is Touba, far out in the dusty badlands of the Senegalese sub-Sahara, very different from the relatively lush countryside in the vicinity of Dakar.

But back in 1981 that 116th Street strip, which has come to include approximately 10 West African restaurants, three mosques, and innumerable stores selling small appliances, religious books, and hair-braiding services, was nonexistent. And when I traveled up to Harlem in search of the restaurant on 114th that David had stumbled on, I found it closed every time. I could see the door under the townhouse stairway that led to the ground-floor space and tell that it had been a restaurant, but no one ever answered my knock.

Soon there were other sightings of impromptu Senegalese restaurants. Senegalese men of the Wolof tribe were the foot soldiers of West African mercantilism in New York in the '80s. Largely here on student visas, these temporary immigrants often furtively sold counterfeit designer watches or handbags, lurking in obscure corners around Times Square and in other places where large numbers of tourists were likely to be seduced by such a seeming bargain. Many purchasers doubtlessly thought the goods were authentic. Aside from the counterfeit merchandise, the commerce was completely on the up and up; indeed, the temporary salesmen, soon known for their natty clothes and stylish demeanor, were the flower of Senegalese youth, and but for a severe downturn in Senegal's economy, they might have been working back in Dakar as bank clerks or government functionaries.

Despite the ephemeral nature of their stay in New York, these individuals needed to eat, and they wanted their own comfort food. As Muslims, they also needed to eat halal. The typical tribal-style repast back home—a single meal per day, supplemented before and after by judicious snacking—occurred around 2:00 in the afternoon. And thus it was that some bright bulb at the Lucky Star Deli just west of Times Square figured out that, after the normal noontime sandwich rush, the place could do another two hours of business by serving West Africans. So they hired a Senegalese cook, and soon immigrant men were lining up in front of the deli around 2:00. The guys would score their cheb and eat it crouching by the side of the street, in a public park, or at a nearby SRO hotel, where the immigrants often lived four or five to a room. Back then there were probably a dozen such hostelries in the immediate vicinity of Times Square, which was at the time a seedy district of discount movie theaters where bums slept away the day in the ratty plush seats and every block beckoned with a peepshow.

Soon after Lucky Star Deli started serving Senegalese fare, I waited in line on West 50th Street with the African street vendors and grabbed a round aluminum carry-out container of cheb. Their version was rudimentary, just a whisper of cheb rather than a shout: the fish fried but unstuffed, only three vegetables, and rice that had been deprived of palm oil, though still colored with a dab of tomato paste. Still, it was a start. And it was scrumptious as far as it went. There was a table or two in the deli itself, and tall dark-skinned Wolof men sat at every spot, each with his own individual cheb. It was five dollars or so, and the serving was humongous. Bluefish had been substituted for whatever small chum had been deployed back home. The bluefish was cheap, and it was a touch that years later might have been praised as locavoristic.

Lucky Star Deli enjoyed a vogue for about three years, at which time a startling thing happened. I had become friends with a Senegalese guy named Abdoulaye Kamara who worked as a security guard in a fancy apartment building just west of Chinatown on Broadway. His excellent English made him a de facto ambassador between the French- and Wolof-speaking Senegalese and the world of Anglophone New Yorkers. One day at Lucky Star, he excitedly told me about an apartment in an SRO hotel on 46th Street in Hell's Kitchen where a mother and daughter named Bettye and Fatou M'Baye were cooking

Senegalese fare. While the vast majority of West African immigrants to New York had been men, this pair were the rare Senegalese women who'd made it to the city. I later discovered they had been invited by the Senegalese United Nations consulate as a sort of humanitarian effort to feed the watch and handbag vendors who swarmed the streets—and were often the sons of influential Senegalese back home.

What a sight awaited me as I entered the premises for the first time! The front door, which had been left open a crack, gave way to a living room in which men wearing robes and skullcaps sat around communal platters of cheb at several points around the room, some perched on folding chairs, some sitting cross-legged on the floor, eating with their right hands. There were over 20 diners crowded into the cramped space, and their numbers waxed and waned as the afternoon went by. Whenever one stood up to leave, another would sit down at his place. A couple of guys were perpetually kept waiting in the airless hallway of the decrepit residential hotel.

Meanwhile the two women worked furiously in the thumbnail-sized kitchen, and I remember a bedroom, too, where counterfeit goods were piled high, along with the folded carts with which the salesmen transport them. The cheb was great, the bluefish properly stuffed, six vegetables present, and the smell of palm oil spread through the room. I was as happy as a pig in slop. The *Times*, getting wind of the phenomenon, sent itinerant reporter Sara Rimer, who published a piece under the title "For the Determined, the Search for a Rare Taste of Senegal," dated August 1992, carefully concealing the exact location of the apartment.

In the piece, Kamara was interviewed, and he claimed his mother made cheb with 15 vegetables, which I later deemed to be something of an exaggeration, but who knows? I was referred to as "a struggling rock musician who earns a living as a secretary at a Manhattan real estate company." Rimer also prominently mentioned my food zine *Down the Hatch* and even gave my phone number, so readers could subscribe. For a few days

I was inundated with phone calls, but I managed to dissuade most of the callers from subscribing. I could only stuff so many envelopes per quarterly issue.

Eventually, the SRO pop-up closed down—or rather it moved after a few months to another location that I couldn't find. I'd hear rumors from time to time, but it never lasted long in any one place. Bettye and Fatou finally disappeared from the underground Senegalese dining scene; I heard later from Kamara that they'd become homesick and gone back to Dakar.

At this point, around 1993, a few full-blown Senegalese restaurants began opening up, principally in Harlem and Brooklyn's Fort Greene. The latter had been a center of the city's Nigerian population, who'd been here for five years, arriving around the time of an oil boom in their home country. A couple of storefronts harboring import-export businesses had been established on Fulton Street by the Demu clan, and eventually a deli was established called Demu Café, run by Ganiu M. Demu, whose pigtailed daughters were often seen playing around the deli. The place was a block south of Brooklyn Tech High School near South Oxford Street. It introduced Nigerian mashes and palm-oil-laced soups to the city for the first time, though later a menu of bagels and other western breakfast items was added. The only remaining vestige of Brooklyn's first Nigerian neighborhood is Buka, a restaurant near the corner of Fulton Street and Cambridge Place in adjacent Clinton Hill. It still serves such Nigerian arcana as tree snails and goat heads on a regular basis.

Dropping into the midst of the Demu empire in Fort Greene in 1993 like a giant nut from a magic tree was Keur N'Deye. It was run by a Rastafarian dude who'd lived in Dakar, and it was certainly the first West African restaurant in town to behave not as a tribal clubhouse or national meeting place for expats but as a full-blown bistro, ready to wow diners with an unfamiliar cuisine. There was yassa and mafe, of course, and nems, the Senegalese version of Vietnamese spring rolls made with beef instead of pork. But there was also a cheb that I complained about when it was first served, not because of any flavor issues, but because it was served deconstructed, with the vegetables, fish, and rice on separate plates.

Ten years later, a Francophone West African presence remained in Fort Greene, but the ambitious restaurateurs were more likely to open actual French bistros, often with a single Senegalese dish or two and the balance of the menu things like steak frites and îles flottantes. In Harlem, Senegalese restaurateurs tended to open French pastry shops instead. And nowadays, Nigerian restaurants will more often be found in East New York, Brooklyn, or Saint Albans, Queens.

But we hadn't heard the last of the Lucky Star Deli, even though that institution was moribund by the late '90s. How would the Senegalese who were not in Harlem or certain Brooklyn neighborhoods that boasted Senegalese restaurants get their cheb? Well, in places where the salesmen congregated, including the Wholesale District around 28th and Broadway, and the tourist-oriented stalls around Canal and Broadway, women began selling tribal Senegalese dishes from shopping carts lined with black plastic garbage bags to provide heat insulation and concealment, taking their cue from the Pueblan tamale sellers around the Port Authority. Around 2:00 in the afternoon they'd appear with mafe or cheb, or less frequently yassa, and ladle out servings surreptitiously due to the operation's questionable legality. Occasionally, one would sell Guinean food instead, leaf-based sauces dotted with lamb and served over Uncle Ben's rice.

While Keur N'Deye had been a trailblazing Senegalese restaurant, inspired by bistros and offering slightly elevated prices to a crowd of Senegalese and other West Africans, college students, and Fort Greene entrenched bohemians and artists, both black and white, another even more curious experiment in African restaurateuring occurred in 1999. Behind the Port Authority Bus Terminal on Ninth Avenue, a region perpetually rife with small "testing the waters" ethnic restaurants, appeared a place with the verbose name of Chez Gna Gna Koty's Senegal Goree Island. It was helmed—and named after—the cook who'd labored so effectively for years at Lucky Star Deli, Gna Gna Diene, as she spelled it, whose name sounded like the refrain of a '60s pop song.

Suddenly, we had one of the longest Senegalese menus seen either here or in Dakar, and a real attempt to ferret out a regional dish or two from places like the Casamance, a sliver of territory below the Gambia, a former British colony that splits Senegal in two, and Saint-Louis, a French colonial city on the northern coast. She delighted Eric Asimov, then the *New York Times* "$25 and Under" restaurant critic, who noted, "The chef and owner, Gnagna Diene, says she will cook whatever you like. But the pride of Chez Gnagna (pronounced NYAH-nyah) is in its Senegalese stews, hearty well-flavored meals that are rich and comforting."

Among the more obscure Senegalese dishes served was dakhine, lamb stewed in peanut sauce with onions and beans, a dish typical of the Casamance. Another was soupikandia, a rich sauce of fish and okra spooned over polished rice. Still, a cookbook by Monique Biarnès, *La Cuisine Sénégalaise* (1972), which I picked up during my first visit to Senegal, offers 80 common recipes, of which we've only seen a dozen or so in over nearly 30 years of Senegalese cooking in New York.

LITTLE WEST AFRICA

By 1995, two blocks of Harlem's West 116th Street, between Sixth and Eighth Avenues, had developed a thriving West African community, of which the Senegalese predominated, with a constantly shifting proportion of Guineans, Malians, and immigrants from the Ivory Coast, with the occasional Ethiopian and Somali. In the early days there was an Ethiopian grocery, and a Somali café where the cooks all came from Yemen and largely served Yemenite food (roast lamb shanks, potato curries, rotisserie chickens) to a constituency that was mainly Somali but came to include other halal-eating East Africans. At the same time as Chez Gna Gna Koty's was operating in Hell's

Kitchen, Fort Greene was getting its own South African restaurant, Madiba, and a handful more would follow in the next two decades. Nevertheless, the city remained severely deficient in East African fare (which includes Kenyan, Somali, Tanzanian, Eritrean, Ethiopian, and Sudanese), aside from perhaps 15 boringly similar Ethiopian restaurants. (Though occasionally a Kenyan restaurant will temporarily appear in Jersey City.)

Indeed, 116th Street has managed to harbor at least three or four Senegalese restaurants at all times during the last 20 years. The longest running is Le Baobab, but Africa Kine has been there a long time, too, starting in a small space on the north side of 116th and moving across the street into bigger digs a few years later. While Le Baobab (named after the iconic West African tree said to grow upside down with roots pointing skyward) is a darkened clubhouse with the shades drawn tight and masks, textiles, and maps lining the walls, Africa Kine is more like an upstairs nightclub of ancient Harlem vintage, with plush booths and a view of a small dance floor, though no alcohol is served. Both have a similar menu of cheb, mafe, yassa, and a few other dishes, plus Franco–West African–North African fare that runs to grilled lamb chops (dibi), braised and roasted whole fish with mustard relish, roasted guinea hen, and—odd man out—spaghetti with tomato sauce.

Gradually, as Harlem's Senegalese restaurants have evolved, the menus have ballooned, and an odd phenomenon has occurred: restaurants that once served a handful of dishes have started segregating their lunch and dinner menus, with quasi-French-style grilled lamb and fish predominating in the evening, relegating their tribal dishes to lunch. Which makes sense in a way, since the tribal dishes were originally consumed around 2:00 p.m. But if you go to, say, Africa Kine for dinner, it doesn't hurt to ask for the tribal stuff, since sometimes a little cheb or mafe remains in the evening.

Some Senegalese places have resisted this trend, perhaps realizing that, to outsiders at least, the French-leaning food is rather narrow and boring, and hence tribal fare should be offered as the heart of the menu at all hours. One such place is Joloff, named after the historic tribe that dominated parts of West Africa starting in the 14th century. They left behind a dish called Joloff rice, and you can find it on the menus of Nigerian and Ghanaian restaurants, a brown pilaf dotted with meat, a far more meager production than cheb. It may have inspired modern cheb, or maybe modern cheb inspired it—either way, the Joloff tribe eventually gave rise to the Wolofs, who now dominate Senegalese politics and culture.

Joloff opened 20 years ago right on Fulton Street in Clinton Hill. Like Keur N'Deye, it was aimed not only at Africans but at African-Americans and adventuresome boho diners as well. In those days, Fort Greene and Clinton Hill were a hotbed of cultural interracialism in the post-hippie era. Joloff offered a broad range of Senegalese tribal dishes and little in the way of French ones, which was good. It also had a prominent vegetarian component due to the Rasta sentiments of founder Papa K. Diagne, once again reflecting a Rastafarian presence in Dakar dating from the time of Bob Marley's 1979 West African tour, which galvanized many followers. The food at Joloff can be a bit pallid, though, so if you're timid about spicing, this is the place for you. As the website warns, "Unlike a lot of other West African restaurants, we understand the value of a healthy lifestyle and wholesome food." Many Senegalese recipes are thus offered in tofu variations, and the notoriously greasy Vietnamese nems are cooked with a vegetarian filling in a less-greasy manner.

Perhaps sadly, Joloff was forced to move from its prime corner Fulton Street location to Bedford Avenue in Bedford-Stuyvesant a couple of years back. Luckily, the place persists, but with a revamped menu that includes much more of the French stuff.

Five years ago, an unusual type of Senegalese restaurant opened on East 100th Street in Manhattan, just east of Park Avenue in a laid-back neighborhood far from the tumult of West 116th Street and its storefront mosques and teeming markets. La Galette was run, not by Sufis, but by Catholics, a

Francophilic group back home who occupy some of the highest socioeconomic positions. The dining room was conventionally stylish, the prices elevated, and the food consisted of elegantly plated tribal fare—including yassa made with citrons and fish croquettes—plus Parisian bistro standards, such as a fine croque madame. Ultimately, the higher prices and unfamiliarity of much of the food doomed La Galette, and it closed after just three years in business.

What, ultimately, does Senegalese food represent to New York? For 30 years the menu has lingered on the fringes of the city's restaurant scene, easy enough to find if you were willing to travel and seek it out, but easy to ignore if you never wondered what all those watch and handbag salesmen were eating. The food was more exciting than that of most nations. What diner who loved peanut butter sandwiches wouldn't want to get up to her elbows in mafe, with its rich peanut sauce dotted with chunks of chicken or lamb? Who wouldn't revel in the culinary glories of cheb or in its historical underpinnings? While gourmet versions of a few West African dishes sometimes pop up in upscale Harlem eateries like The Cecil and Marcus Samuelsson's Red Rooster, these dishes have not been widely experimented with by chefs, nor have they appeared on many non-African menus, which is a shame. So far, West African fare represents one of the city's greatest gastronomic "missed opportunities."

Unlike the Nigerians, who arrived more slowly but stayed longer, a good half of the Senegalese population has disappeared in the last few years, and the number of Senegalese restaurants has gradually dwindled to around eight where once there must have been 16 or so. But gastronomic ideas have a way of lingering and taking root long after their most obvious evocations, like annual flowering plants, have taken root and died. Let's hope we'll see mafe, yassa, and cheb on some East Village bistro menu sometime in the future. The Lower East Side restaurant Dirty French, which seeks inspiration in former French colonies, has lately managed to miss Francophone West Africa entirely—to its own deficit.

FOUR PLACES TO EAT CHEB

1. AFRICA KINE
256 WEST 116TH STREET, MANHATTAN, 212-666-9400

This place looks like a nightclub complete with a downstairs dance floor, upstairs restaurant, and coat check beneath a sweeping stairway. The staff is friendly and agreeable, though you don't get much of a feel for Senegal in the sprawling premises.

2. LE BAOBAB
120 WEST 116TH STREET, MANHATTAN, 212-864-4700

This is a classic West African New York City restaurant, with the shades drawn tight, decor crammed with masks and maps, and a clubhouse feel that will appeal to the most adventuresome diners. The tribal fare like cheb is marginally better than that at Africa Kine.

3. JOLOFF
1168 BEDFORD AVENUE, BROOKLYN, 718-230-0523

This Rasta-run boîte fiddles with Senegalese food to make it "healthier," yet unreconstructed versions of many dishes are available. The staff is very visitor-friendly, and a crowd of mixed races patronizes the place.

4. KEUR SOKHNA
2249 ADAM CLAYTON POWELL JR. BOULEVARD, MANHATTAN, 212-368-5005

Like Le Baobab, this is an old-guard café, reminiscent of the way West African restaurants were when they first arrived in the city.

HERE'S A SENEGALESE-RUN FRENCH PASTRY SHOP:

PATISSERIE DES AMBASSADES
2200 FREDERICK DOUGLASS BOULEVARD, MANHATTAN, 212-666-0078

Excellent French pastries with the occasional Senegalese tribal set meal offered.

AND A FEW OTHER AFRICAN CUISINES:

1. WAZOBIA

611 BAY STREET, STATEN ISLAND, 718-682-1781

Mashed tubers, roots, and plantains, with palm-oil-laced sauces, to be eaten with the fingers, plus alcoholic beverages, all at slightly elevated prices, is the lure of this visitor-friendly Nigerian spot, but beware the upsell!

2. FATIMA

789 FRANKLIN AVENUE, BROOKLYN, NO PHONE

This holdout in a quickly yuppifying Crown Heights presents authentic Guinean fare, leaf-driven sauces and all, over rice, in a steam-table format so you can preview your food.

3. PAPAYE

2300 GRAND CONCOURSE, BRONX, 718-676-0771

Right on the Bronx's Grand Concourse and thus easily accessible by subway, this long-running Ghanaian spot is a delight, with color pictures of the menu offerings prominently displayed. Spoon on the hot sauce!

4. BUKA

946 FULTON STREET, BROOKLYN, 347-763-0619

Vestige of a decades-long presence in Fort Greene and Clinton Hill, this Nigerian restaurant is deep and comfortable and offers a menu that includes northern and southern Nigerian dishes. Check the chalkboard outside for startling specials, such as tree snails.

5. MAIMA'S

106-47 GUY R BREWER BLVD, QUEENS, 718-206-3538

The matriarch Maima is still the cook at this Jamaica, Queens, Liberian establishment, with a menu that shifts by the day. Any of the pepper soups will burn your mouth off—in a good way.

6. ABIDJAN

1136 BROADWAY, BROOKLYN, 347-787-4320

The rice- and mash-based dishes vie for your attention at this long-running Ivory Coast boîte, open late into the evening, with some French dishes thrown in for good measure. But don't expect more than a handful of choices to be available at one time. Athieke (manioc stodge, something like couscous) served with a fried red snapper is sometimes called the national dish.

THIEBOU DJENN, OR CHEB
SERVES 4 TO 6

Traditional cheb employs dried stockfish to give the rice a fishy depth; we use anchovies to the same effect.

FOR THE FISH:

1 (2-pound) bluefish, gutted and scaled (if you can't find a bluefish this small, you can also use a large porgy or bluefish fillets)
3 garlic cloves
2 Scotch bonnet peppers
$\frac{1}{4}$ cup chopped cilantro
$\frac{1}{4}$ cup chopped parsley
4 scallions, chopped
2 teaspoons kosher salt
$\frac{1}{4}$ cup vegetable oil, for cooking the fish

FOR THE RICE:

$\frac{1}{4}$ cup palm oil
5 garlic cloves, minced
2 small or 1 large white onions, chopped
$\frac{1}{4}$ cup tomato paste
2 ounces tamarind paste
3 anchovy filets
$1\frac{1}{2}$ teaspoons cayenne
$3\frac{1}{2}$ cups chicken stock or water
Salt
1 medium eggplant, sliced into 2-inch pieces
1 large carrot, cut crosswise into quarters
6-inch piece yucca, peeled and sliced into 2-inch pieces
1 small turnip, cut into quarters
8 small okra pods
2 cups long-grain white rice

1. Rinse the fish inside and out with cold water; dry well with paper towels. Cut 3 deep crosswise slits into each side of the fish.

2. Put 3 garlic cloves, the Scotch bonnets, cilantro, parsley, scallions, and 2 teaspoons kosher salt in a food processor and pulse until a rough paste forms. Rub the paste all over the fish, stuffing it into the slits and the belly, too. Refrigerate the fish until the rice has started to cook.

3. In a large sauté or cast-iron pan, heat the palm oil over medium-low heat. Add the minced garlic and the onions, reduce the heat to low, and cook until softened, 8 to 10 minutes. Add the tomato paste, tamarind paste, anchovies, and cayenne and cook, stirring to break up. Add the chicken stock or water and bring to a simmer. Season well with salt.

4. Add the eggplant, carrot, yucca, turnip, and okra. Simmer the vegetables; as each piece becomes tender, transfer it to a plate and keep warm.

5. Once all the vegetables are removed from the pan, add the rice and stir well. Bring the liquid to a simmer, reduce the heat to very low, cover, and cook for 15 to 20 minutes. Turn off the heat. Remove the lid and arrange the vegetables on the rice, then set the lid back on top. Let the rice and vegetables steam in the residual heat for another 10 minutes.

6. Meanwhile, as soon as you add the rice to the pot, remove the fish from the refrigerator and put a large sauté pan over medium heat. Add the vegetable oil, let it heat for a minute, then carefully add the fish (cut the fish in half if needed). Fry the fish for about 8 minutes, then flip and fry on the other side, another 8 minutes or so. Test for doneness by sticking a small paring knife into the thickest part of the flesh. If the tip of the knife feels cold, continue to cook for 5 or so more minutes, flipping the fish from side to side. (Fillets will cook more quickly.) To serve, place the fish on top of the vegetables and bring the entire pan to the table.

PASTRAMI

Pleasantly unctuous, smoky, salty, and so pink it's almost magenta, pastrami is something of a mystery meat. Sliced thickly by hand, it takes to rye bread like a dolphin to clear blue water. In the United States we commonly associate it with Jewish delicatessens, but the meat is linked to Jews nowhere else, according to the *Oxford Companion to American Food and Drink* (2007): "Although not originally a specifically Jewish food, pastrami is exclusively Jewish in the United States (and unknown in other English-speaking Jewish communities)." Perhaps, with this bald assertion, the editors are not including Montreal's Mile End among English-speaking Jewish communities, where a pastrami cognate called "smoked meat" is relished.

What is pastrami, anyway? First and foremost, it's a means of preserving beef by brining the cut for periods ranging from a day or two to several weeks, and then covering it with a spice rub that contains coarsely ground black peppercorns and coriander seed and smoking it. This is a fairly unique process, since meats are more commonly either smoked or brined, not both. The smoking is what mainly distinguishes pastrami from corned beef, another staple of Jewish delis in New York, but a meat also embraced by the Irish. Although pastrami is nearly always made from brisket—a cut found below the chuck on the breast of the animal—it can also be made with other cuts, including the short plate (right behind the brisket and below the ribs) or the top round (found highest on the rump) and even, nowadays, from other animals including salmon and duck.

According to the most common story, pastrami supposedly originated in Romania (though as we shall see, in a far different form), and it was Romanian Jews who brought it to America—to New York City in particular—probably late in the 19th century. Around 75,000 Jewish-Romanian immigrants came to the U.S. between 1881 and 1914, the majority toward the latter part of that timespan as the Austro-Hungarian Empire was collapsing. More settled in Pennsylvania and the Midwest than in New York. Our own most famous (some might say notorious) dining institution identified with them is Famous Sammy's Roumanian Steakhouse, which has been on the Lower East Side's Chrystie Street since 1975, replacing two previous Romanian restaurants on the same spot. (Note the diverse spellings of *Romanian*, which also included *Rumanian*.)

According to a rave review of Sammy's Roumanian in the *New York Times* by Mimi Sheraton dated 1982, the meats primarily offered were Romanian tenderloin (skirt steak), meatballs, chopped liver, rib steak, "mush" steak (thin-sliced rib eye), broiled veal chops, broiled chicken, and boiled beef flanken. Then and now, Sammy's Roumanian serves no pastrami.

A Jewish-Romanian restaurant of an older vintage was Moskowitz and Lupowitz, described in Ronald Sanders's *The Lower East Side* (1979) as a place "where one could eat in a murkily romantic East European atmosphere to the sound of gypsy violins." It was apparently a rather formal spot, with tuxedo-clad waiters and white linen tablecloths—though maybe that was considered something of a shtick.

According to the blog *Jeremiah's Vanishing New York*, Moskowitz and Lupowitz was founded in 1909 by Joseph Moskowitz, a child music prodigy on the cimbalom—a type of zither—and the restaurant didn't bite the dust until 1966. It was located on Second Avenue and East Second Street in what is now referred to as the East Village but would have been recognized then as the Lower East Side. In fact, it was at the foot of a strip known as the Yiddish Broadway, so-named for its collection of Yiddish-language theaters. In its heyday, Moskowitz and Lupowitz hosted the likes of Milton Berle and Sid Caesar.

A 1962 menu advertised on eBay shows a wealth of dinner meats, some a bit odd by today's standards, including calf's brains, lamb's tongue, capon, rib steak, boiled chicken, steer liver, sweetbreads served with french fries, roast duckling, boiled beef, turkey, and something called "carnatzels," which I had trouble identifying. A quick post on Twitter led the Culinary Historians of New York to summon Lara Rabinovitch, who replied that it was a type of slender Romanian sausage. It was apparently skinless, made with lamb and beef, something like Balkan ćevapi. But once again, no pastrami. How could this be if pastrami was a meat so closely associated with Romanian Jews?

But the mother of all Jewish-Romanian restaurants was apparently Greenberg's Roumanian Casino, located on Broome Street near Allen, in a space that now houses Yan's Foot Reflexology Center, showing how the neighborhood has changed. Founded in 1894, Greenberg's is referred to in Lawton Mackall's *Knife and Fork in New York* (1949) as "the oldest Roumanian restaurant in the city . . . unpretentious but excellent; no entertainment except for your palate," suggesting that other Romanian restaurants probably featured something of a Catskillian comic floor show, as Sammy's still does today.

Mackall goes on to list a selection of dishes, which again doesn't include pastrami but does feature chopped liver, frozen calf's feet (it's unclear what "frozen" refers to), gefuelt kiska (apparently, similar to the stuffed guts called "derma"), broiled sweetbreads, more carnatzlach, captushala ("liver broiled on steak"), and mamaliga (beef goulash with cornmeal mush—essentially polenta, and still found in non–Jewish-Romanian restaurants in Long Island City and Sunnyside). But why, if Romanian Jews brought pastrami to the States, was this smoked meat not found in their restaurants?

The food writer Calvin Trillin, himself a fan of the Jewish-Romanian restaurant canon, which he must have first experienced when he arrived in New York from Kansas City in the late '50s, boasted of having eaten at Greenberg's and told me several jokes he'd learned there. Unfortunately, the only one I can remember isn't appropriate to repeat.

To find a trace of pastrami on the non-deli menus of midcentury, it's necessary to seek out the rare Jewish-Chinese restaurant on the Lower East Side, such as the long-defunct Bernstein on Essex, as mentioned in the 1972 *New York Times Guide to Dining Out in New York*. There amid dishes with names like lo mein Bernstein, chow mein Bernstein, chopped liver, and stuffed cabbage, "Roumanian pastrami" was prominently featured as an entrée. In fact, the slogan for Bernstein on Essex, which was open as late as 1996, when Jewish food expert Claudia Roden visited it, was "The King of Pastrami."

Maybe Danny Bowien's modern use of pastrami in a Chinese context in his celebrated kung pao pastrami wasn't so unique after all, though Bernstein on Essex seemed to have kept its Jewish and Chinese dishes carefully separated—no fusion permitted!

Maybe pastrami was considered the exclusive province of Jewish delis, which had more of a German identification than an Eastern European one and served a grab-and-go sandwich cuisine distinct from the sit-down fare found at Romanian restaurants. Indeed, as we shall see, the modern form of pastrami may well have been invented by the German-Jewish deli men like those at Katz's, altering it substantially from its European form, though perhaps using some of the same spices. Or maybe pastrami was considered outside the purview of fancier Romanian-Jewish restaurants, or simply considered not appropriate, too pedestrian. Indeed, since the meat arrives at most delis today already cured and smoked (one apparent exception is Liebman's in the Bronx), there's really nothing chefly to be done to pastrami. All it needs is a post-delivery poaching and slicing on the part of the deli.

It is for similar reasons that pastrami almost never appears in Jewish cookbooks, though it is a bona fide and particularly beloved Jewish-American staple: you don't make pastrami, you buy it. Even among the delis that serve it today, there's a certain mystique that veils its origin, both actual and figurative. Katz's Delicatessen, for example, refuses to divulge where in Brooklyn its pastrami comes from, or the precise process by which it's made. Is there an element of paranoia at play? Was competition among pastrami purveyors so fierce at one time that sources and methods were concealed out of necessity? Maybe. By contrast, while pastrami now seems special, its mention in the last chapter of A. J. Liebling's *Between Meals* suggests disparagingly that in the '50s, pastrami was the quick and all-too-common lunch of salesmen, who'd eat several sandwiches quickly in one sitting. Indeed, during this era pastrami was not only a meat found in Jewish delis but one that had migrated onto the menu of diners and common lunch counters with no particular ethnic affiliation.

PASTRAMI DIASPORA

While pastrami can be found in other American cities with Jewish populations and hence Jewish delis (Zingerman's in Ann Arbor, Michigan, and Langer's in Los Angeles readily spring to mind), it is in New York that the meat is most available, not only in the two dozen or so old-fashioned Jewish delis that remain and flourish, but also in bodegas and bistros across the city. Pastrami constitutes a signal part of New York's culinary fabric; it has become one of the meats most associated with the city, along with New York strip steak and Nathan's franks.

Pastrami has also started popping up in unexpected places. One of the best is Danny Bowien's kung pao pastrami at Mission Chinese, mentioned previously, which he developed at his restaurant in San Francisco's Mission District but which found its most meaningful expression on the Lower East Side. Amazing how well little pink nuggets of charred pastrami go with Sichuan peppercorns and peanuts. Maybe we've been making a mistake all these years by treating it exclusively as sandwich fodder.

Recently, pastrami burgers became something of a minifad, appearing in restaurants as diverse as Bowery Diner (an upscale bistro, now defunct) and Schnitzel Express (a kosher sandwich shop). Most are really just a regular burger with thick slices of pastrami flopped on top, though Mile End mixes its smoked meat (the Montreal version of pastrami) into the ground beef. Given that pastrami almost qualifies as barbecue, allying it with a burger is akin to slapping on some bacon, while remaining kosher style. As Jonathan Gold said of Langer's pastrami in the *Los Angeles Times*, "The long-steamed pastrami, dense, hand-sliced and nowhere near lean, has a firm, chewy consistency, a gentle flavor of garlic and clove, and a clean edge of smokiness that can remind you of the kinship between pastrami and Texas barbecue."

During the last decade, we've seen sliced pastrami featured in a ramen soup with miniature matzo balls at Dassara Brooklyn Ramen in Cobble Hill, pastrami pot stickers at Brooklyn Wok Shop in Williamsburg, and pastrami egg rolls at Red Farm, the West Village Chinese restaurant aimed partly at Jews, handily fulfilling the fusion promise that Bernstein on Essex once opted out of. Meanwhile, pastrami and deep-fried pickles proved a popular app at the upscale chain 5 Napkin Burger.

A breakfast cart on 72nd Street on the Upper West Side introduced a penurious pastrami sandwich—a single thin slice on white bread—among its other offerings for $1.75, perhaps the cheapest pastrami sandwich in town, and not really all that bad. A little pastrami can go a long way. Science chef Wylie Dufresne of the trailblazing WD-50 (now defunct) grates pastrami over a dish of homemade rye pasta at Alder, his slightly cheaper spot in the East Village. On the opposite end of the culinary ambition spectrum, short-lived taco stand Super Linda offered a pastrami taco on the edge of Tribeca—then promptly closed, leaving us sadly pastrami taco–less, at least momentarily. Los Angeles boasts pastrami burritos in profusion; we can only drool in admiration.

Bagel stores in Park Slope, Brooklyn; the Upper West Side

of Manhattan; and Forest Hills, Queens, routinely offer bagels with fried eggs, pastrami, and American cheese in blatant contravention of kosher principles. But the mother of all refectories in that regard is the burgeoning Subway chain, which has installed hundreds of locations in the five boroughs during the last decade, becoming ubiquitous in nearly every neighborhood. Their compulsory take on this New York sandwich is an overstuffed hero roll of their own manufacture piled high with thin-sliced pastrami and topped with melted provolone. Not quite Jewish-Italian and not quite good.

Still, Subway has confirmed the fact that, if you're in New York City, pastrami can appear almost anywhere.

THE SEINFELD CONNECTION

Pastrami's association with New York above all other locations (even Romania) is demonstrated by the city's greatest TV show, *Seinfeld*. In episode four, season nine, entitled "The Blood," George contrives to make sex more pleasurable by scarfing a pastrami sandwich and watching television during the act, popping out at intervals from under a blanket as he and his girlfriend, Tara, are engaged in foreplay. When she sees him munching and strenuously objects, he tries to convince her that pastrami was an integral part of a scene in the steamy *9½ Weeks*: "Oh yeah yeah, don't you know they used pastrami in that movie *9½ Weeks*? Remember the pastrami scene?" She replies with a curt "No," and George continues indignantly, "Well, maybe it was *Ghostbusters*? Wherever it was, it worked!"

Later in the episode, by way of explaining his failure with Tara, George memorably admits to Jerry at Monk's Cafe that he "flew too close to the sun on wings of pastrami." Eventually George finds himself again eating a pastrami sandwich, this time with Elaine's friend Vivian in her kitchen. He immediately perks up when she confesses, "I find the pastrami to be the most sensual of all the salted cured meats. Hungry?" After that they sink to the floor in a lewd embrace.

And in the famous "I'll have what she's having" scene from *When Harry Met Sally*, pastrami may also be involved—though Sally is clearly eating a turkey sandwich at Katz's Deli, Harry appears to be eating pastrami during the loudly faked orgasm. However, his matter-of-fact munching suggests that the pastrami has no erotic appeal, at least for him.

Yet, in its deep-pink salinity, there is something sensual about pastrami, isn't there? As an aphrodisiac, I'd take a pastrami sandwich over a raw oyster any day of the week.

A FIRST NIBBLE OF EAST VILLAGE PASTRAMI

It wasn't long after my arrival in the East Village in 1977—moving into a tenement on the south side of 14th Street just west of Avenue C, well in advance of the hipster hordes—that I began exploring the neighborhood. I first discovered the concentric walkways of Tompkins Square, a Victorian landscape that made you want to engage in a counterclockwise promenade, parasol swinging by your side. Apart from a junkie or two passed out on the antique benches, the leafy park filled with old-growth elms and oaks and London plane trees was relatively serene during that era, though I was later to find out it had been the site of draft and political riots in 1863 and 1874; a century later, a modern riot occurred there in the late '80s as cops tore down a shantytown that had grown at the north end of the park. I remember it as a collection of salvaged-wood hovels built close together, cook fires sending up smoke in the early morning as I wheeled my daughter, Tracy, to daycare on East Third Street between Second and First Avenues, known then as the Hells Angels block.

In my early rambles, I quickly discovered the mini–business district on the west side of the park, which was to house the neighborhood's first upscale restaurant in the late '80s, a place called the Pharmacy, at the corner of 9th Street and Avenue A, where Doc Holliday's now resides. The district consisted of a three-block strip that also housed two prominent old-timers:

Odessa, a Ukrainian diner offering Eastern European commonplaces like pierogis and goulash alongside more standard
diner fare; and Leshko's, considered by my growing group of
music-minded friends to be the more proletarian of the two and
hence the more desirable. I think the prices at Leshko's were
about 50 cents cheaper, which explains, perhaps, why Odessa is
still on the west side of Tomkins Square today while Leshko's
is long gone.

I also quickly discovered Saint Marks Place with its hold-
over hippies and beats, excellent pizza parlors, and cheap movie
theaters; and the stretch of Second Avenue that contained a
few faltering examples of eateries associated with the Yiddish
Broadway. The towering theater at 12th Street and Second
Avenue—soon to be known as Entermedia and later to return
to movie use as Village East—had been one of those theaters, and across the street had been the last incarnation of the
Café Royale, where Isaac Bashevis Singer held court. Across
the street and down a block was the 2nd Ave Deli, opened in
1954 by Abe Lebewohl, a Holocaust survivor. It was the East
Village's best Jewish deli, based upon a technicality. That technicality was that Katz's Delicatessen, located on the south side
of Houston Street, was across the street from the boundary of
the East Village as it had been defined by real estate promot-
ers in the 1950s. The 2nd Ave Deli had a room dedicated to the
long-forgotten Yiddish starlet Molly Picon. There were stars on
the sidewalk out front, like the Hollywood walk of fame, only
for celebrities of the Yiddish theater.

I first stumbled into the deli in 1978. Here was a place that
was not afraid to display its bulging dermas (the name basically
means "intestines") and other facets of Jewish poverty cuisine I
wouldn't dare try for several more years. Adventuresome eaters are self-made, not born. Showcasing Lebewohl's left-wing
spirit, a virtual United Nations of meat carvers worked behind
the counter in the front window, sawing away at big hunks of
deli meat with mechanical slicers. The process of getting your
takeout order—I never considered actually eating there, the

clientele seemed too old and alien, as if arriving on a spaceship from an earlier era—was slow and ponderous. In 2006 a large rent increase closed this razzmatazz of a deli and it moved up to Murray Hill the next year, where it still stands and is said by some to still be good.

Eventually, I realized that the pastrami—usually the most superior of the deli meats—was not as good as the corned beef at 2nd Ave Deli. So I'd visit only if I was in a corned beef mood. In 1996, Lebewohl was shot during a nighttime robbery as he climbed into the deli van with the day's receipts. The murderer was never caught, but it changed the neighborhood forever. No one wanted to walk into the deli and not see Abe there, his glasses down on his nose, his bald head with fringes of unkempt gray hair, like some character from Dickens. The square across the street in front of Saint Mark's Church has been named for him.

KATZ'S, THAT'S ALL!

Eventually, I found myself plunging into the Lower East Side. In those days, bohemians like myself and my friends considered the hardscrabble terrain of downtown Manhattan our natural range; we often boasted that we'd never been north of 14th Street, though we secretly climbed on the subway every morning to get to our midtown jobs. But our terroir was pretty much limited to the East Village, with occasional incursions into Soho, which was then a dark precinct of decaying cast-iron architecture with little in the way of restaurants and retail businesses (the exception: Fanelli's Cafe, where you could get a hamburger and a beer)—but plenty of underground performance spaces and fly-by-night galleries that we delighted in patronizing. Loft parties in Soho back then were "everyone's invited" affairs.

But the Lower East Side remained largely unknown to us. So it was, in my rambles, that I found myself walking down Avenue C one Saturday morning. Hitting Houston Street, I hung a right. As I passed Essex—the southward extension of Avenue A—I spotted a faded metal sign emblazoned "KATZ'S That's All!"

THAT'S ALL WHAT? I WONDERED.

As I got closer, I spotted another sign on the same building, this one trailing down Ludlow Street—"Wurst Fabric KATZ'S Delicatessen," it further proclaimed. Using my schoolboy German, acquired through compulsory classes in Minneapolis elementary schools, I understood that "Wurst Fabric"—which sounds like a place that manufactures poor-quality textiles—meant "Sausage Maker." How quaint, I thought, as I ventured closer.

Big windows flaunted come-ons concerning salamis. One urged, "Send a Salami to Your Boy in the Army." Since there hadn't been an overseas conflict in a while, I wondered what war it referred to. Years later, as I began to have an ear for New York accents, I realized like a freight train had slammed into my head that *army* was supposed to rhyme with *salami*.

The deli had a door right at the corner that led you to a square metal podium that had apparently once been a ticket dispenser, now out of commission but unremoved. There, a guy stood with a roll of rectangular tickets, something like movie tickets but covered with consecutive numbers. According to an arcane system, each person must take a ticket, and as viands are acquired at counters on one side of the room, that ticket is checked off with a grease crayon that details everything you've bought, with a scrawled total adjusted as each new dish is added. Tax is tacked on and a grand total determined as you stand in line at the cash register after your meal. If you lose your ticket, a fine of $50 is supposedly assigned. As you sit deliriously enjoying your pastrami, it's common to temporarily lose track of your ticket, and a brief panic ensues.

The room was vast, with an L-shaped extension that veered around a corner to the right. There were tons of Formica-topped tables arrayed in the center for the common folk, and a line of Waitress Only tables along one wall for the swells. The ceilings were high, the lighting fluorescent, the walls composed of cheap wood paneling, deeply stained with grease. The place seemed to be mired in the 1930s, though I later learned the establishment dated to 1888; there was an air of well-worn poverty and working-class resignation about it. Later, when I went to one of the few remaining plebeian restaurants in Paris known as *bouillons*, where cheap meals were provided en masse for factory workers, I realized that Katz's was our equivalent. This was long before it became an agreeable species of tourist attraction that slices 15,000 pounds of pastrami per week.

The carvers, who stood behind a high glass counter, were earnest guys. On my first visit, they were nearly all elderly Lower East Side Jews. When I went recently, they were mainly Lower East Side Puerto Ricans. While the carvers at 2nd Ave Deli cut their meats on automatic slicers, these guys wielded fearsome knives, like some Semitic tribe fighting the Romans. And they cut the meats thick. They'd spear cuts of meat— pastrami, corned beef, and plain uncured brisket—with long forks, lift them out of centrally located water baths, and rush them to their slicing stations, triumphant. Tubs of cucumber and green-tomato pickles stood at the ready at each station, along with loaves of rye and white and bags of "club rolls": crusty, torpedo-shaped, blunted at both ends.

Each carver seemed eager to assemble your sandwich, and it was always something of a dilemma whom to pick. Most folks who wandered into Katz's chose their carver according to the length of the line that snaked from his station. Each carver observed a sacred ritual as he prepared your sandwich. First he requested your specifications, say, a combination of pastrami and corned beef with mustard on rye bread (my perpetual favorite). The guy pulls a couple of pieces of rye from its archaic wax-paper package—which led me to wonder, even then, "Who still sells rye wrapped in wax paper?"

Next, he brushes each slice of bread with grainy mustard using a cavalier flick of the wrist, though some carvers refuse to put the mustard on your sandwich on the grounds that each table in the dining room has a bottle of mustard on it. If mustard were applied now, the bread might go soggy before you had a chance to dig into it—especially if you stood in another line for a beverage. Or if you decided you needed some of Katz's truly awful and mealy steak fries, which come from another station. The compulsory beverage order, by the way, is a can of Dr. Brown's Cel-Ray soda, flavored with celery. After you've tasted one can, you may never order another—it's terrible!

Back at the carving station, your guy slides the requested cut or cuts of meat in front of him and ostentatiously trims a little fat from it here and there, making sure that you see he's still leaving lots of fat. He begins slicing in earnest. He pulls out a plate and puts a couple of slices on it, then slides it onto the raised glass counter for you to take a taste. This free taste is a quintessential part of the experience. Then he finishes cutting and places the symmetrical stack of meat slices on the bread. He pauses a moment, as if reconsidering, and finally cuts a few more slices and places them on top of the other slices perpendicularly, as if to emphasize the surfeit of meat he's just given you. He adds the second piece of rye on top and straightens the whole thing, as if it were about to teeter.

Next, he inquires what kind of pickles you want, and slaps them on a plate. You then hand him your ticket, and he scribbles some numbers on it. At this point, you're expected to put a tip in his paper cup. Since the sandwich will cost $16 or so and is sufficient for two normal eaters, especially if you get extra pickles, you should give him a dollar. But wait a minute! What good is a tip after the whole process is completed? It's not going to improve anything about your sandwich at that point.

Accordingly, one day I invented the Katz's pre-tip, whereby you put a dollar or two in the tip cup just as you're placing your sandwich order. The carver will then nod appreciatively and assemble a sandwich approximately 30 percent larger than the usual rather large sandwich. And often, extra pickles. I'll sheepishly admit that others may have invented this improvement, too. But I've been encouraging patrons to practice the pre-tip at least since the first time I wrote about Katz's, which was around 1990 in my food fanzine *Down the Hatch*.

What did Katz's mean to me in those first years of eating there in the late '70s and early '80s? A hell of a lot. It was my first connection with New York's ancient food culture. I can remember being floored the moment I looked across its great expanse, aimed directly at working-class immigrants, a place where being fed had been shorn of its every pretension, where big plates of food were not intended for tourists, foodies, curiosities seekers, or slummers from further uptown. A place as indigenous to Houston Street as the soot-clogged air, a place that belonged there as certainly as does a car in a suburban garage. Katz's forcefully reset my mind's default where New York City food was concerned, and every time I eat a sandwich of any sort I must forever compare it to Katz's.

Yes, someday the wrecking ball will come down on this august institution, or a condo will be constructed directly on top and the space "modernized"—and New York City will be desperately poorer for it.

WHERE PASTRAMI THEORETICALLY CAME FROM

Later, as a restaurant critic at the *Village Voice*, I became aware of pastrami cognates from the Old World and how dissimilar they were from the juicy, red, gently warmed, thick-sliced pastrami we enjoy today. I figured out that pastrami as we know it had probably not been carried from Romania as a fait accompli but modified and improved here by German-Jewish immigrants so as to be nearly unrecognizable from its original form.

In December 1996, while grazing on a platter called "assorted meet" at Café Caspiy, an Azerbaijani joint on Brooklyn's Avenue U, I stumbled on a form of dried beef called *basturma*. It was deep red and oily, sliced paper thin, and ringed with yellow fat that crumbled to the touch. And it was served at room temperature. "Wow. 'Basturma' sounds like the same word as 'pastrami,'" I exclaimed to the group of misfit diners I'd managed to drag along with me to the far reaches of Brooklyn. "But it hasn't been smoked," I continued, "though the edges have been rubbed with spices. But the spices are different."

Of course, once you stumble on this sort of thing a first time, you start seeing it everywhere. A few months later, as the weather turned warm, I found basturma at one of those sidewalk cafés frequented by expat Russian Jews at Brighton Beach, Brooklyn, as strolling accordionists played "Those Were the Days" and children cavorted on the boardwalk, doing handstands and cartwheels in spite of the danger of slivers. In a 1997 *Voice* review, I noted: "Basturma ($4) generates much excitement among the Russian diners: thin slices of air-dried beef generously veined with fat, with the funk of Italian soppressata."

I soon was spotting basturma in every Turkish, Balkan, and central Asian restaurant as well, more often spelled *bastirma* or *pastirma*. One thing these thin-sliced meats had in common was that they were all very fine grained and seemed to be made from a more delicate cut than brisket. Indeed, this form of cured beef is said by some to have originated in the Ottoman Empire, which spread Turkish cuisine throughout adjacent areas of Europe, Asia, and North Africa for six centuries, ending around 1908.

How was this basturma made? According to *Eat Smart in Turkey* (1996), a travel guide by Joan and David Peterson, the product is "dried, salted meat cured with a paste called *cemen*, which consists primarily of red pepper, fenugreek seeds, and garlic." Yes, it's pronounced "semen," and cumin is another frequent component. A further element of basturma production is pressing. Indeed, the word means "pressed meat" in Turkish. It was traditionally air dried for 15 days in the hot winds of the Anatolian plains and carried by Turkish horsemen bent on conquest as they rode through the Caucasus Mountains and central Asia, the meat tucked between the saddle and the body of the horse, which must have improved the flavor tremendously. This is presumably how basturma made it to Romania: on the back of a sweaty horse.

I must have eaten three dozen versions of the Anatolian dried meat in the ensuing years. The Bulgarians and Serbs call it *pastarma*; the Greeks, *pastourmas*; the Azerbaijanis, *bastirma*; the Arabs, *basterma*; and the Romanians, *pastrama*. In Yiddish, it's *pastromeh*. In Turkey, Lebanon, Syria, and Egypt, the dried meat is most often eaten with eggs at breakfast. In the Turkish restaurants of Bay Ridge, Brooklyn, bastirma is used as a topping for large-circumference, flat pitas that are presented as a competitor for pizza.

So how the hell did our pastrami descend from Turkish basturma via Romania, when the two products have nothing in common except curing and beef? Claudia Roden, in *The Book of Jewish Food* (1996), bears me out on this point: "One of the great inventions of the American deli was pastrami. It is said to be of Romanian origin, but it is entirely different from the cured meats with a similar-sounding name that you find in Turkey, Romania, and the Balkans."

Stick with me here, because this is going to be one of this book's most contorted and convoluted theories.

BRISKET, THAT'S ALL

As I imply in the barbecued brisket chapter, smoked brisket is the queen of barbecued meats, even though it has recently been suffering some stiff competition from cudgel-sized beef ribs. Well, in a recent piece on *Texas Monthly*'s barbecue blog, the magazine's barbecue critic, Daniel Vaughn, did some amazing research, the upshot of which was to demonstrate that the earliest Texas barbecues—we're talking mid- to late-19th century here—were open-pit, public-picnic affairs in which whole steers were smoked. Later, when butchers such as Kreuz Market started doing barbecue on premise, they, too, tended to use the entire animal, selling it bit by bit with no prejudice toward one cut or another; all were available and relished by someone.

According to Vaughn's theory, U.S. Army specifications for

meat to be fed to troops resulted in cuts of beef being differentiated and separated for commercial purposes in the mid-20th century, or perhaps earlier. Butchers would sell these desirable cuts en masse to the government according to specifications promulgated by the USDA in the years after World War II. Vaughn further posits that this period, the 1950s, is when Texas barbecues began to focus on brisket as being a cut of meat eschewed by the military and hence leftover for the meat markets to put to their own usage. He goes to some trouble defining how the increased usage of briskets in the barbecues of Texas forever changed the barbecue terrain of the Lone Star State.

But he also investigates who was selling and advertising smoked brisket in Texas at a much earlier time and finds that it was Jewish butchers who did so in newspaper advertisements as early as 1910, from shops that also stocked smoked whitefish and kosher sausage. He found the brothers Alex and Moise Weil of Corpus Christi, Texas, not only selling smoked brisket in 1916 but also a product called "pastramie." He also mentions that the Weil brothers—who were selling products such as pork sausage and pork headcheese, so were certainly halfhearted kosher butchers, unless kosher was less serious a commitment than it is now—were descended from a father who emigrated to Texas from Alsace, France, in 1867, suggesting that Texas pastrami has nothing whatsoever to do with Romania.

Rather, due to the timing, it's fun to think that maybe New York pastrami as we know it—corned beef rubbed with spices and smoked—might have originated in Texas via Jewish butchers who preferentially handled the brisket over other cuts and doubtlessly looked for new ways to market it because of the favor brisket had historically enjoyed among Jews in Germany as well as Eastern Europe. According to the advertisements unearthed by Vaughn, Jewish butchers had already made the leap to smoking briskets, Texas style, so they might have first decided to experiment with smoking corned beef as well. And hence might pastrami as we know it have been born.

While this theory is far-fetched, perhaps, it might be proven by looking into correspondence that has been preserved from the era, or perhaps just by demonstrating that there was extensive regular communication between Jews in New York and Texas. Given that many early Jews in the South and Southwest had been traveling tinkers and later clothing salesmen, it's not too difficult to imagine that a taste for smoked corned beef somehow traveled from Texas to New York about the time pastrami as we know it popped up as New York City's most characteristic meat in the early 20th century.

NINE PLACES TO EAT PASTRAMI

1. KATZ'S DELICATESSEN

205 EAST HOUSTON STREET, MANHATTAN, 212-254-2246

The greatest deli in the world. Get a pastrami on rye or a club roll with mustard and your choice of pickles. I usually get a sandwich of corned beef and pastrami, and lately I've been known to occasionally get plain brisket, because that's great, too. Also, don't miss the knoblewurst, a thick garlic sausage, on rye with mustard and sauerkraut.

2. JAY AND LLOYD'S KOSHER DELI

2718 AVENUE U, BROOKLYN, 718-891-5298

This deli was founded by a pair of third-generation deli men in 1993, but it seems much older. They, too, are somewhat coy about how their pastrami is made, hinting that it is smoked with schmaltz, or chicken fat, an ingredient central to Jewish cooking.

3. 2ND AVE DELI

162 EAST 33RD STREET, MANHATTAN, 212-689-9000

Founded by Abe Lebewohl in 1954 and once a fixture of the East Village's Second Avenue, the deli was driven to Murray Hill by spiraling rents. The newer premises is smaller, but the pastrami is just as good according to some, though sliced by machine, rather than by hand. Hey, some people like it sliced thin. Not me. The corned beef is as good as before. Kosher.

4. SARGE'S DELI

548 THIRD AVE, MANHATTAN, 212-679-0442

Founded by a police sergeant in 1954, Sarge's is famous for its overstuffed sandwiches and matzo ball soup. The machine-sliced pastrami is a little saltier and a little less smoky than usual. It's damn good anyway. Pickles and slaw in profusion are placed upon the tables. Open 24 hours.

5. LIEBMAN'S KOSHER DELICATESSEN

552 WEST 235TH STREET, BRONX, 718-548-4534

For over 50 years Liebman's has been a fixture of the Bronx's far northern Riverdale neighborhood, in a region of tree-shaded shopping streets. This exceedingly old-fashioned deli boasts that the pastrami is made right on the premises, which means there must be a smoker installed somewhere.

6. MILL BASIN KOSHER DELICATESSEN

5823 AVENUE T, BROOKLYN, 718-241-4910

This wacky kosher deli, located in a seaside Brooklyn community with wharves and houses on stilts, doubles as an art gallery. The pastrami is rich and more peppery than most, and in 2008 my colleague at the Village Voice, *Sarah DiGregorio, proclaimed its pastrami sandwich the best in New York City. I won't go quite that far, but it's damn good and notably overstuffed.*

7. PASTRAMI QUEEN

1125 LEXINGTON AVENUE, MANHATTAN, 212-734-1500

This Upper East Sider moved from Queens to Manhattan over a decade ago, and I swear the sandwiches got smaller, but the pastrami is still exemplary, and it has many advocates. If for some reason you don't eat beef, the turkey pastrami is an interesting substitute. Kosher.

8. CARNEGIE DELI

854 SEVENTH AVENUE, MANHATTAN, 212-757-2245

Opened in 1937 and conveniently located in midtown not far from the big hotels, Carnegie has become one of the city's culinary tourist traps. Don't get me wrong, the pastrami is good, and you can get it not only in a sandwich but also in omelets, hash, and various other configurations. And it's piled to mind-boggling heights, which is not necessarily a good thing unless you bring a friend and share it—it doesn't taste good cold two hours later.

9. MILE END DELI

53 BOND STREET, MANHATTAN, 212-529-2990;
97A HOYT STREET, BROOKLYN, 718-852-7510

Its specialty is Montreal "smoked meat," delivered in prim and pristine little sandwiches on traditional rye bread. Owners Noah and Rae Bernamoff go to pains to distinguish this red cured meat from pastrami, touting its superior taste. The process of creating it sometimes involves dry curing rather than brining, and the rubbed-on spice mixture contains garlic and mustard seeds as well, resulting, for me at least, in a sweeter and less smoky flavor. Having this Canadian specialty available alongside actual pastrami has been one of the great gastro pleasures of the last decade.

PASTRAMI

This great cured and smoked brisket, central to the menu of New York Jewish delis, may have originally been inspired by Texas barbecue.

$1\frac{1}{2}$ cups black peppercorns
$\frac{1}{2}$ cup coriander seeds
$\frac{1}{4}$ cup mustard seeds
$\frac{1}{2}$ cup red pepper flakes
4 bay leaves
1 tablespoon allspice berries
2 cups kosher salt
1 teaspoon pink curing salt (or sea salt)
6 garlic cloves, smashed to a paste
$\frac{1}{2}$ cup packed light brown sugar
1 beef brisket, around 8 pounds

1. Working in batches, grind the peppercorns, coriander seeds, mustard seeds, red pepper flakes, bay leaves, and allspice in a spice grinder until coarsely ground, transferring them to a large bowl as you go.

2. Add the kosher salt, curing salt, garlic, and sugar to the ground spices, mixing well.

3. Find a container that will hold the brisket and will fit into your refrigerator; a giant, sturdy zip-seal bag will also work. Rub the spice mixture all over the brisket, covering all sides, corners, and crevasses. Transfer the meat with all the spice mixture to the container, cover tightly, and refrigerate. Every day for the next 10 to 12 days, turn the brisket over and reapply any of the cure that has fallen off.

4. After it has cured for this period, smoke the brisket in a smoker, low and slow, 6 to 8 hours. Or use a Weber or other enclosed barbecue grill, cooking over indirect heat, placing an aluminum pan of water alongside the coals to catch drips and adding soaked wood chips to the hot coals for smoke (replenish the wood chips or charcoal as needed). The brisket should reach an internal temperature of 160°F. Refrigerate the brisket overnight or up to 1 week.

5. When you are ready to eat, place the brisket in a large roasting pan with 2 cups of water at the bottom and steam-roast at 300°F for 2 hours. Remove from the pan and slice by hand.

MASALA DOSA

O nce, it was among the city's most obscure dishes. In fact, there was only one place in town that served it. Around 1982, an Indian friend I'd known in Wisconsin who was doing post-doc research in physics at NYU, Raghu Raghavan, pulled me aside and whispered conspiratorially, "There's an Indian restaurant uptown that does dosas."

"What the hell is a dosa?" I parried. Though I'd been living in New York City since 1977 and was already deeply into the ethnic food scene, I wouldn't start writing about it until 1989, when I published the first food fanzine, *Down the Hatch*. Nevertheless I hung on his every word as he replied, gesturing with a roll of his hands. "It's a sort of sour crepe wrapped around a potato mixture with spices and nuts in it," he explained.

"That doesn't sound like any Indian food I've ever heard of," I replied.

"That's because all you've ever eaten is northern Indian," he snorted pityingly. "South Indian is much lighter, starchier, and more vegetable-y."

Back then, Indian food in New York was mainly confined to the meat swimming in gravy found at slightly upscale Punjabi palaces in midtown, where the decor was dark and ornate, the air smelled faintly of incense, and waiters a shade too obsequious would give your plate a prolonged and ostentatious polishing before they set it down before you, as if afraid you might consider Indian restaurants unhygienic. The alternative was a short row of wonderful but decidedly downscale restaurants on a single block of East Sixth Street in the East Village that had appeared around 1975, with such unappetizing names as Anar Bagh and Purbo Rag. By the 1980s, the strip was expanding and several had taken to putting turbaned sitar and tabla players in their front windows to attract diners; later they used touts who would aggressively try to coax you into restaurants from their sidewalk posts.

These East Village places (several, including Mitali East, Raj Mahal, Panna II, and Gandhi, still exist) peddled humongous, nearly identical all-in meals centered on chicken, beef, or lamb—then considered exotic by many diners—in ginger-heavy sauces that came in several shades of brown. You spooned the meats from metal vessels, accompanied by rice, poori, or chapatti; a caddie of chutneys and dals; and a choice of samosas or mulligatawny as a starter. Sometimes dessert was included, with the entire meal costing less than five dollars. The food delighted us, not only for its ability to fill you up more cheaply than almost any other restaurants in town, but also because the fare was unspeakably rich and meaty compared to similarly priced budget meals. Only the Ukrainian steam table places in the nabe competed in the same meat-for-the-money category.

We later discovered these Indian establishments were mainly run by Bangladeshi immigrants who originated in a single small town, hence the similarity of the menus. A decade later at their peak I counted 21 of these places on East Sixth Street and the adjacent avenues. Late in the '80s a couple of these restaurants caused a sensation by introducing tandoori chicken to a city that had experienced little of it previously. These places defined Indian food (and cheap dining to a large extent) for a generation of hipsters who were then remaking the East Village into one of the city's most notorious neighborhoods.

A few days after I spoke to Raghavan, Gretchen and I, along with a group of our punky friends who dwelled in the same rundown tenement at 630 East 14th Street, found ourselves at Madras Woodlands, the restaurant Raghavan had mentioned. Located on 44th Street just north of Tudor City, it seemed to hang on a precipice above the United Nations like something out of *Lost Horizon*. The interior I remember as elegant, and my friends and I must have presented quite a spectacle in our all-black attire to the diplomats and Indian businessmen who frequented the place.

We were nearly flabbergasted to find that the entire menu was vegetarian, since we'd been expecting something similar to what was served on East Sixth Street. But what amazing vegetarian food it was! If we'd eaten vegetarian food before at all, it was the hippie cuisine that originated in the '60s. That food was all garden vegetables and brown rice—with flavor limited to a squirt of soy sauce or tamari—while this was rife with lentils, kari (curry) leaves, black mustard seeds that popped in the mouth like tiny firecrackers, and powerful curry spices. It was a real assault of unfamiliar flavors much more interesting as a prototype for meat-free eating than anything we'd imagined existed.

We oohed and aahed at Madras Woodlands that evening back in 1982 as we got our first glimpse of the masala dosa: a humongous starch cylinder the size of a rolling pin colored sienna brown, fantastically crisp and piping hot. Raghavan had told us we must eat it with our fingers. As instructed, we tore off little swatches of the thing—which sat on a shiny stainless-steel salver—and munched thoughtfully. The wrapper was crisp and buttery and slightly tart, entirely agreeable and like nothing we'd ever tasted before. The inside was mellow and starchy, with depth charges of spiciness and a nuttiness from the cashews planted here and there. It was entirely delectable, and we tore it to pieces in three minutes flat.

Had it been 10 years later, we might have compared the taste of the wrapper to Ethiopian injera. But that cuisine was then unknown to us, so we found ourselves completely out to sea as far as analogs went. That evening we also ate soups and pilafs and vegetarian curries that we thoroughly enjoyed, but what stuck in our minds—and established an unquenchable yearning that begins the moment you finish your first—was that magnificent taste of the masala dosa. Little did we suspect that the dosas, along with the idlis and uttapams we were also tasting for the first time, were a harbinger of a pan–South Indian cooking set to arrive in New York over the next three decades, a series of dishes relished all over India at breakfast and lunch that would eventually become one of New York's most exciting cuisines.

The Madras Woodlands we visited turned out to be part of a worldwide chain of hotel-based Indian restaurants that served a slightly upscale version of this standard South Indian vegetarian menu. According to the website of a Hyde Park, New York, branch that still miraculously exists, the UN branch founded "in the 70s" introduced this type of Indian food to New York for the first time. In an aside, Milton Glaser and Jerome Snyder wrote in their *All New Underground Gourmet* (1977), "If this restaurant is meant to be the spearhead of an American gastronomic colonization, it's off to a great start." Little did they realize what a slow-moving colonization it would prove to be.

The Manhattan branch lumbered along, gradually losing customers and growing slightly seedy, till it closed in 1989. Another rendition appeared briefly in 1990 on 49th Street between First and Second Avenues, nearly as good as the original. But the fledgling *Zagat* guide wrote of it dismissively, "It's low on ambiance and service, is 'amateurish at best,' but the prices are reasonable and the Southern Indian food is an 'unusual' change of pace." Damning with faint praise! I eventually learned from a former *Zagat* editor who'd gone to work as a listings editor at the *Village Voice* that *Zagat* employees pretty much wrote all of the supposedly crowdsourced copy in the spot reviews, leading me to wonder, did *Zagat* try to smother the dosa in its infancy?

WHAT IS A DOSA, ANYWAY?

There are many regional cuisines in South India, each with its own characteristics. Hyderabadi cooking, for example, is very proud of its biryanis—rice pilafs probably inspired by Persian cooking; while the food of Kerala at the southern tip of the subcontinent is awash in fish and coconut milk. But one dish that unites all the southern regions is the masala dosa, of which every city and town seems to have its own variation. To confuse matters further, those invented here are sometimes retrospectively given Indian place names, when a certain *masala* (spice mixture) associated with a town or region is used in the preparation of the dish, or simply to flatter immigrants from that region and attract them to the restaurant.

The dosa—the crisp pancake that forms the outside of the masala dosa—is created from a batter that, somewhat unexpectedly, is made with rice and small black urad dal, which is yellowish after the skin is removed, one of the myriad types of lentils available in India. Both rice and lentils are ground up raw and mixed with water and allowed to ferment with adventitious yeast and bacteria. Yes, simple exposure to air provides the organisms that cause the batter, over a period of 24 hours, to bubble up, increase in volume, and change its flavor and texture. This process is brilliant food chemistry, since it results in both grain and lentils being rendered into a form in which they can be cooked in a significantly shorter time, thus conserving energy while adding loads of flavor.

After fermentation, this batter is ladled onto a round greased griddle called a *tawa*. The dosa maker makes swirling motions with the ladle, spreading the foamy batter into great corrugated concentric circles. The dosa is cooked on the bottom side to brownness, while the top side, which will eventually be the interior of the rolled pancake, remains pale in color, since it never touches the griddle. The dosa master lifts up the edges of the finished pancake with a spatula, and if it's to be served unfilled, rolls the South Indian flapjack up for delivery to the table. Sometimes the dosa is folded into a triangle instead.

If the pancake is served unfilled, it's called a *dosa*, *paper dosa*, or *sada dosa*, one of a dozen dosa variations found in a typical South Indian restaurant. Any dosa filled with a potato mixture may be called a masala dosa, with the word *masala* used as a synecdoche to describe the entire filling. The conventional filling is made with potatoes, onions, and sometimes cashews or pistachios. The flavorings in this filling may include black mustard seeds, tiny Asian cumin seeds, and kari leaves—tiny, shiny, green astringent leaves that have almost no connection to curry powder. Confusingly, sometimes an actual masala (referring to any dry spice mixture) is spread inside the pancake while it cooks, and extra ingredients—such as fresh green chiles for added hotness—can become part of the filling.

Nevertheless, until recently masala dosa variations never ventured far beyond several standard configurations. One alternate type, called a *rava dosa*, is made with an unfermented batter something like cream of wheat, resulting in a crisp lattice-like pancake with no sourness. These are often listed alongside the regular masala dosas on the menu, with a similar choice of fillings.

Whatever the filling composition, part of the masala dosa's aesthetic involves not spreading the potato mixture too evenly inside the wrapper, as you might do with a French crepe or Russian blintz, but rather leaving it in a single lump in the middle. This encourages people to share one communally with their fingers, hands politely darting into the center of the table to tear fragments of the wrapper and scoop up little wads of potato. Sharing a dosa is often a good idea, since they've gotten larger and larger over the years, and one is often more than a single diner can eat, especially if other dishes are consumed as part of a communal meal.

I once bought a masala dosa at Sapthagiri—a vegetarian Indian restaurant still going strong in Jersey City, just across the Hudson River from Manhattan—which was over two feet in length, so that the waiter smiled broadly as he carried it in and we marveled at its size. Many dosas here are cooked especially large for their shock value, but the wad of potato in the middle remains relatively small. The largest on record in the New York area so far was at the now-defunct South Indian restaurant Tamil Nadu Bhavan, which advertised a "5-foot family dosa" for $19.93 in 2008. At the time, I noted in a *Village Voice* review, "It's so big, you could wrap a good-size child up inside. The menu warns: 'Not for takeout.'"

THE MASALA DOSA'S MURKY ORIGINS

I've gotten into fights with other Indian food aficionados over the topic of how the masala dosa came to be. Pick up a book like *Indian Food: A Historical Companion* (1994) by Professor K. T. Achaya of the Indian National Science Academy, New Delhi. Flip to the exhaustive index and you'll find no mention of the dosa. This is because Achaya regarded it as too newfangled for inclusion. (The samosa also gets the cold shoulder from the professor, even though its tetrahedral shape makes this hand-held Indian empanada one of the most interesting foods in the world, geometrically speaking.)

Achaya does mention a related dish called *idli*—another food made from a fermented mixture of raw rice and urad dal and invariably available in places that serve masala dosas, but more appetizer or snack than main course. Instead of being spread into a pancake, the batter is steamed into small, soft, white, puffy disks, porous and spongy and tasting like new-mown hay. Dipped in coconut or cilantro chutney, they absorb the condiment and are rendered sublime. Achaya notes that a poet mentions idlis in 1485. That doesn't mean that the poet's version is the same as the ones we have today, he says, which contain rice: "There are references to other moon-like products made only from urad flour." So the antiquity of the contemporary dosa and idli is limited by the appearance of rice in India, which was sometime after 1485. But the professor at least establishes that fermentation was a common practice in South Indian cooking going back many centuries.

Another issue in dating the masala dosa is the potato, though the dosa as a simple rolled or folded pancake is fully functional without its filling. The spud originated in South America, and thus isn't indigenous to India. Though Indians were cooking with sweet potatoes as early as 1615, the white potato doesn't seem to have appeared until around 1675, and there's no mention of it being cultivated until 1830, when English colonialists initiated the practice. So the masala dosa as it has come down to us is certainly less than 170 years old, and probably considerably younger, since the spud spread slowly across the South Asian subcontinent.

One can't help but notice that the French had an Indian "concession" (small colony) in the southern coastal city of Pondicherry from 1674 to 1954. And I wonder if the dosa, which originated during that time frame, wasn't inspired by the French crepe. But say that to any self-styled Indian food expert, and you're likely to hear a fierce denial, paired with a claim that the French had no influence whatsoever on Indian food. Indeed a blogger at *Club Mahindra* made a point of scouring the modern city of Pondicherry to see if he could find crepes being served anywhere—there weren't. Except for the masala dosas right under his nose!

THE SLOW PROGRESS OF THE DOSA IN NEW YORK

Like a small but hearty sapling, and in spite of *Zagat*'s dim view and the difficulty of finding it, the masala dosa gradually grew in Gotham. Where it took root in Manhattan won't come as much of a surprise: a three-block stretch of lower Lexington Avenue centering on 28th Street. Part of an area officially known as Murray Hill, it's been waggishly called Curry Hill since at least the mid-1980s. Back then it consisted of two Indian groceries and three restaurants, with an appliance store and sari house thrown in. It seemed to be gradually dwindling as a neighborhood in response to real estate pressures. Would it survive? My friends and I wondered.

It never was much by the standards of other Indian micro-neighborhoods in the New York region. But it was of a piece with similar strips in Jackson Heights and Floral Park, Queens, and in Iselin and Jersey City on the other side of the Hudson River. These neighborhoods boasted South

Asian shopping strips teeming with Indian, Pakistani, and Bangladeshi stores and restaurants, serving as a destination for unique Indian goods found at few other retail establishments. These specialty goods ran from newspapers and paperback books in Hindi, Urdu, and Tamil; sumptuous silk saris and other festive wear for the ladies; gold jewelry destined to be included in a bride's dowry; unusual vegetables such as karela (a bitter green gourd with sharp points), tinda (looking comically like a tiny cucumber), and the long, sinuous bottle gourd; as well as the full range of lentils and spices in bulk that are so necessary to Indian cooking. These commercial neighborhoods served as destinations for Indian shoppers, who often didn't live in the immediate vicinity but flocked to these streets once a week to load up their SUVs.

As I said, real estate pressures in Manhattan being what they were, Curry Hill was one of the smaller examples of an Indian shopping neighborhood, but if you hoped to cook relatively authentic curries or buy your spices cheaply in bulk, this three-block stretch centered on 28th Street became your destination—and the same is still true today. A pioneering café in Curry Hill was a place with the rollicking name of Curry in a Hurry, founded in 1975 and still in existence, and there were two more restaurants, including a formal sit-down place called Annapurna. During the 1980s I worked nearby as a photo editor and book dummier at Betty Binns Graphics, where I laid out textbooks and museum catalogs by sticking trimmed galleys to cardboard flats using hot paraffin. Exhausted as I was by noon and covered with sticky wax, Curry Hill was a godsend for me and my fellow employees at lunchtime.

Madras Mahal appeared in 1985, named after the coastal South Indian city now called Chennai. As I recall, the place started mainly as a carry-out window selling masala dosas, but quickly expanded into a full-service restaurant offering other Indian vegetarian specialties from Gujarat and northern India. But, while the dosas served at Madras Mahal were relatively unique, the strangest thing of all was that the place was officially kosher and advertised as much, the certification obtained by simply inviting in a rabbi who could perform that function and paying his fee. Since no meat, pork or otherwise, had ever crossed the threshold, this was presumably a pro-forma process. Soon, other vegetarian kosher South Indian restaurants began popping up in Curry Hill. You never saw many yarmulke-wearing observant Jews eating in these places, though as a marketing gimmick, it was fairly successful. There was no plate polishing in these places; for many diners the kosher certification also telegraphed wholesomeness.

What was the significance of these changes in Curry Hill? Well, for one thing it represented the first significant incursion of South Indian food into Manhattan, but in limited form. While the multiple cuisines of South India and the related food of Sri Lanka would eventually blossom in fuller form in places like Jersey City, eastern Queens's Union Turnpike, and along Victory Boulevard in Staten Island, the presentation of the dosa and its ilk here in their kosher-certified form was an important first step in the introduction of South Indian food to the general populace. And it ushered in a whole host of other appearances of the vegetarian cuisine of South India in the metro area.

As Indian food lovers of every stripe as well as tourists flocked to Curry Hill, it became less of an Indian shopping neighborhood and more of a regional dining destination. The collection of Indian food stores with Kalustyan's (as the name suggests, owned by an Armenian) as its flagship has remained steady over the last decade. But the sari stores and other establishments aimed only at Indian immigrants are long gone.

Many of the old Curry Hill restaurants are now closed or closing, as a new wave of more expensive and glitzier eateries take their place, some serving the newly faddish Indian-Chinese and Indian-Thai food. Others offer a host of other regional cuisines, such as Hyderabadi (Biryani Pointe) and Gujarati (Bhojan, already closed, replaced by a Bengali place called Haldi). Madras Mahal persists, however, and in imitation of the kosher Indian places, Curry in a Hurry began serving dosas in the early '90s. They still do. Their dosas are refreshingly simple and small, as they probably still are in India.

But the masala dosa was not depending on Curry Hill for its growth, though many westerners were to sample it there for the first time and fall in love with it in the '80s. In the '90s the availability of dosas in the metropolitan area was to increase tenfold. On Bowne Street in the southern part of Flushing, Queens, a Hindu temple dedicated to Ganesha—covered with bas reliefs of the elephant-headed deity—appeared in 1977. Nearly two decades later, in 1996, a canteen materialized outside called Dosa Hutt. (There had long been a secret dining room open to the public inside the temple basement, if you were willing to remove your shoes and had the balls to walk in.) I learned about Dosa Hutt from the photographer for my book *Secret New York* (1999), Linda Rutenberg, while she was in town from her home in Montreal working on the colorful square-format photos for the book. Rutenberg called me excitedly to report she'd found a very interesting small restaurant outside a wonderful temple—very off the beaten track.

By 1993 I had begun writing biweekly ethnic food reviews for the *Village Voice*, and this new place seemed like a perfect subject, so I was soon there and feasting on dosas and idlis, which were particularly zippy and fresh tasting compared to the ones I'd had earlier. And the uttapams (flat pancakes related to dosas, but much thicker and often studded with chiles) were hotter than I'd ever tasted before, so hot that I gulped water as I ate and eventually started to hiccup. The secret of the superior idlis, dosas, and uttapams at Dosa Hutt was the make-up—not of the batter, but of the diners who frequented the place. Nearly all Indians and Sri Lankans, they were very demanding as far as their dosas went and never hesitated to approach the counter and complain if their order was not perfect.

To say the place was picturesque is an understatement: it was indeed like a ramshackle structure out in the Indian countryside, with mismatched furniture, a couple of secluded nooks for dining, and a step-up-and-order counter, behind which could be seen an army toiling to produce the labor-intensive South Indian vegetarian menu. (Aside from the stray special, you never found any curries there, though other southern specialties like curd rice, lemon rice, and the wonderful farina porridge called *upma*, something like a bumpy cream of wheat laced with herbs and spices, were available.)

It was at Dosa Hutt that I got my first glimpse of the contraption—something like a cement mixer, but lower to the ground—in which the dosa, idli, and uttapam batters were mixed, bubbling and sputtering. While I've always been delighted by the place, the hilarious review blog *NY India* observes disparagingly, "Dosa Hutt is not the kind of place you'd want to take your date to if you want to make *headway* with her." The place is still open and as good as ever—well worth the pilgrimage on the 7 train and 15-minute walk down Kissena Boulevard.

Dosa Hutt was perhaps the first restaurant in town to specialize exclusively in dosas, idlis, and uttapams. The dosa master seen in the kitchen, Thiru Kumar, occasionally took his turn at the counter and chatted up the customers, especially if he saw non-Indians, whom he gladly educated in the South Indian menu. We'll be seeing more of him later in this chapter. My favorite dish at Dosa Hutt continues to be the butter dosa, drenched in ghee. This dosa is said to have originated in the southwestern Indian state of Karnataka. It came with sambar, a sort of thin spicy soup that can be used for dipping or sipping; a delightful, freshly made coconut chutney; and a cilantro chutney thinned with yogurt.

Chutneys are an inevitable accompaniment to dosas. In Jersey City, a creamy peanut chutney sometimes replaces cilantro chutney, and you occasionally see a chutney made with tomatoes, showing, if nothing else, how the South American tomato has finally had an impact on southern Indian cooking. In a Sikh neighborhood along 101st Street in Richmond Hill, Queens, Dosa Hutt spawned an imitator, Dosa Hut (with one *t*). Eventually another Dosa Hut opened in Jersey City. Both places are still open. By the millennium, dosas had become firmly implanted in the popular imagination, among foodies at least. And I found myself so addicted that I'd go out of my way to eat one at least once or twice a month, even as ethnic food in the city continued to become wildly more diverse, and there were always more new cuisines waiting to be checked out.

At about the same time that Dosa Hutt was flourishing in Flushing, Jackson Diner was the sole peddler of dosas in western Queens, where an Indian shopping neighborhood three times the size of Curry Hill had been in place since the '70s. In 1983, the eatery was founded in a former diner at the corner of 37th Avenue and 74th Street, at the end of a block-long Indian business strip, which eventually spilled onto 37th Avenue and adjacent streets. The Sikh proprietors retained the name of the old diner despite serving a strikingly non-diner menu aimed at pleasing northern and southern Indian tastes, including a limited range of dosas and idlis and a substantial quantity of other Indian vegetarian fare.

If you tried dosas for the first time in the '90s it was probably at Jackson Diner, which grew in fame and eventually moved into larger and less amusing digs down the street that looked nothing like a diner. There's now a branch in Greenwich Village that omits dosas from its menu entirely. Despite the presence of dosas at the Jackson Diner in Jackson Heights and at one other restaurant, the food in the neighborhood has remained relentlessly northern Indian, suggesting that the expected incursion of South Indian immigrants that was to be seen elsewhere in the city never really happened there. In fact, now the neighborhood is gradually being taken over by Himalayans from Tibet and Nepal.

Now that the cat was out of the bag dosa-wise, many New Yorkers had the opportunity to sample the South Indian treat, but it would be another decade before the greatest accumulation that the metropolitan area has yet seen appeared across the river in Jersey City, easily accessible on the PATH train via the Journal Square station. But first, let's offer a taxonomy of the dosa and its siblings and cousins:

A DOSA ROLL CALL

BANGALORE DOSA: *A spicy red masala is applied to the inside of the wrapper*

BUTTER MASALA DOSA: *The dosa is soaked in butter and then stuffed with potato*

CHANA MASALA DOSA: *A dosa stuffed with a classic northern Indian chickpea curry*

CHEESE PLAIN RAVA DOSA: *A cream of wheat wrapper with Velveeta melting inside*

DOSA OR PAPER DOSA: *Just the fermented rice-and-lentil wrapper, rolled or folded up*

GHEE MASALA DOSA: *Cooked in the clarified butter called ghee (otherwise, most dosas are vegan)*

GHEE OR BUTTER IDLI: *Idli served in a bowl sluiced with ghee, or alternatively, butter*

GUNPOWDER DOSA: *Similar to the Bangalore dosa, with explosive heat inside in powdered form*

IDLI: *Made with the same batter as dosas, little spongy Frisbees of tart bread*

IDLI MASALA: *Pieces of leftover idli broken up with a spice powder*

IDLI VADA: *A popular breakfast combo of idli, vada, and chutney, served on a banana leaf*

MASALA DOSA: *The same wrapper as a dosa with a dollop of seasoned potatoes inside*

MYSORE MASALA DOSA: *A spicier version of masala dosa, with all the other elements in place*

PANEER DOSA: *A regular dosa filled with the pressed ricotta-like cheese called* paneer

PESARATTU: *Like a dosa, but with ground-up mung beans and cilantro in the wrapper*

PONDICHERRY DOSA: *Wildly spicy, perhaps to bedevil the French, with fresh chiles and raw onions*

PONGAL: *A breakfast porridge made of rice and lentils*

RAVA DOSA: *A lacier wrapper made with farina plus some rice flour, unfermented*

SADA DOSA: *A synonym for plain dosa*

SPRING DOSA: *Perhaps inspired by pasta primavera, with fresh steamed veggies inside*

TAMIL NADU KARA DOSA: *The missing link between the crepe and the dosa, filled with caramelized onions*

UPMA: *A porridge made from cream of wheat ramified with spices*

UTTAPAM: *A thick flat pancake made from a similar fermented batter to the dosa, but with the fillings cooked inside, sometimes called an Indian pizza*

VADA OR MEDU VADA: *Little fermented-batter fried savory doughnuts made with two kinds of lentils*

DOSAS INTO THE NEW MILLENNIUM

The biggest event in local dosa history came about a decade ago in Jersey City's Little India. Up until that time, that magnet shopping neighborhood was dominated by Gujarati immigrants, and the restaurants reflected this. Chowpatty was foremost, a colorful joint with a beach/jungle theme that presented the vegetarian fare of Gujarati Hindus and Jains, centered on an array of crunchy shoppers' snacks known as *chaats*, and a series of all-in vegetarian meals served in little cups on glittering stainless steel platters called *thalis*. Often, each dish on a thali highlighted a different vegetable of those favored in Gujarat—India's relatively impoverished westernmost state. Black-eyed peas and cornbread are eaten there, making the food seem a trifle southern, but most of the vegetables used are pods, gourds, melons, and cucurbits.

Little India is a three-block stretch of Newark Avenue just north of Journal Square. It starts at Kennedy Boulevard's highest point, then rapidly descends westward toward the swampy Meadowlands, with its knotted highways heading into the city. No one I've talked to is sure how the neighborhood started, but I'm pretty sure the original Indian inhabitant—the area used to be Italian—was a Mr. Singh, who took over a rickety, two-story green variety store that still stands on Newark Avenue. The store, which boasted a vertical sign something like that of a movie theater, looked like it was built in the '30s or '40s. Inside, you could barely walk between aisles of helter-skelter merchandise that ran from jumbled housewares to Indian religious icons to sports-themed T-shirts to Garbage Pail Kids bubble gum cards. Going inside the store was fascinating, but as you moved toward the dusty and darkened rear, you felt like you might never emerge into the sunlight again.

This ownership of a notable store, and its gradual turning toward South Asian usages, must have attracted other businesses, including the supermarket chain Patel, a name almost universal in Gujarat. In the '80s there were at least a half dozen

unrelated businesses on the avenue named Patel, part of a burgeoning strip that included jewelers, sweets shops peddling
milk-based sweets, over a dozen restaurants, and assorted appliance stores, newsstands, paan sellers, and Hindu temples. There
was a Muslim presence in the neighborhood, too, most obvious
through a pair of butcher shops, but also in the ownership of
several of the restaurants that served halal cuisine.

But suddenly, the Gujaratis moved on and in their place came
a wave of South Indian immigrants from places like Hyderabad
(pronounced without the first *a*) and Chennai. In fact, both
those cities came to be represented by multiple restaurants
peddling regional South Indian fare. But the most prominent
feature of the dining scene had become the total invasion of the
dosa and its bubbly fermented relatives. Two restaurants—Sri
Ganesh's Dosa House and Dosa Hut—offer expansive menus
of masala dosas running to nearly 50 varieties, dispensed via a
pleasantly weird ordering system whereby you first tell the guy
at the counter what table you intend to sit at, as designated by
numbers hoisted above each table on metal rods.

Order your dosas, idlis, and uttapams and sit down, and
when the number of your chosen table is called, go the counter
and grab your order. Or at least part of your order, since if you
request six dishes, you'll be called to the counter six times to
fetch them. These convivial places also offer unlimited free sambar that you ladle from a crock pot in the rear of the room. Sri
Ganesh's Dosa House also boasts an elaborate shrine to the ele-
phant god, surrounded by fruit offerings in bowls right beside
the ATM machine.

But masala dosas are also available in over half of the 20-odd
restaurants that now grace Newark Avenue and surrounding
streets, and the selection runs to dozens upon dozens of varieties. One of the newer restaurants, Chennai Flavors (now closed),
slung such New World choices as a cheese dosa made with
Velveeta, and also a pizza dosa made with Sargento supermarket mozzarella and bottled pasta sauce. It was awful. But this is
apparently how Indian parents coax their American children to

come to the restaurant with them. "I hate Indian food," the kid says, "I want a hamburger!" And the mom replies, "If you come to dinner with us, you can order a pizza dosa, darling!"

In the last couple of years, along with this wealth of dosas, New Yorkers have gotten a truer and more complete picture of South Indian regional cooking, more rife with meat and poultry than we'd ever imagined. In fact, only 25 percent of South Indians are vegetarians, though the popularity of the masala dosa among all the new South Indian immigrants suggests that even the most ardent meat lovers also love dosas. Nevertheless, the presence of meaty biryanis hailing from Hyderabad along this strip has given the dosa its stiffest competition since Sri Ganesh's opened a decade ago.

THE CASE FOR MEATLESS DOSAS

There have been other "improvements" on the dosa in the New York region besides the pizza dosa. With branches in Soho and the Upper West Side, Hampton Chutney Company offers dosas stuffed with things like avocado; spinach, jack cheese, and roasted tomato; kalamata olives; smoked turkey; and fresh tuna. These places treat the dosa like any other wrap, and thus do something of a disservice to one of the great food traditions of the world. The dosa needs no meat.

But what is the significance of the dosa to New Yorkers in the 21st century? Gestated on three continents—including potatoes and chiles from South America, grains and pulses and cooking techniques from South Asia, and now size, execution, and innovation in New York City—the masala dosa has come of age in America, and in doing so has become one of the city's most compelling dishes. It was brought here by immigrants and has been adapted by New Yorkers in several significant ways. Yes, we have made the dosa our own, incorporating unique spice mixtures, new fillings, serving it as street food, cheesing it up for our immigrant children, or generating restaurants that are temples to this great stuffed pancake.

Nothing brings this point home more than the homely cart of Thiru Kumar, once the chief dosa maker at Dosa Hutt. Driving from his home in Staten Island—where a dosa-loving Sri Lankan community thrives—he parks his cart on the south side of Washington Square Park in Greenwich Village every day except Sunday. From that post he peddles vegan dosas (he uses no butter) in several permutations, and a line of supplicants stretches down the block. Each dosa is crafted by hand, the batter made the previous day spread on a double griddle, a good scoop of potato mixture added at the last minute before being folded up and then cut in half to fit in a Styrofoam container, served with homemade sambar and fresh coconut chutney.

To see legions of students, hipsters, and business people on their lunch break chowing down on masala dosas right in Washington Square demonstrates that, if nothing else, the dosa has finally arrived as a real New York specialty, and one with a bright future. And if vegan food can be this tasty, maybe there's hope for that, too.

EIGHT PLACES TO GET DOSAS

1. SRI GANESH'S DOSA HOUSE
809 NEWARK AVENUE, JERSEY CITY, NEW JERSEY, 201-222-3883

The mother of all dosa purveyors offers dozens of variations in a rollicking dining room with the elephant-headed god as its focus.

2. MADRAS MAHAL
104 LEXINGTON AVENUE, MANHATTAN, 212-684-4010

Curry Hill's original dosa purveyor is still going strong and is certified kosher, too.

3. NY DOSAS
WASHINGTON SQUARE SOUTH, MANHATTAN, 917-710-2092

Dosa superstar Thiru Kumar crafts dosas to order at this vegan cart, sold with an array of Sri Lankan juices and sodas.

4. DOSA HUTT
4563 BOWNE STREET, QUEENS, 718-961-5897

Well worth the 15-minute walk from the 7 terminus at Main Street in Flushing, with the Ganesh temple an added attraction.

5. SAMUDRA
75-18 37TH AVENUE, QUEENS, 718-255-1757

Jackson Heights finally gets its own dedicated dosa parlor, among the meatier northern Indian (and Himalayan) fare of the neighborhood.

6. CURRY IN A HURRY
119 LEXINGTON AVENUE, 212-683-0900

The original Curry Hill café offers edible-sized dosas and a dining room with a panoramic view of the neighborhood.

7. CHUTNEYS
827 NEWARK AVENUE, JERSEY CITY, NEW JERSEY, 201-222-9909

An expanded range of dosas and other South Indian homestyle dishes served with an extraordinary selection of chutneys, some powdered.

8. SAPTHAGIRI

804 NEWARK AVENUE, JERSEY CITY, NEW JERSEY, 201-533-8400

A full range of dosas and vegetarian specialties from all over India, in a comfortable and semi–elegant setting.

MASALA DOSA

SERVES 4 TO 6

Be forewarned: This takes three days to make.

FOR THE DOSA:

1 cup white rice
$\frac{1}{4}$ cup split yellow lentils (chana dal)
$\frac{1}{4}$ cup split red lentils (masoor dal)
Pinch of turmeric
2 teaspoons kosher salt

FOR THE FILLING:

3 large Yukon gold potatoes, peeled and cut into $\frac{1}{2}$-inch pieces
2 tablespoons vegetable oil
5 tablespoons ghee or clarified butter (substitute vegetable oil
    to make this vegan)
$\frac{1}{4}$ cup cashews
1 tablespoon finely chopped fresh ginger
2 hot green chiles, finely chopped
1 tablespoon curry powder
1 teaspoon whole mustard seeds
$\frac{1}{2}$ teaspoon turmeric
1 large white onion, chopped
1 carrot, shredded
Salt

1. First make the dosa. Combine the rice, both lentils, and a pinch
    of turmeric in a medium bowl. Cover with an inch or two of water
    and let sit out for at least 8 hours, or overnight. Drain the soaked
    solids and transfer them to a blender. Add ½ cup water and the
    salt and blend, adding slightly more water if needed to get the

blades going. Once the mixture is blending comfortably, add water by the tablespoon until you have a medium to light batter, similar to a loose pancake batter. Blend for a full 3 minutes; the batter should be very smooth. Pour the batter into a bowl with room for it to expand, and let it sit out, uncovered, overnight or for up to 24 hours to ferment. The batter should then be bubbly and have increased substantially in volume; if not, let it ferment for a couple more hours.

2. To make the filling, boil the potatoes in a large pot of water until just tender, then drain and set aside. In a large sauté pan, heat the oil with 1 tablespoon of the ghee or clarified butter over medium-low heat. Fry the cashews in the fat, shaking the pan often, until they are golden brown, then remove with a slotted spoon and set aside.

3. Add the ginger, chiles, curry powder, mustard seeds, and turmeric. Fry the spices, stirring constantly, until fragrant, 1 to 2 minutes. Add the onion and carrot. Season the mixture well with salt and cook until the onion softens, 8 to 10 minutes. Add the potatoes, mixing everything together. Cook until the potatoes are soft and the spices are incorporated. Stir in the cashews. Taste and add more salt if necessary. Keep warm.

4. In a large skillet, preferably cast-iron or nonstick, heat ½ teaspoon ghee over medium-high heat and spread to coat the surface. Using a ladle, pour about ¼ cup of the dosa batter into the pan, spreading it over the entire surface with the bottom of the ladle, like a crepe. If the batter is sticking too much or won't spread easily, whisk in a little water. When the edges curl upward and the dosa is browned, transfer it with a spatula to a plate and cover with a kitchen towel to keep warm. Continue making dosas, adding ½ teaspoon ghee to the pan before each, until all of the batter is used up.

5. To serve, place ½ cup of the potato mixture in the center of each dosa and roll up. Serve immediately.

FRIED CHICKEN

I first started gobbling New York fried chicken around 1980, three years after I moved to the city. Most of the restaurants I visited to that end were in Harlem or Bed-Stuy, Brooklyn. They tended to be simple cafés run by black women in their 60s and 70s who had migrated from Georgia and North Carolina as youngsters around the time of the Great Depression. Their style of fried chicken was a spare one—usually cooked in cast-iron skillets, the bird pieces very lightly coated with breading, so the skin did all the crunch work. But, man, was their fried chicken good!

One of the places that wowed me was called Margie's Red Rose Diner, pronounced with a hard *g*. Located on 144th Street in the upper reaches of Harlem, it sat across the street from the hardscrabble Drew Hamilton housing projects just off Frederick Douglass Boulevard. The place was small and cramped, and Margie presided behind a carry-out counter, a tall woman in a flowered apron, her hair permed in big curls piled on top of her head. (Later she would affect a much shorter, primmer cut, like Twiggy.)

A kitchen could be seen through a door on her right. Occasionally, one of the neighborhood kids would serve as waiter, but Margie did nearly all the work. The main feature of the decor was an amazing jukebox, glowing with neon and stocked with soul singles from the '60s, from James Brown to Aretha Franklin to the Jackson 5. I remember Fontella Bass belting out "Rescue Me" one day as I ordered. There was more obscure stuff, too. The interior of the café was painted dark red, and there was a vase with a red plastic rose on each small table.

Margie took a liking to me right away. She thought she recognized me from a religious revival she'd attended, and said to me, "I knew your father. He was a godly man and a great minister to his flock." I tried to set her straight, to tell her my dad wasn't a minister but a chemical engineer from Chicago who was, if not an atheist, at least a freethinker. But she would have none of it. Every time I'd go up to Harlem for her wonderful fried chicken, she'd greet me almost gleefully with, "I remember you. You're the preacher's son." Years later, I realized she was already going a little batty back then, and identifying me with a religious personality was the only way she could explain why a white guy—and later, groups of his friends—were appearing in her small Harlem café. In 2000, Margie's Red Rose Diner served as a backdrop for the Sean Connery flick *Finding Forrester*. So if you want to see it as it was back then, pull the movie up on Netflix and take a gander.

What was Margie's chicken like? The pieces were smallish, cooked to a deep amber, with skin as crisp as a Dorito. The skin didn't hang off the pieces either, but remained perfectly intact. From my own dubious chicken-frying experiences, I'd say such a result was difficult to achieve, taking great perseverance and the gingerly use of tongs. Flecked with black pepper, the bird was well salted, too. The sides included the usual soul food standards of collard greens flavored with fatback (later, smoked turkey wing was substituted for the fatback as a supposed health measure, as cooks were taught to be ashamed of the greasy opulence of their culinary output), coleslaw swimming in mayo, a mustardy potato salad dotted with sweet pickle relish and on the way to becoming yellow mashed potatoes, cornbread from a box, and really great mac and cheese. Not only was the elbow macaroni presented in a cheese-laced béchamel, planks of mild cheddar were laid across the top to enhance the luxuriant cheesiness.

During that decade I stumbled on several similar places and

became a big fan of the African-American school of southern cooking, which constitutes one of the great culinary matriarchies among the city's historic cuisines. I estimated then that there were at least a dozen of these places left in Harlem—many dating from the '50s and '60s, and often on side streets. Sylvia's Restaurant (founded in 1962), still serving the skanky pork intestines called chitterlings but on weekends only, was the most celebrated example. But it had already become a giant tourist trap by the 1980s, nothing like the holes-in-the-wall in which I was scarfing my fried chicken, tearing the skin off with my teeth and chewing it up first. And there were probably twice as many old-fashioned soul food spots in Brooklyn, along an axis that ran from Fort Greene to Ocean Hill. Occasionally you'd find one isolated in the Bronx, in neighborhoods like Crotona Park and West Farms, and in Saint Albans, Queens.

The best fried chicken to be found in Brooklyn was at Mitchell's Soul Food on Vanderbilt Avenue in Prospect Heights. The menu, as spare as Margie's, included smothered pork chops, smothered chicken, fried whiting, chicken livers, barbecued chicken (baked in barbecue sauce, not really smoked), oxtail stew, and sometimes—in a tip of the hat to the Caribbean residents of the neighborhood—curried chicken and jerk chicken. The sides were pretty much the same as at Margie's. The soul food café menus of the time were certainly compact, running to fewer than 10 mains and a handful of sides. There were no apps. In this way, the women who ran them could serve as manager, cook, and waiter simultaneously.

I've watched the waters of gentrification eddy around Mitchell's. The place has remained steadfast over the decades and is miraculously still open, now surrounded by trendy bars, boutiques, and eateries that want to extract $50 from your wallet per meal and more. A dinner at Mitchell's, with free cornbread, remains under $10. I've hyped the place going on 25 years. But gentrification has done some good things to Prospect Heights: at Mitchell's, the acrylic glass barrier has come down between the kitchen and the dining room, and seats have been added in the kitchen itself, in a postmodern touch that allows you to survey the action as your meal is prepared.

Another favorite in Brooklyn was affiliated with the Carolina Country Store on Atlantic Avenue in Stuyvesant Heights, which is what the easternmost section of Bedford-Stuyvesant—or Bed-Stuy—is called, where the Long Island Rail Road tracks in the middle of the street fling themselves up a small hill and then into the ground.

The name Carolina Country Store telegraphed a fact that gradually dawned on me as the century wound down: while the African-American residents of Harlem tended to come from Georgia, those in Brooklyn neighborhoods like Fort Greene, Clinton Hill, and Bedford-Stuyvesant often hailed from North or South Carolina. The Carolina Country Store supplied nostalgic products from back home: grits, fresh collards, old-fashioned candy formed into ribbons by obsolete machinery, black-eyed peas, cornmeal ground at little mills in small southern towns, off-brand baking powder biscuit mixes, smoked and brined pig parts from snout to tail that sat in buckets on the floor, and colorful sodas that tasted mainly like bubble gum.

A guy who ran a secondhand store across the street let me know how those products got there. According to him, elderly black Brooklynites often returned to the Carolinas during the 1980s because Brooklyn was violent and living there was expensive. Moving vans would take their furniture and other household items back to the Carolinas, and, rather than returning empty, the trucks would refill with whatever southern goods the drivers could sell up North—sometimes collards, double-yolk eggs, watermelons, or heavily smoked and salted bacon, sometimes dry goods and candy. In that way a small fleet of generally old and rickety trucks made dozens of trips per year.

The Carolina Country Kitchen (recently closed; the store remains open) began as a concession inside the store; it specialized in several types of pork sausages, frying them in cast-iron skillets and placing them in buns. A line of customers often ran out the door. Then the restaurant component was spun off and relocated slightly further east on Atlantic Avenue, to a strip mall that seemed comically modern in a neighborhood where the houses, shops, garages, and warehouses dated mostly to the '20s and '30s. Now centered on fried chicken, the new menu included all the soul food standards. Yes, there seemed to be an unwritten consensus as to what all of these establishments served.

Margie passed in 2009. A year later, her daughter and her son-in-law, a police lieutenant with the Metropolitan Transit Authority, reopened the place, which had moved a few doors down the street while Margie was still alive. The rose-themed decor was not retained, and neither was the jukebox. In addition, the bone-in fried chicken that had been Margie's glory was replaced with chicken nuggets and chicken filets. I asked Margie's daughter, Koko, why she no longer did full pieces of fried chicken. "It's not what our customers want nowadays," she said—sadly, I thought—"and it's much easier and cheaper to fry the chicken cutlets than fried chicken. Maybe someday we'll make fried chicken again."

Most of the old soul food places in Brooklyn and Harlem have closed down, so that there are only a half dozen left in both locales altogether. Like human beings, these women-run cafés had lifespans, often contingent on the age of the original entrepreneurs and the willingness or not of their offspring to keep the institutions afloat. Cooking day in and day out among clouds of grease is not something most college-educated kids want to pursue. Unless they're *Top Chef* contestants, that is. And the low-fat craze that surfaced in the late '70s, though the movement has since been discredited, made the populace permanently fearful of fried foods. Even now, full-fat dairy products are still scarce in supermarket aisles. And for a time, fried chicken disappeared from menus all over town, as skinless and boneless chicken breast—often poached into total blandness—took its place.

Gradually, as the new millennium dawned and low fat was partly forgotten, new soul food places opened up with menus that also included wraps and meal-sized salads and "healthy" manifestations of southern cooking, often about as flavorful as a tennis shoe. These had none of the lipidity and homeliness of the original spots, and mounted menus filled with buzzwords. Most of those, too, went out of business, leaving us impoverished in a cuisine that had seen the city through the heyday of the Harlem Renaissance and the Black Power movement of the '60s and to the dawn of the hip-hop era. As the Fat Boys rapped in their 1985 hit, "All You Can Eat":

> *Well, I'm a stuff my face to a funky beat!*
> *We're gonna walk inside, and guess what's up:*
> *Put some food in my plate, and some Coke in my cup*
> *Give me some chicken, franks, and fries*

The national franchise restaurants that invaded the city by the hundreds during the real-estate-friendly Giuliani and Bloomberg administrations took their toll on the city's soul food spots, too, as chains like KFC and Popeyes set up shop in high-priced storefronts in Times Square, along 14th Street in the East and West Villages, on 125th Street in Harlem, in downtown Brooklyn, and on Bed-Stuy's Fulton Street, usurping part of the venerable African-American menu with similar prices and incessant advertising.

Meanwhile, in the most impoverished neighborhoods, chains such as Kennedy Fried Chicken and New Texas Fried Chicken were opened by immigrant Afghanis. The halal fried chicken was quite good, and it was clear that the recipes had been learned at the knees of African-American cooks. In the name of efficiency, deep fryers replaced the original cast-iron skillets. In places like the Lower East Side, Chinese restaurants took to frying chicken in the soul food style in woks, underselling all competitors with a solid product, along with french fries rather than the fusty-seeming potato salad. To coat the chicken, these places often used crushed corn flakes. In the long run, there was probably more fried chicken being produced during the lead-up to the current era than there was before—it just wasn't being cooked by aged black women born and reared in the South.

WHERE FRIED CHICKEN ORIGINATED

Since 1980 or so, I've been pondering the convoluted international route by which fried chicken made it to United States, and how it gradually became ubiquitous on New York menus. Even now, after three decades of fried chicken vilification for its supposed unhealthiness, the website MenuPages lists 3,587 restaurants that serve it in various guises—not all of it the soul food article, of course. In fact, fried chicken deserves to be counted among the city's most popular dishes in perpetuity. By contrast, MenuPages lists only 1,767 places (out of a total of twenty thousand or so total restaurants listed for New York) that serve hamburgers. Hamburgers!

As the widely accepted story goes, the dish originated with African cooks who, as enslaved persons, worked in plantation kitchens down South. As with other recipes such as fried okra, roasted yams, black-eyed peas, grits, and stewed collard greens, fried chicken is said to have originated in Africa. The West African antecedents of these other dishes are quite clear, since the raw materials are native to or were available in West Africa during the 17th and 18th centuries. But what about fried chicken?

Indeed, on a trip I took to West Africa in 1979–1980, I kept careful track of the food I ate in Senegal, Mali, Benin, and Burkina Faso (then known as Upper Volta). In those days, as far as chicken went, you had two choices: you could buy it, feathers and all, in the local outdoor market, or you could find it already grilled over scraps of wood in open pits by the side of the road. At the time these chickens cost two dollars apiece, limiting their purchase to the wealthy. Each of the four countries also had its own chicken specialties (for example, Senegal's poulet yassa, chicken stewed in mustard and onions), but none involved breading the bird and frying it. Africans tend to cook chicken and game birds (and bats, for that matter) in stews that can accompany rice or fufu—tubers or plantains mashed to a bouncy constituency—starches that form the largest part of the meal.

In fact, I never ate or even saw fried chicken in two visits to West Africa, the second of which occurred in 1984. As a dish that supposedly originated there—according to legend, at least—it had executed something of a disappearance. A decade later I was to find myself visiting and reviewing dozens of West African restaurants in all of New York's five boroughs, mainly Nigerian, Ghanaian, Senegalese, Ivorian, Guinean, Sierra Leonean, and Liberian places. These modest establishments, usually just a single small room with African paintings, masks, and wooden carvings on the walls, filled with the rich smells of palm oil, dried stockfish, and peanut soup, invariably offered fried chicken.

But that didn't necessarily mean that the dish had been familiar back home. As I was to find out, putting it on the menu functioned in two distinct ways. First, to lure the already resident African-Americans who lived in the neighborhoods the new West Africans were moving into, places like West 116th Street in Harlem, University Heights in the Bronx, and Fulton Street in Brooklyn's Bed-Stuy. The relationship between the two groups tended to be fraught, and the presence of fried chicken on the new West African menus formed a sop and tribute to the entrenched soul food spots, which in turn had a certain familiarity to the West Africans due to the food's culinary underpinnings. Fried chicken played a conciliatory role, not to mention a commercial one, bringing curious outsiders into the clannish West African establishments with something familiar.

Second, fried chicken was provided so the children of the new immigrants could feel like they were eating something American, rather than West African. This happens to nearly all immigrant cuisines: eventually something like a hamburger will appear on Mexican, Jamaican, and even Thai menus, to induce kids, who generally eschew the food of their immigrant parents, to consent to eat with them.

Why had fried chicken disappeared from West Africa? Well, perhaps chickens and the fuel needed to fry them had simply become too expensive, much as hog barbecues in parts of South Carolina have recently been replaced by fried chicken places in many small towns for economic reasons. I found that out during a trip to South Carolina in 2012, during which my friend Melissa McCart (currently the food critic at the *Pittsburgh Post-Gazette*) and I drove hundreds of miles to track down barbecues listed in *The Palmetto State Glove Box Guide to Bar-B-Que* (1997) and discovered few that still remained. In many towns, the sole eatery was now a fried chicken joint.

There was lots of other frying happening in West Africa, however, during my visits in 1980 and 1984. In Bamako, the capital of Mali, my wife, Gretchen, and I feasted on plantain-flour fritters fried on the side of the road by a woman in a wraparound print dress called a *panya*. She formed hard dough into irregular globes and fried them in a charcoal-heated wok using palm oil, which made the fritters very red. We also ate plenty of french fries during both trips, a staple of the open-air French steakhouses aimed at foreign-service types that constituted one of the few kinds of refectories available to the hungry traveler. These cafés, open at the sides to afternoon breezes in a climate often stultifyingly hot, were decorated with objects that flaunted their French origin (I remember Picasso reproductions and miniature Eiffel towers). It was like something out of Graham Greene, and the steaks were tasty but tough.

Frying fritters in a shallow lake of oil can be done in five minutes or so, while frying chicken properly can take 20 minutes or a half hour and take five times as much oil. As I mentioned previously, few West Africans can afford to buy large amounts of fuel of whatever sort, and in the sub-Sahara, forageable wood has become nearly nonexistent. Hence, fried chicken, either at home, in restaurants, or by the side of the road, has not persisted to the present day, but may have been more common during an earlier era. In the 1982 *Nigerian Cookbook*, published by Macmillan in London but distributed widely in Anglophone

West African countries, out of hundreds of recipes, only a tiny paragraph is devoted to frying chicken. This fried chicken was very much like our own New York recipe, only the result was then incorporated into other dishes. You made your soup to dip your fufu in, then you would dump the cooked chicken into the potage, almost as an afterthought.

It's also possible that the coastal West Africans who'd learned how to fry chicken in the first place had simply disappeared from the continent, perhaps by being transported to America. We know that those who knew the art of growing rice made more desirable candidates for slavery, so why not those who could fry chicken, too?

MAYBE THANK THE IBERIANS (AND THE JEWS)?

My theory for the last decade or so has been that the method of frying chicken and other proteins in hot oil reached the west coast of Africa via Iberian mariners in the 16th century. I believe those mariners got it from Sephardic Jews, for whom it was the signature cooking method. In Judaism, emphasis on oil as a precious substance goes back to biblical times; indeed, Hanukkah, or the Festival of Lights, celebrates the primacy of oil in the culture. Anyone who has visited the Roman ghetto—a Jewish settlement by the Tiber River that originated in ancient times, predating the Inquisition—knows that frying is the most celebrated cooking style of Italian Jews. Their most famous dish, *carciofi alla giudia* ("artichokes Jewish style"), may date to Roman times, when there were 50,000 Jews living in Rome and the vicinity.

The recipe for baby artichokes in the Jewish style treats the vegetables in much the same way that chicken is treated in our favorite fried chicken recipe, simply cooked in fresh oil to supreme crispness, maybe with a light dusting of flour, maybe not. Nothing like the thick breading that one often finds on fried foods. So, according to my theory, a Jewish frying method common in Spain and Portugal was learned by gentile Iberians during the time of the Inquisition, who brought it with them on visits to the coast of West Africa, where it became popular with the local population. To show how earlier colonial influences like this can continue to exist: on the Senegalese island of Gorée, one of the most notorious slave embarkation points, West African women of the Fulani tribe were sometimes seen still wearing the headscarves and full aprons characteristic of Portuguese peasant dress of the 16th century—at least they still did in 1980.

Portuguese and Spanish mariners could have taught coastal West Africans how to fry, and some tribeswomen could have carried the method to the United States on slave ships. But Africans were not the only ones to pick up the Jewish-Iberian method of cooking. It turns out the Iberians were rather free with their frying lessons. They apparently showed the Japanese how to fry around 1542, when they established trade contacts with Japan. The immediate result was tempura. (Note that *tempura* is not a Japanese word, but a Portuguese one.) The fried pork cutlets called *donburi* followed, apparently inspired centuries later by Wiener schnitzels said to be all the rage in late-19th-century Tokyo.

The Sephardic genesis of fried chicken was further suggested circumstantially by a couple of factoids. As late as the 19th century, fish and chips in Britain was known as "the Jewish method of cooking fish." According to *Wikipedia*: "Deep-fried fish was first introduced into Britain during the 17th century by Jewish refugees from Portugal and Spain, and is derived from pescado frito. In 1860, the first fish and chip shop was opened in London by Joseph Malin," a Portuguese-Jewish shopkeeper. But while the breaded and fried fish constitutes a Sephardic contribution to British cuisine, french fries (or "chips")—first mentioned in print in *A Tale of Two Cities* (1859) by Charles Dickens—were apparently of Scottish origin.

On my second visit to Senegal, I'd traveled down the coast from Dakar to Fadiouth, an island composed almost entirely of seashells, boasting granaries on stilts to keep the rats out of the

wheat. Fadiouth is the site of a 17th-century Portuguese cemetery, one of the few tourist attractions in that part of Senegal,
and one which I sought out due to my interest in Iberian trad-
ers and their culinary influence around the world. Only as I
write this have I discovered that the Portuguese cemetery I visited was really a Portuguese-Jewish cemetery. This modifies my
theory, so now I can say the Jews may have brought their chicken-
frying method directly to the West Africans, with no gentile
intermediaries.

FRIED CHICKEN REACHES AMERICA

Still, the idea that fried chicken is at heart a Jewish dish is a
disputable one. All the evidence is circumstantial. Take a
look at John Mariani's *The Encyclopedia of American Food and
Drink* (1983), and you'll see it attributes southern fried chicken,
as the book calls it, to English speakers: "The Scots, and
later Scottish immigrants to the southern United States, had
a tradition of deep frying chicken in fat, unlike their English
counterparts who baked or boiled chicken." Yeah, sure.

On the other hand, dipping into *The Thirteen Colonies
Cookbook* (1975), which collects recipes from a number of wealthy
homemakers from all 13 colonies during the 30-year run-up to
the Revolutionary War, we find only a single fried-chicken
recipe, attributed to Baltimore—then, as now, a city almost more
southern than northern. Still, the paucity of recipes for fried
chicken, a dish we know to have been wildly popular, suggests
that fried chicken was a vernacular dish and not a showy or
effete one. In other words, perhaps there are few recipes because
everyone already knew how to make it and did so all the time.
The simple recipe was apparently particularly popular with both
freed and enslaved blacks, for whom chickens were relatively
easy to raise and provided a good source of nourishment.

The source of the recipe in the cookbook was Margaret
Tilghman Carroll, a white woman who lived on a Baltimore
estate called Mount Clare, a sprawling Georgian house of pink

brick located in the center of town. She'd married a wealthy barrister, Charles Carroll, in 1763, and immediately began remaking the estate with random furnishings that showed the breadth of tastes and pursuits undertaken by the era's wealthy: expensive damask tablecloths for throwing lavish dinner parties, furniture imported from France, card tables in profusion for gala card get-togethers, a distilling apparatus specifically engineered for making rose water, and a microscope. That the wealthy were interested in the subvisual world during that era blows my mind. Like the 1950s, it was a scientific age.

Margaret Tilghman Carroll, like Thomas Jefferson, was also a committed gardener and manager of her own estate. She wrote out many of her recipes in longhand in her "receipt book," as recipe books were then called. (Fried chicken's first appearance in a published cookbook in America was in *The Virginia Housewife*, which was first published in 1824.) Her fried chicken recipe is just the sort we've been talking about: a three-pound bird well salted and peppered, then dusted with flour and fried, in this case in bacon fat. The account of Carroll's life indicates that she had 36 servants for the house and its 848-acre grounds, which included greenhouses and orchards overlooking the Patapsco River. She was also said to have an English housekeeper, which was apparently a sign of great status. But where did she get her chicken recipe? And were her servants black or white? History suggests that in Maryland, where slavery persisted even after the Emancipation Proclamation, and 40 percent of the inhabitants were black, her "servants" were actually probably "slaves."

Eschewing the Scotch fried chicken theory, *World of a Slave* (2010) by Kym S. Rice and Martha B. Katz-Hyman provides an alternate attribution to African-American enslaved females who became associated with chicken as early as the 1730s in the South, selling raw chickens as well as fried ones, as fried chicken became first a street food and eventually a festival food among African-Americans. The surplus of lard as a result of widespread hog farming in the South supposedly provided another impetus for treating frying as the favored means of cooking chickens. Apparently with frying, the hog begat the bird.

TYPES OF FRIED CHICKEN

It is significant that the idea of fried chicken in colonial Maryland, in modern Nigeria, and in New York beginning a century ago was a spare recipe that involved only a salting and peppering, a light flouring, an intact skin, and simple frying in hot fat, with lard preferred in some of the earliest extant recipes. This was also presumably the standard form of fried chicken in the Carolinas and Georgia—all seaboard locations—prior to the arrival of the recipe in New York almost a century ago.

What motivated the black population to migrate to northern cities starting in the 1920s, bringing their chicken recipe with them? According to a book by civil rights historian (and sometime bandmate of mine) Philip Dray called *At the Hands of Persons Unknown* (2002), racially motivated terrorism of blacks by whites was at an all-time high during that period, and lynching was its most gruesome manifestation. From that time until the civil rights era of the 1960s, bombings, burnings, and lynchings with the motivation of suppressing what in many counties constituted a majority of the population, was on the upswing. Many African-Americans reacted by fleeing northward, to locales where black communities had already been established. One such, at the southeast corner of Bedford-Stuyvesant, was Weeksville. It dated to 1838, when the population was mainly freed slaves from the Carolinas. A single country lane of rambling frame houses with front porches preserves the 19th-century, small-town feel of the place, which seems much like the rural South even today. Pay it a visit, and bring along a carry-out box of fried chicken.

It turns out that when African-Americans migrated to the North in the '20s and later, they often went straight north rather than on the diagonal, so that the black population of New York, as I've said before, came mainly from Georgia and the Carolinas.

Chicago communities tended to originate in Mississippi, which is why the Windy City has such a strong blues tradition. Could it be that our style of cooking chicken might be considered the country's most ancient, brought to the Eastern Seaboard by slaves and kept in something like its original form, a method so versatile that even the finished product could function in a number of ways, including as an add-in to other dishes, stews, and so forth?

There are many methods of frying chicken across the United States, though most originated in the South. As Eugene Walter put it in the Time Life book *American Cooking: Southern Style* (1971):

> *Any attempt to prescribe the best way to prepare fried chicken is likely to start the Civil War all over again . . . Southern cooks disagree on just about every step in the frying process. Some of them salt and pepper the chicken pieces then dredge them in flour, while others put the flour, salt, and pepper—and sometimes paprika—in a brown paper bag and shake the chicken pieces in it. A Middle South variant soaks the pieces in buttermilk, then does the bag trick, and after that dips the chicken in cream and returns it to the flour mixture before frying; all this, it is claimed, makes an especially crunchy crust.*

Some cover the chicken with a lid during part of the cooking time, some leave the cooking vessel uncovered for the entire period. Some advise putting a little cinnamon in the flour, others remove the skin and brine the bird. In my fried chicken travels, I've seen all of these methods and many more. Which is why it's so amazing that a distinctive New York style of cooking chicken, based on ancient models, has persisted—southern, African, Jewish, and Iberian all at once.

WHITHER NEW YORK FRIED CHICKEN?

When I first encountered fried chicken in New York in the '80s, the bird was in its death throes. In restaurants and private homes, skinless, boneless, flavorless, godless chicken breast was elbowing fried chicken out of the way, as I mentioned before. You can still see this tendency in supermarket poultry cases, in the pink jiggling masses of deboned and deskinned chicken parts. With a populace gripped by fat paranoia, soul food places went out of business left and right, and everyone seemed to forget the number one principle of fried chicken: the crisp skin is the best part.

But every food attitude eventually begets its opposite. And the Age of Foodism, which began around 2000, led ambitious chefs, home cooks, and bloggers to reconfigure just about every familiar recipe and imbue it with the new values of sustainability, seasonality, and locavorism. As a new spirit of culinary adventure seized the country, fried chicken, too, was reinvented. And nowhere was this movement more profound than in Brooklyn, where traffic-clogged streets and trash-strewn green spaces seemed the antithesis of organic farming and humanely raised meat.

One paradoxical result were the urban farms that seemed to rise on every empty lot in places like Greenpoint and Red Hook, at first producing quick-growing, low-maintenance crops like herbs and lettuces, but eventually extending to squashes, pulses, and even fruit trees. Hipsters started raising chickens in their backyards, and for the first time in decades, birds not intended for Santeria sacrifices were flourishing in private hands.

Honey, too, from rooftop beehives at hilariously elevated prices became common, and farmers' markets flourished throughout parts of the city offering fruits, vegetables, baked goods, and meats with varying degrees of localness. *Heirloom* became a buzzword, and paying premium prices for produce became a point of pride. As evidence of this seismic shift in the way the city perceived farms and food, a former municipally owned petting zoo in the remote eastern reaches of Queens was rebranded the Queens County Farm Museum and soon was selling spectacular produce at the Union Square Greenmarket, as the mother of all farmers' markets was called.

Into this burgeoning milieu stepped Pies 'n' Thighs. It had

the sort of homely rep valued at the time, a "tie on the apron and let's make food like grandma made" attitude, only incorporating the latest gastronomic principles. Williamsburg became the epicenter of this type of cooking. There, Pies 'n' Thighs was founded in 2006 by Steven Tanner and Sarah Buck. He was a Georgia native and she was from California, and they moved into an improbable location early in the year: the tiny rear kitchen of the Rock Star Bar, a hardscrabble workingman's tavern on Kent Avenue. It was directly across the street from the long-closed Domino Sugar factory on the decaying East River waterfront, which for decades had produced the tiny sugar packets used in diners across the country. Later that same waterfront became a maze of glassy high-rise condos.

The Rock Star Bar had last been decorated during the psychedelic era and had a bikers-on-acid feel; the tiny improvised rear kitchen was filthy, with pots and pans and pies teetering on every available surface, even placed directly on the cracked tile floor. There were a couple of twirling barstools in the kitchen, but things were always parked on them, so you had to find a place to reposition the offending object before you could sit down. Most patrons carried their food into the dark and musty barroom, others sought out the fenced-in backyard in fine weather. Indeed, 2006 became the summer of great chicken. Tanner manned a smoker out back, doing decent pulled pork. Buck made the pies. I got the impression, when I reviewed the place for the *Village Voice*, that the pair collaborated on the chicken.

How was the bird? Well, it was degrees different than the traditional, unfussed-over poultry we were accustomed to finding in soul food places. And it partook of the eclecticism of chicken recipes that had evolved all over the South throughout the 20th century, partly propelled by women's magazines. As southern food experts John T. Edge and Ellen Rolfes noted in *A Gracious Plenty* (1999), "There is no such thing as Southern fried chicken. Instead, there is chicken fried in the South, and the variations are as myriad as the cooks." They could have been

speaking about south Williamsburg, too, because the newfangled fried chicken at Pies 'n' Thighs was baroque compared to
the city's earlier, sparer recipe.

The key to this new chicken, let's call it hipster chicken, was
brining. Brining was usually accomplished in a simple mixture of water and kosher salt. But sometimes brining solu-
tions became more complex and idiosyncratic as cooks strove
to outdo each other bird-wise. The brine was osmotic: it had
the effect of swelling the chicken with moisture, also adding a
salty flavor to flesh that would normally have been more bland.
In the worst instances of overbrining, the breast developed a
texture like marshmallow. If you're one of those folks for whom
"tender" is always a positive feature, no matter how extreme,
then brining is for you. At newcomer Root & Bone in the East
Village, the brining solution is sweet tea, resulting in a product
cloying in its sweetness.

In many cases the skin would be removed to facilitate brining—
but also, I suspect, because skin is a colossal pain in the ass to
the fryer of chickens. The missing skin would be replaced by
some sort of crunchy coating, invariably denser and greasier
than the intact skin would have been. Sometimes buttermilk
would be employed, which created blackened patches on the
surface of the chicken where the buttermilk came into direct
contact with fat—in other words, over-caramelizing or burning.

I didn't entirely approve of brining fried chicken at the time,
and I still don't, though I loved the hell out of Pies 'n' Thighs's
fried chicken. And the catfish and pulled pork were fine, too.
The pies tended to be of the icebox variety, better in summer
than in winter. The place enjoyed a tremendous underground
reputation that soon saw long lines wending out the door and
congratulatory pieces written in *New York*, *Time Out*, and other
publications and websites. Of the Kent Avenue establishment,
Peter Meehan—the post–Eric Asimov "$25 and Under" critic,
later editor of *Lucky Peach*—enthused in a *New York Times*
piece, "In Pies 'n' Thighs Mr. Tanner and Ms. Buck have cobbled together a restaurant that makes their loves clear: good

Southern cooking and great baked goods. . . . It's a compelling combination, well executed and put forth with real heart—the sort of restaurant that's hard to find, especially in the big city, but easy to love once found."

But the whole shebang was over almost before it started. In 2008, less than two years after it opened, the city's Department of Health and Mental Hygiene swooped in and closed the place permanently. And there wasn't a dry eye in Williamsburg. But the chicken ball had already started rolling. Pies 'n' Thighs reopened uphill two years later near the bicycle exit from the Williamsburg Bridge, sans Steven Tanner. The new place was immediately thronged every afternoon and evening and remains the hottest ticket in Williamsburg dining to this day. Two other partners joined Buck, both adept at the sort of quasi-southern cooking that had become a Brooklyn signature.

Tanner decamped to Egg, which specialized in breakfast, adding fried chicken as a highlighted lunch special. Later he started the Commodore, a dive bar with a nautical theme and mixed drinks to match on Metropolitan Avenue. One of his signature dishes there was a spicy fried chicken biscuit, which re-created the glory days of the crusty Pies 'n' Thighs bird in more spectacular fashion, with the vinegary burn of Louisiana-style hot sauce. And the chicken was organic. Soon, chicken biscuits (made with boneless chicken parts and hence easier to prepare) started popping up everywhere.

Meanwhile, fried chicken rolled over New York like a herd of Teletubbies, with Williamsburg and Carroll Gardens as its epicenters. Largely in emulation of Pies 'n' Thighs, fried chicken places started opening helter-skelter. Sweet Chick debuted at North Eighth and Bedford, reviving the famous dish chicken and waffles. The combo had been invented for late-night jazz sessions at Wells Supper Club in Harlem, which opened in 1938. Nat King Cole and Sammy Davis Jr. were regulars. The waffle, of course, was a Dutch invention, making it particularly apropos to Dutch-named Harlem and the permanently Netherlandish (via street signs and neighborhood names) New York, which had once been known as New Amsterdam. Though Thomas Jefferson is popularly credited with importing the first waffle iron from France, my guess is that there were already plenty of them in New Amsterdam in the 17th century.

Meanwhile, as Sweet Chick was making us love breakfast and lunch at the same time, beatbox rapper Doug E. Fresh set up his own waffle-and-chicken shop in Harlem on Adam Clayton Powell Jr. Boulevard, called Doug E.'s. There he served miniature waffles along with full-size pieces of chicken and bubble packs of syrup in a fast food setting. The place closed after four years, but has now reopened.

Sweet Chick is still going strong. Not to be outdone, the Blue Ribbon guys (the Bromberg brothers, Bruce and Eric) started their own fried chicken franchise at the southern end of Second Avenue in the East Village. They left the skin intact, but added a thickish crust and spicy red coating of chili powder. The owners of Hill Country Barbecue also got into the act, spinning off Hill Country Chicken right on Broadway a couple of blocks north of Eataly in the Flatiron District, offering two types of fried chicken, one with skin, the other without. Just last year, they opened another branch in downtown Brooklyn.

In the East Village, more fried chicken started appearing at the Cardinal in 2011, served with a thick crunchy coating clearly inspired by Pies 'n' Thighs, which reopened the same year. The year after that, Bobwhite debuted way over on Avenue C, cooking its fried chicken in the old New York City manner and offering not only a chicken dinner but a chicken-on-biscuit sandwich in emulation of the Commodore. The place billed itself as a "lunch and dinner counter" and had as much seating at the tiny bar as at tables, one of an increasing number of micro-eateries that were setting down in the East Village, the small size in response to real estate pressures. In November 2012, Bobwhite was badly damaged by a wall of water from Hurricane Sandy that swept down Avenue C and left businesses and housing projects without fresh water for over a week and Bobwhite with a flooded basement. It was weeks before the place reopened.

Another feature of the fried chicken explosion was its inclusion on many bistro menus. Carroll Gardens led the way with places like Buttermilk Channel (named after the estuarial finger separating Brooklyn from Governor's Island in New York's Upper Bay) and Seersucker. Both served some semblance of revamped southern cuisine—a movement, though it can be traced to the Brooklyn fried chicken revolution, that also had roots in Gage and Tollner, a downtown Brooklyn institution that ran from 1879 to 2004. At one point during the last 15 years of its existence, the chef was Edna Lewis, an iconic African-American cookbook author and doyenne of southern cooking, originally from Virginia. The place had always had a southern bent; Lewis only accentuated it. Even a 1964 menu, as posted by the blog *Lost City* in 2012, affords pride of place to our beloved bird: "Fried Chicken with Bacon and Corn Fritters . . . $3."

FRIED CHICKEN DIASPORA

While we've mainly paid attention to African-American and hipster fried chicken, all sorts of other ethnic versions had been circulating in New York, often in the restaurants of immigrants. I drove around the city with John T. Edge in 2002, prior to the publication of his book *Fried Chicken: An American Story* (2004), with the intention of showing him that not only were some ancient traditions of southern fried chicken still being maintained here, but also that other cultures has seized upon the bird and sent it flying in different directions.

If I recall correctly, we first visited Margie's Red Rose Diner, then went on to a Georgian (former Soviet Union) restaurant in Brooklyn where chicken tabaka was being prepared—a flattened, fried bird paved with crushed garlic, and really one of the world's great fried chicken recipes. We also sampled some Dominican fried chicken that had been previously soaked in vinegar, making a very tart version of the dish. Caporal Fried Chicken, now defunct, was located in Hamilton Heights in the very northern reaches of Harlem, and the logo featured a yellow smiling chick with twin six guns holstered on each hip.

Whether these two errant versions were inspired by the type of fried chicken associated with African-Americans and the South, or whether these recipes had spontaneously occurred or been delivered by the Spanish or other colonial influences separately, is beyond my clairvoyant powers. Fried chicken is a great idea. Maybe several different groups invented it independently. Other immigrant groups that jumped into the act included the Koreans, who brought a number of their franchises first to Murray Hill, Queens, and then to Manhattan, around 2007. The Korean style of fried chicken—which involves a skin stiffened with sugar and optional chile peppers in the glaze, and two fryings—was developed after Americans introduced the dish to Korea during the Korean War. It comes accompanied with a daikon slaw that is often strangely flavored with vanilla.

My favorite fried chicken in town remains that of a humble Palestinian deli at the corner of Fulton and Clinton in Clinton Hill: Yafa Deli. The chicken is displayed in a glass case on the counter kept warm with a light bulb. It's fried a few pieces at a time, very lightly breaded. The chicken is so good, it's almost started a cult, and the owners are very proud of it. They make no bones about where they got the recipe: not from the Iberians, not from the Jews, but from "Black friends living in the neighborhood," the owner of the store beams. Neighborhood types—Pratt students, African-Americans, newly arrived hipsters and yuppsters—rush into the cramped store late into the night to score a piece or two of delicious, bare-bones, well-salted-and-peppered fried chicken, the kind New York has always done best, at least since the 1920s.

SIX PLACES TO GET GREAT OLD-FASHIONED-STYLE FRIED CHICKEN

1. MARGIE'S RED ROSE DINER

275 WEST 144TH STREET, MANHATTAN, 212-491-7685

The Harlem classic, now making a boneless version of Margie's original.

2. MITCHELL'S SOUL FOOD

617 VANDERBILT AVENUE, BROOKLYN, 718-789-3212

This Prospect Heights fixture is miraculously still open, and still great.

3. YAFA DELI

907 FULTON STREET, BROOKLYN, 718-789-8630

Palestinians make great chicken, using the classic Brooklyn recipe.

4. CHARLES' SOUTHERN STYLE KITCHEN

2839 FREDERICK DOUGLASS BOULEVARD, MANHATTAN, 212-281-1800

Located in far northern Harlem, this wonderful fried chicken place started out as a truck.

5. CARMICHAEL'S DINER

117-08 GUY R. BOULEVARD, QUEENS, 718-723-6908

This classic diner in Rochdale, Queens, serves southern fare, including classic fried chicken.

6. DOUG E.'S

2245 ADAM CLAYTON POWELL JR. BOULEVARD, MANHATTAN, 212-368-4371

Started by beatbox rapper Doug E. Fresh, this jazzy Harlem storefront dispenses good fried chicken and miniature waffles.

SEVEN PLACES TO GET GREAT NUEVO-FOODIE-STYLE FRIED CHICKEN

1. PIES 'N' THIGHS

166 SOUTH FOURTH STREET, BROOKLYN, 347-529-6090

This place started the Brooklyn fried chicken revival in the shadow of the Williamsburg Bridge.

2. THE COMMODORE

366 METROPOLITAN AVENUE, BROOKLYN, 718-218-7632

This bar with a nautical motif makes a wonderful fried chicken sandwich.

3. THE CARDINAL

234 EAST FOURTH STREET, MANHATTAN, 212-995-8600

This East Village bistro specializes in Carolina cuisine, and chicken is a focus.

4. BOBWHITE LUNCH & SUPPER COUNTER

94 AVENUE C, MANHATTAN, 212-228-2972

A small lunch counter with celebrated fried chicken over in Alphabet City.

5. BUTTERMILK CHANNEL

524 COURT STREET, BROOKLYN, 718-852-8490

This bistro, a stone's throw from the Gowanus Expressway, dips their chicken in buttermilk prior to frying, as the name might imply.

6. WILMA JEAN

345 SMITH STREET, BROOKLYN, 718-422-0444

In the same nabe as Buttermilk Channel, this snack bar also uses buttermilk, and the chicken is quite good.

7. SWEET CHICK

164 BEDFORD AVENUE, BROOKLYN, 347-725-4793; 178 LUDLOW STREET, MANHATTAN, 646-657-0233

Leading the waffle-and-fried-chicken revival, Sweet Chick offers the bird brined in the style of Pies 'n' Thighs.

FRIED CHICKEN
SERVES 4 TO 6

This favorite recipe represents an evolved attitude toward the bird; with its buttermilk dip, it would be very much at home in a modern Brooklyn bistro.

1 ($3\frac{1}{2}$- to 4-pound) chicken, cut into 8 pieces
(or any combination of parts)
4 cups buttermilk
5 tablespoons kosher salt
$\frac{1}{2}$ teaspoon cayenne
2 cups peanut oil
$2\frac{1}{2}$ cups flour
$\frac{1}{4}$ cup cornmeal
1 teaspoon freshly ground black pepper

1. If the breast pieces are especially large, cut them in half. In a large bowl, mix together the buttermilk, 2 tablespoons of the salt, and the cayenne. Add in the chicken parts and submerge. Ideally, cover and refrigerate for at least 3 hours or overnight, but if you don't have the time, you can proceed with frying.

2. Heat the oil in a large cast-iron skillet over medium-high heat. Meanwhile, make the mixture for dredging. In a plastic shopping bag (double-bag it, in case it tears) combine the flour, cornmeal, black pepper, and remaining salt. Shake the bag to combine. Pull pieces of the chicken from the buttermilk, letting most of the liquid drip off. Place the chicken in the mixture, a couple pieces at a time, gather the bag tightly to close, and shake well to coat, about 15 seconds per batch.

3. Once the oil is hot (350°F on a deep-frying thermometer; a pinch of the dredge mixture should sizzle), lift the dredged chicken pieces from the bag—without shaking off too much coating—and into the oil. Don't crowd the pan—cook in batches if necessary. Fry the

chicken, turning every couple of minutes, until golden and crispy, about 10 minutes for the breast pieces and 13 minutes for the rest. If the oil begins to smoke, lower the heat slightly. Drain the chicken on a wire rack and proceed until all the pieces are cooked. Serve immediately.

PAMBAZO

To understand the lush Mexican sandwich called *pambazo*, we have to travel back in time a little over three decades, to New York in the post–Vietnam War era.

At the end of the 1970s, at least according to census records, there were only 6,700 hundred Mexicans living in New York City out of a total population of 7.9 million. And there were virtually no Mexican restaurants. Well, that's not completely true. There were perhaps 20 places that called themselves Mexican. Nearly all of these served not mainstream Mexican fare or Mexican regional cuisines (as Rosa Mexicano would begin doing in 1984) but some semblance of Tex-Mex. This collection of dishes had originated in northern Mexico and had been adapted by Mexican immigrants for their new surroundings in Texas, mainly in the 1950s. Of this early New York set of Mexican restaurants, several, like the still-remaining Tio Pepe in Greenwich Village, were Spanish restaurants (serving paella and whatnot) that discovered they could easily serve newly popular Tex-Mex as a sideline. The downside was that the Mexican food they served often tasted a little Spanish.

The Mexican fare at these restaurants was similar to what I was exposed to when I lived in the Lone Star State from 1967 to 1972: enchiladas made with American processed cheeses; tamales smothered in canned chili gravy; fajitas (invented at Ninfa's in Houston circa 1970); tacos made from flour tortillas or U-shaped hard-shell corn tortillas; nachos, supposedly created in the late '40s by a guy named Ignacio "Nacho" Anaya in a border town across from Eagle Pass, Texas; and quesadillas made from a pair of flour tortillas glued together with refried beans and cheese, quite unlike the ones made with a single large round of hand-patted masa dough, as they do it in Puebla and other southern Mexican states. But I get ahead of myself.

IT ALL STARTED WITH CHILI CON CARNE

The heart of Tex-Mex cuisine was a dish over a century older than most of its brothers, one still invented in what would become Texas, but at the time was still part of Mexico. One theory suggests that, using the limited roster of ingredients available to them, chili con carne was invented by chuck-wagon cooks for their cowboy and caballero customers, a reddish-brown, one-pot tuck-in of oily beef stew flavored with dried red chiles and cumin, plus herbs and wild garlic that could be plucked from beside the cattle trails. An advantage of this chili con carne was that a batch could be endlessly added to—extending it indefinitely—and tasted better and better by this process.

The exact time the dish appeared on chuck-wagon menus is uncertain, but the combination of chiles and cumin brands it as quintessentially Mexican. Supposedly it migrated from the cattle trails into the cities, becoming a poverty food for the underclasses. According to Richard J. Hooker in *Food and Drink in America: A History* (1981), the dish was well known in San Antonio in the second half of the 19th century, made with meat scraps by the poorest of its citizens. By the 1880s, there were ladies in San Antonio known as "chili queens" who ladled the savory stew from swarthy calderos, first at Military Plaza, then at Market Square after an edict by the city fathers in 1887. At the time it constituted the city's predominant street food.

But the dish is probably at least 50 years older than Hooker suggests. According to Frank H. Bushick, writing in *Glamorous Days in Old San Antonio* (1934):

The chili stand and chili queens are peculiarities, or unique insti-
tutions, of the Alamo City. They started away back there when the
Spanish army camped on the plaza. They were started to feed the
soldiers. Every class of people in every station of life patronized them
in the old days. Some were attracted by the novelty of it, some by the
cheapness. A big plate of chili and beans, with a tortilla on the side,
cost a dime.

That would place the dish in San Antonio when the Spanish
army was still in occupation, meaning before 1836. Note that the
chili was served separate from the beans, which is still the modern practice in the most traditional Texan settings.

And an announcement in the *San Antonio Light* of September
12, 1937, suggests an origin even earlier than the time of the
Texas Revolution (1835–1836), in the 1730s, when the city of San
Antonio was first founded as San Fernando de Béxar and the
women of the 16 original families were fond of a spicy Spanish
meat stew: "Recent action of the city health department in
ordering removal from Haymarket Square of the chili queens
and their stands brought an end to a 200-year-old tradition. The
chili queens made their first appearance . . . after a group of
Spanish soldiers camped on what is now the city hall site . . .
The greatest of all the queens was no Mexican but an American
named Sadie." The really amazing thing, though, is that this
ancient street food has come down to us in something like its
original form—a pungent meat stew, today served either with
or without beans.

Chili con carne's first real national exposure came in 1893,
when a booth mounted by the city of San Antonio appeared
at Chicago's Columbia Exposition. By all accounts, the San
Antonio Chili Stand—consisting of trencher tables laid out
across a vast open courtyard formed by the exposition's elegant temporary buildings, with actual carts ladling chili into
bowls—was a huge success. It introduced folks from all over the
country to a dish that had previously been only a local specialty.

The chili con carne craze took root in a number of ways,

though much more gradually than fads like Cronuts do today, spanning decades rather than days. Recipes appeared in cookbooks and ladies' magazines, and by the 1920s, canned chili con carne filled supermarket shelves, made by companies like Wolf Brand of Corsicana, Texas. Its founder, Lyman T. Davis, had been selling chili from the back of a cart since 1895. Davis named the company for his pet wolf, Kaiser Bill.

By the mid-1920s, the brand was being promoted with a pickup that had a cab shaped like a can of chili, with a wolf padding around in a cage on the vehicle's flatbed. Who wouldn't want a bowl of chili after seeing something like that clatter by? By 1936, 43 years after the Columbia Exposition, Hormel Foods of Austin, Minnesota, had begun canning chili and distributing it nationally, one year before the same company introduced Spam. That was the brand my mother bought and kept in our cupboard when I was a kid in Edina, Minnesota, in the 1960s. She'd open a can with her whizzing electric can opener for Saturday lunch, and my twin brothers and I would sprinkle broken saltines over the top. It was considered exclusively a time-saving luncheon dish, not something fit for, say, a dinner party. We loved it but didn't realize the richness of chili history. And it was probably the only time we'd tasted cumin, which seemed strange and exotic to us. Naturally, the chili canned for national distribution contained no heat.

WHEN MEX WAS TEX-MEX IN GOTHAM

So let's take a closer look at the Mexican fare available in New York in the early '80s, most of which was inspired by Tex-Mex cuisine, which had as its core element chili con carne. Not only was chili featured among the appetizers on Mexican menus, it also served as a sort of unifying principle for the combination plates that formed the heart of this citified cuisine. Typically, you'd have a choice of three selections—say a chicken enchilada, a chili relleno (spelled with the anglicized *chili* instead of the Spanish *chile*), and a hard-shell taco or a tamale. The oblong platter—usually served on some pastel shade of Fiesta-ware—came sided with yellow rice containing frozen mixed vegetables alongside red beans or refried beans scooped from a can. Chili gravy—really just a thinned-out chili con carne, often also from a can—would be poured over the platter, and grated cheese or cheese food product scattered over that. The Mexican combo platter was at the time one of the world's great comfort foods, with San Antonio flare.

Many of the city's Tex-Mex places were located in the Village or elsewhere downtown, where dining out assumed a raffish tone and any meal was considered by New Yorkers from further uptown as something of a walk on the wild side. Typical was Mexican Village on Thompson Street, of which Craig Claiborne wrote in the *New York Times* in 1968, "If you like Mexican food with Texas overtones, however, you will proba-bly like the restaurant." He must have, because he gave it two stars. Such a high rating for an inexpensive greasy spoon would be unthinkable now. Brooklyn Heights and Staten Island were other hot spots for this sort of restaurant.

In fact, a popular Mexican restaurant in Staten Island had the unlikely name of Montezuma's Revenge. Milton Glaser and Jerome Snyder wrote in the *All New Underground Gourmet* (1977) that the place also served paella and French onion soup, but once again, the specialties of the house were the platters: "In a special category are the predicable Mexican combination plates of enchilada (beef, chicken, or cheese), burrito, tostada, and chalupa," suggesting that by the '70s, Tex-Mex was already a culinary commonplace in New York City.

I have a special place in my heart for this cuisine and am glad it still exists here, though it's now relegated to the fringes of the city's foodist scene. One reason the fare persists (and it can be truly awful) is the boat-sized frozen cocktails diners expect to find, making the suggestion of a visit to a Tex-Mex joint a code for "I'm going to get sloshed on sweet frozen margaritas." One such establishment is Caliente Cab Company, a flatiron-shaped barn prominently positioned in the West Village at the intersection of Seventh Avenue South and Bleecker Street, which boasts a giant overflowing margarita protruding from the second story of the façade.

I once sat at a table next to the kitchen and stared in awe as the "chef" opened can after giant number-10 can of refried beans, tomato sauce, and chili gravy, then poured them into the buckets of an elephantine *mise en place*. Thankfully, much better evocations of this cuisine still exist, including El Cantinero, one of my favorite restaurants in the Village, where the fajitas sizzle with fresh strip steak and shrimp, the chile rellenos are just-fried, the tamales shaken from a can (as they should be in this context), and the enchiladas—now retrofitted to use mild cheddar instead of Velveeta—come smothered in the same canned chili gravy I enjoyed as a teen in Texas, spicy and salty. And laced with cumin.

BACK TO THE FUTURE

At first, there were rumors that the cause was massive layoffs at a Volkswagen plant in the city of Puebla. Immigrants from the Mexican state of Puebla—the state has the same name as its capital—began arriving in New York around 1985, initially in a trickle and almost unnoticed. By the end of the decade, they were appearing in waves and quickly came to dominate entire employment sectors. But contradicting the layoffs theory, most of these newcomers had clearly not been city folks; some didn't even speak much Spanish. It turned out the newcomers were mainly rural and mainly agrarian, from the mountainous and arid southern part of Puebla, bordering Oaxaca.

The names of the towns they came from would soon be emblazoned across Mexican delis in all five boroughs: Tulcingo del Valle, Atlixco, Tehuitzingo, Zacapala, and Izúcar de Matamoros. At first these delis appeared in Sunset Park, Brooklyn; Corona, Queens; and East Harlem; neighborhoods where Spanish had long been the predominant language of the Dominican and Puerto Rican denizens, and the new immigrants found their mother tongue easily understood. Soon, they were everywhere.

The real reason these immigrants came here was an extended drought that lasted most of the 1980s and spanned a broad swath of southern Mexico, decimating the corn and bean crops and slaughtering livestock. A bigger question, and one that has never been successfully answered, is why the hard-pressed Pueblans moved to New York instead of, say, California or Texas. But their impact on the dining scene in the city was to be cataclysmic. Later joined by immigrants from Guerrero and Morelos, the Mexican population in the city zoomed to a half million by 2011.

Not only did the immigrants have a profound impact on the city's bodega culture and soon thereafter on our street food, they also tended to find work in fancier restaurant kitchens. Side by side with Ecuadorians, they came to dominate the food-prep lines due to their propensity for working long hours and ability to tolerate crappy working conditions (including the excess heat of restaurant kitchens, which must have felt something like home). According to the Fiscal Policy Institute, as many as two-thirds of these Mexican newcomers were illegal, but that doesn't detract from the overwhelming contribution they made to the city's dining scene at both the high and low ends. As the *New York Times* admitted in a 2012 analysis of Mexican workers living crowded into a single building in Bensonhurst, Brooklyn: "As they have filled the city's restaurant kitchens and building sites, they have acquired a reputation for an extraordinary work ethic."

But as restaurant workers, the Mexicans were largely invisible. Starting in the late '80s, their most visible institution became the bodega, a small convenience store principally stocking ethnic groceries and staples like milk and margarine, with neophyte Mexican owners often replacing earlier Dominican and Puerto Rican ones. These began appearing not only in neighborhoods where Mexican immigrants lived, but also in places where they found work. As an example, one of the earliest Mexican hot spots for bodegas, taquerias, and beer bars was Manhattan's Garment District, where many of the campesinos worked. The men pushed racks full of clothes through the crowded streets just south of Times Square, while the women cut patterns and sewed, often in sweatshop conditions that seem nearly 19th century. Such garment sweatshops are still prevalent along the border of Bushwick and Ridgewood, with the doors flung open to the streets in the sweltering days of July and August, with the cramped interiors, heaped with textiles on all sides, visible to all.

As with all new immigrants, at lunchtime they craved food that was familiar. Typical of the places they sought nourishment was Matamoros Puebla Grocery, which surfaced around 1995 on Williamsburg's main drag, a stone's throw from the Bedford Avenue subway stop, the first in Brooklyn coming from Manhattan on the L train. The place was named after Izúcar de Matamoros, a small city in western Puebla situated at 5,000 feet with a current population of around 40,000.

At first the store remained mainly a Puerto Rican bodega, as it had been previously, but gradually groceries imported from Mexico—corn husks in bales, dried and canned chiles, bottled salsas and moles, Mexican candy, parti-colored piñatas—came to dominate. A few years later, the place was also selling fresh agricultural products familiar to southern Mexicans, such as green tomatillos; spiny cactus paddles; prickly pear fruits; thick, flat, dark-green papalo leaves; guaje seedpods; and even chayote macho, the strange hairy squash shaped like an avocado. As of this writing, mainstream New York chefs have yet to explore the exciting possibilities of this botanical bounty now available in bodegas all around us.

Soon after Matamoros Puebla in Williamsburg began operating as a Mexican bodega, a counter appeared at the rear of the store staffed by two short ladies in flowered aprons, their hair pulled back in neat buns, laboring 14 or so hours per day, Sundays included, over stew pots that barely fit on the burners of a small, tenement-style, four-burner gas stove. They made tacos, which were soon being enjoyed by the neighborhood's burgeoning hipster population. Like the Mexican immigrants whom the makeshift kitchen had been created to feed, these hipsters also craved delicious cheap eats in a neighborhood where great food at low prices was increasingly harder to find.

While these low-rent hipsters may have been accustomed to the hard-shell tacos made in Tex-Mex joints, at Matamoros Puebla suddenly they were confronted with typical Pueblan ones: two white-corn tortillas, softened on the griddle, then filled with a choice of meats from a list of Mexican culinary commonplaces, such as cabeza (headcheese), lengua (tongue), and ora (pig ears). Indeed, the organ meats were often the tenderest and tastiest, they found, outstripping the more familiar carnitas (pork tidbits), bifstek (beefsteak), pollo (chicken), and carne enchilada (pork in chile sauce). Instead of tomatoes, shredded lettuce, and cheddar cheese, these Pueblan tacos came dressed with chopped onions and cilantro, with a choice of homemade red or green salsa on the side. The hipsters found the green one to be startlingly hot. "Yowza!" they shouted, removing their hats, but happily went on eating.

Using the same tortillas—which were soon being made at tortilla factories that came to line Flushing Avenue in Bushwick—the ladies prepared enchiladas with simple green or red sauces based on dried and fresh chiles and green tomatillos—all sold at the bodega—but also with more complex moles based on pre-Columbian models invented by the Indian tribes from which many of the new Mexicans were directly descended. Speaking of the Indian origins of many immigrants: more than once during the '90s I stumbled on bodega kitchens where the Mexican cooks spoke very little Spanish but Indian tongues instead, communicating with each other in a language I took to be Nahuatl.

When it came to antojitos, the plethora of corn-based snacks that made up much of the city's burgeoning southern Mexican food scene and included Puebla-style tacos and enchiladas based on corn tortillas, these bodega cooks seemed to prefer fabricating the masa-based platforms by hand rather than relying on machine-made tortillas, a real sign of their rural tastes. First to appear were the huaraches, sandal-shaped boats of masa dough that held the usual taco fillings plus opulent quantities of onions, cilantro, crema, and queso seco.

Then followed sopes, picaditas, tlacoyos, chalupas, gorditas, and, especially, quesadillas—not the double-flour-tortilla melt we were accustomed to in the city's Irish bars and Chinese-owned taco joints, but giant, thick rounds of hand-patted masa dough that functioned as hyper-steroidal tortillas when folded around the typical taco fillings. While you needed three or more tacos to make a full meal, one Pueblan quesadilla easily did you. Like the Italians with their myriad forms of pasta, each suited to a particular locale and narrow usage, the Mexican immigrants seemed to have endless ways to pat damp masa dough into unique vessels.

Pueblan quesadillas were popularized at the ball fields in Red Hook, Brooklyn, where on the weekends quesadilla vendors lined up to provide sustenance to an international collection of soccer players, stuffing their hand-patted masa flatbreads with steak barbecued over charcoal, oddly reminiscent of Tex-Mex fajitas. Meanwhile, other Mexican cooks, realizing a vigorous market for Tex-Mex already existed in a city only barely familiar with their own southern Mexican specialties, started making nachos and burritos, too, creating a sort of universal Mexican menu that incorporated Californian and Texan food in a way found probably nowhere else in the world, not even in Mexico.

By 2000 or so, as it had been earlier with neighborhood pizza parlors, it seemed you were never more than a few blocks away from a bodega with a taqueria housed in back. In Coney Island, there was El Jarochito ("Little Rude One," a reference to the place's Speedy Gonzales logo), a lively place founded in 1993 that steamed up an excellent barbacoa (whole baby goat or lamb) on the weekends, a real Pueblan homestyle specialty, while maintaining a full-service grocery in front. Campesinos, sometimes with children in tow, would breeze in, grab a kilo of fresh tortillas and some fresh Pueblan herbs like yerba santa, cilantro, and papalo, along with a pound or two of barbacoa, and then head out to promenade on Neptune Avenue in their colorful serapes and cowboy hats as the birds chirped and previously arrived Russian immigrants stood and gaped.

My favorite establishment of this sort in Hell's Kitchen was Tulcingo del Valle, which began around 2000 as a single narrow storefront selling groceries. It soon began selling tacos and other antojitos from a small space cleared of groceries in the front of the store. By 2008, it had added a dining room next door, accessed from the store via a narrow improvised passageway in the rear and decorated with Aztec calendars, images of the Virgin of Guadeloupe, sombreros, and piñatas that were calculated not to make Mexicans feel more at home but to attract gringo customers. It worked, and soon the place was filled with office workers at lunchtime on weekdays, and it wasn't long before foodies were enjoying salsa-smeared plates of chilaquiles and huevos rancheros for brunch on the weekends.

By 2010, many of these bodegas had been strung together in chains. Bushwick alone had at least three Cholulitas (named after the town of Cholula, a center of Toltec civilization before the arrival of Cortés, on the outskirts of the city of Puebla), my favorite situated on Broadway close to the pop-up, illegal hipster nightclubs around the corner of Myrtle and Broadway. I watched over a period of two years as the grocery part of the bodega withered, as new tables were added in the rear taqueria, then a second storefront was annexed to contain the groceries that had been displaced.

One of the specialties besides picaditas (little hand-patted circles of masa with a ridge around the edge, intended to hold a greater quantity of fillings), huaraches, and tripe soup was a vegetable-heavy beef stew called mole de olla, a delectable potage that outwardly resembled Irish beef stew, though with a different constellation of vegetables. By 2013, I counted at least two dozen taquerias, most descended from bodegas, in Bushwick alone. Some were Pueblan, but increasingly immigrants from

Guerrero and Morelos were opening bodegas, too, and even some immigrants from Mexico City itself. Increasingly, the hegemony of Pueblans was disappearing as a new mix of Mexicans appeared.

THE RISE OF THE MEXICAN SANDWICH

From the very beginning, in addition to tacos, the earliest bodega-taquerias peddled tortas. Though the word *torta* back in Spain signified any flatbread, in Mexico it came to mean a sandwich served on a torpedo-shaped white roll known as a *bolillo*. Another name for this roll was *pan frances*, or *French bread*. A torta made on a French roll was a very urbanized and Europeanized viand to be sure, considering that the sandwich itself was invented in England in the 18th century, though the torta was extensively adapted for Mexican usages.

The sandwich soon spread across Mexico after its early 20th-century introduction. Its chief utility is suggested by the name conferred on it in northern Mexican cities like Monterrey: *lonche*, or *lunch*. Found mainly in urban areas, the sandwich boasted stuffings that ran from typical taco fillings like carnitas and skinless chorizo to prosaic cold cuts like boiled ham and sliced cheese, to—most famously—milanesa de res: breaded and fried beef cutlets. The name suggests these cutlets originated in Milan, though Vienna is more likely. Call them Mexican Wiener schnitzels, one of many Teutonic contributions to Mexican culture. These fillings were typically further heaped with lettuce, tomato, mayo, chipotle peppers, and sliced avocados, the last tremendously ramping up the creaminess, color, and lubrication.

But in the early days of Mexican immigration to New York, bolillos were hard to come by, so the plucky bodega owners of the early '90s grabbed whatever farinaceous cognate they could get their hands on. Often it was a type of roll already being sold by the Dominicans or Puerto Ricans who had earlier owned the bodegas. So it might be a tapered Portuguese roll like those made in Newark's Ironbound and distributed throughout the metropolitan area, very much like a bolillo already; or it might be one of those stunted demi-baguettes made by Italian bakeries; or it might be the so-called kaiser roll—a round Austrian semmel with a twirling pattern on the top, first introduced to New York by the Germans in the late 19th century and persisting as a deli sandwich bread just as popular as rye, whole wheat, and white. The point is that New York's earliest tortas were made on readily available breads, and you can still find tremendous variations in the bread used to make tortas.

The East Village's wonderful Downtown Bakery was the earliest purveyor of tortas in lower Manhattan. As the 1990s dawned, the place had been an Italian bakery turning out the usual butter cookies, bread sticks, pastries, traditional round Italian breads, and demi-baguettes from a narrow storefront. It was the type of small bakery once found on nearly every block of the Lower East Side. But very early in the new decade the Pueblans invaded and made the bakery their own, gradually turning the place into a taqueria. First they naturally started making tortas on the demi-baguettes already in the glass cases. In doing so, they had undoubtedly been influenced by the Italian hero sandwiches so readily available in neighborhood pizzerias; indeed, the range of fillings found in Italian heroes and Mexican tortas overlapped by about one third, mainly in the cold cuts area. In fact, a veal parm hero and a milanesa de res torta were virtually indistinguishable save for the garnishment.

The very elasticity of the torta, the lack of set historic definition in Mexican terms, led the field to be wide open for innovation. One of my favorites quickly became Downtown Bakery's carne enchilada torta, a giant gut bomb of a sandwich, oozing red chipotle sauce and fiery hot. This was an extreme example of the torta's emulation of the hero: the luxurious quantity of red sauce in which the meaty and fatty pork chunks swam seemed like it was intended as a substitute for the tomato sauce in, say, a meatball hero. Eventually, in Bushwick, which was already rapidly becoming one of the city's greatest Mexican strongholds by 2010, I saw a place advertising something called "torta paninis," representing yet another instance of the torta's absorption of Italian influences here in America. To my infinite regret, I didn't snap one up immediately.

In preparation for this book, I ate nearly a dozen tortas to see how the sandwich was faring in its most modern incarnations. I scarfed them in Corona and Ridgewood, Queens; in Mott Haven, the Bronx; in Sunset Park and Ditmas Park, Brooklyn; in Stapleton, Staten Island; and in East Harlem and the East Village, Manhattan. In fact, for a solid two weeks, come lunchtime I was never to be found without a torta in my hands.

The best was sourced at a street stand called Taco Veloz. Located on a bustling stretch of Roosevelt Avenue in Jackson Heights, Queens, with the 7 train clattering deafeningly overhead, the place consists of a broad window on the street with a long metal counter for standing and eating tacos, tortas, and quesadillas. Inside, two women dressed in bulky sweaters and knit caps (this being early February in a harsh winter) hustle around preparing food. I ordered their signature torta—queso de puerco. This lush sandwich is layered with pig headcheese precut in slices that are at once slippery and gelatinous, and occasionally you can make out a bit of ear or lip in the quivering matrix.

The torta fabricator began by slathering brown refried beans on the bottom of the split roll, and then mayo, rather liberally I thought, on the top half. Next she extracted a huge wad of headcheese from her metal tub *mise en place*, putting it in the sandwich. I should point out that the roll was not the usual baguette, Portuguese bolillo, or kaisersemmel, but rather a flat, brown, bouncy bread something like a small Frisbee. It had notably less crumb within its crusts that the usual bread roll, leading me to wonder, is this something the city's Mexican panaderías invented in response to the low-carb craze?

The first handler then passed it to the second, who juggled it in one hand as she added lettuce, tomato, ripe avocado, and plenty of chipotle chiles, enough to create a monstrous burn as the sandwich slid down my throat and sought its way further down my alimentary canal, abetted by the surreal slipperiness of the head-cheese, which added a very mellow savor to the sandwich. A real working-class tuck-in! I wolfed the entire thing down standing at the metal counter, watching the street theater of the milling and passing throngs, mainly Mexican immigrants celebrating a children's holiday that featured sidewalk displays of colorfully dressed dolls representing saints when they were babies, trundled out on trencher tables to lure passersby. I found the baby saint incarnations kind of creepy, just like Muppet babies.

HERE COME THE CEMITAS

Arriving in New York with Pueblan immigrants was another notable sandwich, this one slightly more Mexican than European. And this sandwich was unique to Puebla, rather than spread around, as was the torta, mainly in the country's urban areas. Jonathan Gold first predicted the existence of cemitas here around 2001 like a sage foretelling the coming of a prodigy, leading me to look for them along Fifth Avenue in Sunset Park, which then had the greatest accumulation of newly arrived south-of-the-border immigrants in the city. And I found the roll called a *cemita*—rounded, brown, domed, and sesame seeded—at a bakery on 55th Street. It wasn't a sandwich, just a roll. But it suggested that someone was using them to make cemitas. As with tortas, the cemita is defined by its bread.

Back in the city of Puebla and state of Puebla, the cemita roll contains cactus pulp, which gives it a somewhat spongier texture and moister crumb than plain-flour breads. Originally, the inclusion of pulp had probably been an economic expedient, because in the desert cacti are cheaper than flour. Here, where cactus paddles are a semi-luxury item, cemitas tend not to con-tain much pulp, though I occasionally stumble on a roll that seems to have some fibrous substance mixed in.

The first actual cemita sandwich I found was in 2005 at San Francisco De Asis, a taqueria at 110th Street and Lexington Avenue, now defunct. The interior was draped with Mexican flags and pictures of the patron saint of animals. The cemita, which I carried out, then stood in the street admiring on what was an unusually warm day for May, came stuffed with carnitas.

But the vast majority of the sandwich's filling was dairy and vegetable, including competing layers of smeared ripe avocado, lettuce, tomatoes, onions, chipotle peppers looking something like sun-dried tomatoes, masses of white string cheese, and refried black beans. There was also some crema here and there, distributed in little twitching squirts. Some ran out the side of the bun, not as a testament to incompetent sandwich making, but as a signifier of richness and overabundance. Here was a sandwich both thicker and lusher than the average torta, and priced just a dollar more.

One bite of that first cemita knocked me out, not only through its savory and moist combination of ingredients, but because of another flavor that I for a time was unable to identify. A call to Jonathan Gold in Los Angeles revealed what it was: the small, dark-green, shiny, lobulated leaf called papalo. It had a slightly acrid taste, something like burning rubber, but in combination with the other sandwich fixings, the flavor was heavenly. There's something so satisfying about stumbling on an unfamiliar herb! I felt the same way the first time I tasted cilantro. "It tastes like someone spilled some cleaning fluid in my soup," I had exclaimed to a companion. And then went right on eating. Ditto Vietnamese mint, an ingredient I first encountered at Zak Pelaccio's Fatty Crab in a pork belly and watermelon salad. Once again the taste was nearly indescribable, a combination of cinnamon and mint with a hard edge. The flavor also resembled a well-worn leather wallet.

The cemita is unthinkable without papalo, an herb that still has to be imported. Occasionally, I'll order a cemita and find it contains no papalo. I'm crestfallen. But when I complain to the sandwich maker, she gets all sheepish. The leaf remains hard to find, even in the most well-furnished Mexican markets in East Elmhurst, East Harlem, and Sunset Park, where the best Mexican groceries are. These days, most of the best Mexican food stores don't have taquerias attached anymore. That's partly because we have many more fully functioning Mexican restaurants run by immigrants.

Nowadays, tortas and cemitas stand side by side on the menus of most small restaurants, beer bars, and taquerias run by immigrant Mexicans. Other than the choice of bread and the presence or absence of papalo, there's scant difference between them, except a certain opulence one finds in the cemita that comes with its longer roster of ingredients, mainly the result of Pueblan pride. Both sandwiches have proven to be elastic vessels—capable of holding diverse fillings never imagined back home—in a way that tacos and masa-based antojitos like sopes and huaraches have not. One of the most amazing examples of this is a cemita I recently discovered in the eastern reaches of Jackson Heights.

It was designated on the chalkboard menu "Cubano," seemingly inspired by the Cuban sandwich that is still a staple of the city's dwindling collection of pan-Latin lunch counters such as El Sitio de Astoria and Margon. Normally, the sandwich would be made on a demi-baguette extensively smeared with margarine and mayo and layered with thin slices of pork roast, boiled ham, and white cheese, plus thin pickle spears. Annealed to flatness in a sandwich press, this unctuous beauty, sometimes additionally flavored with garlic, is about the most compact repository of salt and grease imaginable. Needless to say, it's also supremely delicious.

As I encountered the Cubano cemita at Bella Puebla Inc. in Jackson Heights, it had layers of breaded and fried beef and chicken cutlets, a comically thin slice of boiled ham (the only bit of pork in the sandwich), a fried egg, lettuce, tomato, soupy chipotle sauce, papalo leaves, string cheese, and refried black beans, making a sandwich easily four inches in thickness. It became clear as I ate it in the rear of the restaurant sitting on a barstool, that the sandwich was not only a tribute to the original, but a profound one-upping as well. While the Cuban sandwich is monovalent, an essay in pork and cheese, the Mexican counterpart exploded with its tastes and textures. It also cost $8.99, which is the most expensive Mexican sandwich I've ever eaten.

ALL HAIL, PAMBAZO!

You may now breathe a sigh of relief, because we have finally reached the ostensible subject of this chapter, pambazo, sometimes spelled *panbaso* or *panbazo*. The name means "low-end bread," referring to a type of bread enjoyed by the poorest citizens, made without butter or lard so that it has a light, open texture with little solidity. *Pambazo* is also the name of the sandwich made from such a loaf, perhaps the most obscure of the three Mexican sandwiches that have arrived in New York over the last 25 years, revolutionizing the city's sandwich scene.

Some say it arose in the port city of Veracruz on the Gulf of Mexico. And while the torta and cemita have an entire catalog of possible fillings, the lowly, streetwise pambazo has but one in every incarnation I've seen in New York: a hash of potatoes and skinless chorizo, usually topped with a nest of shredded Oaxacan cheese, which is something like a cross between string cheese and mozzarella. The cheese squeaks in your teeth as you bite into it. While the obsessive nature of the fillings deployed in the pambazo is notable in itself, the significant feature of the sandwich is that the lowbrow bread is improved by being split and then immersed briefly in bright-red chile sauce as the sandwich is assembled. That makes it something like Los Angeles's famous French dip. Eating a pambazo is invariably a big sloppy mess, as your fingers get stained red and fragments of potato and sausage tumble out.

I first became aware of the sandwich early in this century at a place occupying some rather low-end real estate on Fourth Avenue in Sunset Park. Then, as now, the more desirable storefronts were found on Fifth Avenue, constituting one of the city's most popular Latin American shopping zones, anchored at its southern end by the Basilica of Our Lady of Perpetual Help.

Restaurante Taqueria Guerrero was one of the city's first visible indicators that immigrants were now flooding the city from Guerrero, in addition to Puebla. It seemed logical, since mountainous and hardscrabble Guerrero was just west of Puebla and had been beset by narco-terrorism since the late '90s, giving its impoverished residents further motive to split.

I say "became aware" because, though "panbaso" was perpetually advertised in the window of the place, they never seemed to have it. The lady who waited on tables and whipped up the food—and who was famously featured in a photo on the marquee of the place, a large woman with a sweet, fair face that had masses of dark hair cascading around it—declined to make one every time I asked. The food she did make, however, was fabulous—pork chunks of stunning diameter in a green mole that seemed to include earthy pumpkin seeds as well as fresh green tomatillos, outsize shrimp in a fiery sauce served only on the weekends, and lots of dishes made with salted and air-dried pork cecina, one of the staples of cooking in Mexico's arid south. It was also the only authentically Mexican place in town I was aware of that hand-patted its own fresh tortillas. (A few upscale places of dubious overall authenticity like Rocking Horse Cafe in Chelsea had previously done it as a gimmick.) These tortillas were used to make a remarkable taco called the Azteca, which featured cecina as well as strips of grilled cactus paddle in a pair of tortillas, sprinkled in the usual southern Mexican fashion with chopped onion and cilantro.

I finally got a real taste of pambazo at a bakery near the basilica, long defunct, around 2003, and I can still remember eating it on the sidewalk outside (there were no tables), leaning over to keep the sloppy mess from dripping on my shirt. I was hooked. From that point, the floodgates opened, relatively speaking, for this rare sandwich. I know of eight or so places that serve them now. But I've developed certain theories about pambazo. While the ostensible origin point for the sandwich was Veracruz, I'm convinced that the examples found here are all from Guerrero. That would explain the timing of the appearance of the sandwich, long after the Pueblans had introduced the torta and the cemita. Another piece of evidence is the nature of the chile gravy utilized. It's made from bright-red guajillo chiles, which are often used in Guerreran cuisine, especially as a topping for enchiladas.

The pambazo is considered both poverty food and street food, not entirely suited to restaurant menus. Which is why, though you may see a sign in a taqueria advertising the sloppy, supremely delicious sandwich, on any given day the proprietors may claim to be unable to make it, either because they don't think you will appreciate it, or maybe because they don't think the sandwich represents the best their homeland has to offer. Pambazo is a sandwich that will perpetually linger in the realm of afterthought as far as food establishments are concerned. Persevere, and you will eventually be rewarded. Finding a pambazo in New York is like stumbling on a gold nugget, and it's also like a sloppy joe your mom may have made you as a child. Close your eyes and chew, but make sure to come prepared to make a mess of your shirt, since no laundry detergent on earth can erase that red chile guajillo sauce.

And the impromptu and ephemeral quality of the pambazo, the sense of something bravely being remade using perhaps not the most distinguished of ingredients, and maybe in absence of raw materials you'd rather be cooking with, reminds me of the Mexican food I first fell in love with in Texas, which evoked an ancient and complex cuisine using a rudimentary and artificial catalog of ingredients. Yes, there is a profound commonality between, say, Tex-Mex dishes and the pambazo. And it tells us about the adamantine persistence of popular cultures from all over the world on the streets of New York.

WHERE TO GET A PAMBAZO

1. EL RANCHITO POBLANO
1228 FLATBUSH AVENUE, BROOKLYN, 718-282-0366

Who'd expect to find a great taqueria in Flatbush, right on its most ancient Dutch thoroughfare? The pambazo is of unusually large size, toasted top and bottom to melt the cheese a little and warm the hash filling. You're going to have trouble finishing the entire sandwich; the leftovers are doubly good at breakfast.

2. EL COYOTE DORMILON
92ND STREET AND ROOSEVELT AVENUE, QUEENS, NO PHONE

This cart offers a decent pambazo, nicely toasted (some might say burned) and with especially large masses of cheese and one of the best versions of the chorizo–potato stuffing. It boasts more lettuce than usual, which might be an advantage depending on your perspective. Uses a bolillo, the bread usually used to make a torta. Not a bad choice.

3. LA MESITA
1513 MYRTLE AVENUE, BROOKLYN, 718-366-8700

This Bushwick newcomer offers what is currently the city's best pambazo. The hash has a spicy kick and is offered in profusion. There could be a little more cheese, but who's complaining? The filling bulges and the sandwich is fabricated with great care.

SIX PLACES TO GET TORTAS AND CEMITAS

1. DON PEPE TORTAS Y JUGOS

3908 FIFTH AVE, BROOKLYN, 718-435-3326

No pambazos, no cemitas, but the greatest collection of tortas—many elaborately stuffed with multiple ingredients—the city has yet seen. The Española Doble contains a slather of refried beans, slightly runny fried egg, slice of ham, plancha-fried cheese, split hot dog, potatoes, bacon, another type of cheese not fried, pickled jalapeños, sautéed onions, tomatoes, and avocados.

2. DOWNTOWN BAKERY

69 FIRST AVENUE, MANHATTAN, 212-254-1757

This Italian bakery turned taqueria in the East Village still uses Italian bread to make tortas, with some surprising fillings from the taco side of the operation, including a carne enchilada torta unlike any sandwich you've ever seen.

3. TACO VELOZ

86-10 ROOSEVELT AVENUE, QUEENS, 718-397-1233

This is the taqueria (really, just a window) to get the marvelously slippery headcheese torta, which you should order by the Mexican name of queso de puerco.

4. BELLA PUEBLA

94-11 ROOSEVELT AVENUE, QUEENS, 718-639-7300

This Jackson Heights spot is one of the city's best vernacular Mexican restaurants and the proud purveyor of the overstuffed cemita Cubano, containing a laundry list of fillings, and spicy as hell.

5. TACOS MORELOS

438 EAST NINTH STREET, MANHATTAN, 347-772-5216

Cemitas are few and far between in Manhattan, and this little East Village spot does some fine examples on rolls that actually contain cactus pulp. My favorite is the potato and chorizo model, overstuffed and outfitted with plenty of papalo leaves.

6. TULCINGO DEL VALLE

665 10TH AVENUE, MANHATTAN, 212-262-5510

This 15-year-old Hell's Kitchen grocery store turned taqueria offers some of the best cemitas, heavy with papalo leaves, refried beans, sliced avocado, and Oaxacan cheese, with your choice of 14 fillings, of which my favorites are huevos y chorizo, lengua (veal tongue cut in strips and stewed to a fare-the-well), and milanesa de res (beef Wiener schnitzel).

PAMBAZO

SERVES 4

Get ready to enjoy one of the world's messiest—and potentially spiciest—sandwiches.

FOR THE CHILE SAUCE:

8 dried guajillo chiles
1 dried ancho chile
1 small white onion, chopped
2 garlic cloves
4 cloves
$\frac{1}{2}$ teaspoon ground cinnamon
$\frac{1}{2}$ teaspoon dried oregano
2 teaspoons salt

FOR THE FILLING:

2 large Yukon gold potatoes, peeled and diced
2 tablespoons vegetable oil
1 pound fresh Mexican chorizo
Salt

FOR THE SANDWICH:

1 tablespoon vegetable oil
4 pambazo rolls (or any soft, oval roll)
2 cups shredded iceberg lettuce
$\frac{1}{2}$ white onion, thinly sliced
$\frac{1}{2}$ cup crumbled cotija cheese
$\frac{1}{2}$ cup crema

1. First make the chile sauce. Remove the stems from the chiles, tear them open, and shake out the seeds; discard the stems and seeds. Place the chiles in a medium bowl and cover with boiling water. Let them sit, submerged, for an hour. Transfer the soaked chiles to a blender with 1 cup of the soaking liquid, the onion, garlic, cloves, cinnamon, oregano, and salt. Blend on high until smooth. Pour the chile sauce into a sauté pan. Bring the mixture to a boil and cook 3 to 5 minutes, stirring constantly. Turn off the heat and keep warm.

2. Make the filling. Boil the potatoes until tender, drain, and set aside. In a sauté pan, heat 2 tablespoons vegetable oil over medium-high heat. Remove the skins from the chorizo and crumble the sausage into the pan. Cook, breaking up the sausage into pieces, until it starts to brown, 8 to 10 minutes. Add the potatoes and cook, mashing up the mixture until incorporated and hot. Taste the filling and add more salt, if necessary. Remove from the heat and keep warm.

3. To assemble the sandwiches, heat 1 tablespoon vegetable oil in a cast-iron or other skillet over medium heat. Dunk each roll briefly in the chile sauce, covering all sides. Add the sauce-dunked rolls to the skillet, 2 at a time, and toast on each side so the exterior gets crisp. Open each roll, fill with some of the chorizo-potato mixture, top with lettuce, onion, cheese, and crema, and place the top back on top, pressing down to adhere. Serve immediately.

BARBECUED
BRISKET

Texas barbecue and me go way back. When I was attending Lake Highlands High School in the north White Rock Lake area of Dallas—this would be back in the late '60s—we'd sneak out around noon into the student parking lot. The steaming expanse of tarmac was presided over by a crusty character known to generations of students only as Zeke, who stood all day in a ramshackle guard box. Even though we technically were not permitted to leave the grounds during the school day, we'd distract Zeke by tossing a rock into a remote part of the parking lot, then pile into one of our rundown Chevys or Fords, positioned next to the exit on purpose, and tear ass out into the street, burning rubber.

We'd trace a route that took us from our suburban enclave west along Church Road, hang a partial left onto Fair Oaks, sometimes reaching speeds in excess of 80 miles per hour as we flew through what was then forest and farmland. I was the Yankee who'd moved to Texas from Minneapolis the year before, forever the outsider, but this crew of misfits drew me to its bosom. Sometimes Mike Drummond—the leader of our pack, a tall lanky guy with a thick drawl given to wearing plaid shirts and torn sneakers, who talked incessantly about sex—would pull a small bottle of whiskey from under the seat and we'd each take a gingerly swig. At Lake Highlands High School, only the football players really knew how to drink.

Our perpetual destination, approximately three miles west, though it seemed like 50, was the tiny town of Vickery. It was really just a blot on Greenville Avenue in a grove of pecan trees within the city limits. We marveled at the antiquity and run-down quality of the place. Even in our limited adolescent imaginations, we understood quaint, and this was it, a vestige of a bygone Dallas where hay wagons were pulled by horses, houses were wood and had front porches with swings, and the shit-kickers—guys who dressed in the full regalia of ten-gallon hats, faded jeans, pointy-toed boots, and giant belt buckles that shone in the punishing midday sun—were somehow still in charge of large parts of the landscape.

Our destination was an icehouse. I don't remember the exact name. Nor did I know why my friends called it an icehouse, except that in the days before refrigeration, this was a place where you got your blocks of ice. When I lived in Dallas, even 7-Elevens were referred to as icehouses. In New York, we'd call them bodegas.

This particular icehouse, the anchor of Vickery and the only business that seemed to still exist, was a concrete block structure presided over by a hugely fat guy who sat on a short stool behind the counter like Jabba the Hutt. He had positioned the cash register so he would never have to stand, selling cigarettes, fried pies, and candy (mainly Hot Tamales, Boston Baked Beans, and Mary Janes) from a seated position. We'd hand him our money, he'd make change, then we'd scoot outside to the shade created by the store, where a tattered guy of indeterminate race dressed in overalls managed a set of ice chests repurposed to keep food hot rather than cold. His skin might have been leather. Flies buzzed around him.

"What'll y'all have, boys?" he'd ask in his tobacco-raspy drawl, pausing at the comma for a wheezy, labored intake of air. We'd reply promptly, using the form of address all high school students were taught to use with their elders: "Four hot links sandwiches, sir." He'd framed the question pro forma, because he knew what we were buying and had indeed already paid for inside, and that was the only thing he sold: the best hot links sandwiches in the world. He made a point of counting the four

of us with a stained index finger, as if we needed precise counting, then began the process of assembly.

He'd take the bright-red links—two to a seeded hamburger
bun—cut them in half through the middle on a tree stump at
his elbow, then cut each of the pieces lengthwise, making four
pieces per sausage. He'd slather the bun top and bottom with
barbecue sauce, then pile the eight pieces of sausage, teetering,
on the bun. The sauce wasn't spicy but the hot links were, with
a grainy texture and livid red exterior—these were certainly not
natural-skinned franks. They had a way-smoky flavor as a result
of being smoked in a charcoal-stoked pit out back of the store,
an almost sour aftertaste, and left a burning sensation on the
tongue. A hot links sandwich hastily consumed in the shade
of a pecan tree, washed down with a bottle of Big Red or Dr
Pepper (which we referred to as "Prune," due to its perceived
flavor), was our lunch at least two or three times a week. Then
we'd pile into the car and drive back to school at a leisurely pace.

We were not the only ones who recognized the picturesque-
ness of Vickery. Bonnie Parker, of Bonnie and Clyde fame, had
apparently once worked at a small café on the south end of town.
When it came time to shoot the movie, Arthur Penn selected
Vickery as the backdrop for a couple of scenes. In fact, what was
left of the railroad siding and the hay wagon sprawled by the
side of the road may indeed have been leftover props from the
film. When we saw the movie soon after it came out in 1967,
we felt almost famous as we recognized the broken-down town
where we ate our 'cue. I can still taste those hot links, peppery
and gritty. They were my first inkling of how wonderful Texas
barbecue could be.

FROM HOT LINKS TO RIBS AND BRISKET

But it took years for me to realize the full scope of Texas barbecue. I attended the University of Texas at Austin from 1968
to 1972—majoring in chemistry and psychology—but returned
home every summer, because that was what college students

were expected to do. My mother, who wanted me to be a pediatrician, managed to secure me a position at Parkland Memorial Hospital and the attached Southwestern Medical School, a branch of the University of Texas. The job entailed, most notably, working as an autopsy assistant, where, at the tender age of 16 (I'd started college early), I was exposed to some very gruesome sights. Parkland was where John F. Kennedy was rushed after the assassination in 1963. And there remained a chastened aura about the hospital still. In fact, it was rumored that the president was still being kept alive in a remote wing. Others fervently believed it was only his brain.

Working at the hospital was a chance to further mix with working-class Texans and fall in love with their foodways. Sometimes I'd eat lunch in the brightly lit hospital cafeteria, where I marveled at a hot vending machine that sold nothing but fried baloney sandwiches on biscuits, oozing grease and mustard. They were good! There was also a steam table where my favorite selection, offered on Thursdays, was Tex-Mex ground beef enchiladas, which came in a metal foil container smothered in yellow cheese and brown chili con carne gravy. A tub at the end of the line provided pickled jalapeño peppers at five cents each. My hospital friends and I would have chile-eating contests, and it was at that time that I first learned the masochistic pleasure of eating chiles. And lots of them.

Other days my friends and I would drive to Spindletop, an ancient Texas bar a block or two north of Harry Hines Boulevard named after the state's first major oil strike, which doubled as a strip club. It was only topless back then, and if you sprang for a beer, the luncheon buffet was free, which seemed like a throwback to the Great Depression. Usually it consisted of fan-shaped arrays of cold cuts and sliced cheese, along with white bread and Miracle Whip and vinegar pickles and canned jalapeños on the side. But on Fridays there'd be something hot, usually elbow macaroni mixed with chili con carne, poured from a can into a sort of Lake Wobegon hot dish. It was served with saltines, and we loved it.

During this era I became familiar for the first time with Texas barbecue in its purest and most original form at Sonny Bryan's Smokehouse. By this I mean brisket, pork ribs, and sausage of one sort or another, long smoked. Folks—including barbecue guru and Dallas resident Daniel Vaughn (himself a transplanted Yankee)—have told me Bryan's is no good anymore, and perhaps they are right, but back in 1969, the place was a revelation. It was a stone's throw from the hospital on Inwood Road, which is how I stumbled on it as I was driving home one day, located in a former gas station repurposed as a down-and-dirty BBQ joint.

There was an upright metal smoker (which by and large had replaced the traditional in-the-earth pits of earlier times) belching hardwood smoke out back, and you could see the chimney over the top of the jazzy slanted roof. The gas station had functioned as a barbecue since 1958, when Sonny Bryan's first opened. But the roots of this Dallas institution go back much further: Sonny's dad, William Jennings Bryan Sr., known as "Red," had run a barbecue in Oak Cliff, a hardscrabble Dallas suburb southwest of the Trinity River, since 1930. And before that his grandfather Elias Bryan, born in Cincinnati, had opened the first of the family barbecues in 1910, also in Oak Cliff. The Bryans were Texas barbecue royalty.

Inside, you were expected to eat your 'cue at grade-school desks that any outsize Texas footballer would have been unable to fit into. You'd place you order at the counter, receive your 'cue, then go over to a sideboard where bottles of homemade barbecue sauce sat in a hot water bath. I said to myself, "This is real obsession: that you'd go to the trouble of making your own barbecue sauce and also insist it be kept warm." That hot water bath was one of the things that made Sonny Bryan's unique. The other was the selection of smoked meats. For one thing, there was ham, pulled pork, turkey, and pulled chicken—all anomalous as far as Texas BBQ goes, but damn good in their own way, especially the ham, which was far smokier than the product shaken out of a can and served on Sundays (back then salt-cured Virginia and other artisanal hams were as scarce as hen's teeth).

But what constituted the bedrock of the menu was the brisket. Streaked with fat, in fact dripping with it, it had only two strong flavors: smoke and beef. This was the real quintessence of Texas barbecue for me. Even then I must have realized that the fat did more than its share of the work carrying the smoky taste that I soon craved: in Dallas barbecues of the day, just as they do it now in New York at the Texas-style Hill Country, you request your brisket either fatty or lean, and the fatty was obviously the smokiest. I'd emerge from Sonny's in a blissed-out state, my lips and chin glistening with grease. It took a while, but that first summer working at the hospital and eating Sonny Bryan's 'cue, I realized that the meat tasted better without the sauce, no matter how much care had been taken in delivering it to you.

The other main attraction of the place was the ribs. But not by the rack. These were relatively stubby as pork ribs went, but full of flavor; in fact they gave the brisket a run for its money. The most delectable system of delivery was the rib sandwich—which just goes to show how soft the meat on Sonny Bryan's ribs could be. A few pork ribs were placed between two slices of white bread in a style used throughout the South, to make what was technically a sandwich, but one with bones in it, which gave you the option to eat the thing any way you wanted. (The same technique is also used for bone-in fried chicken.) You could choose to remove the meat and the sauce by sawing it with your plastic knife to create a more conventional sort of sandwich, or you could take a bite of meat and sauce while the full rib was still in the bread, and gum it around with your mouth, leaving the bone behind. The bread really functioned as a sauce and meat catcher, so that none of the rib's goodness would go to waste, and there would be no pool of sauce left on your plate after the ribs were eaten.

I haven't eaten at Sonny Bryan's in 20 years—not since my family moved to Austin, and I didn't return to Dallas. Besides, I was soon to discover the greater barbecue pleasures that central Texas afforded. Nowadays, Dallas is considered a barbecue haven, I hear. Nevertheless, as a picturesque place to get a first tantalizing glimpse of what 'cue could be, Dallas was just fine for me.

By the way, real hot links like the kind I ate as a high school student are still not easy to find outside of northern Texas and southern Oklahoma. The only place in New York that serves them is Mable's Smokehouse in Williamsburg, Brooklyn. They get their links straight from Oklahoma and smoke them a modest amount of time, so the sausages remain bright red with a little char here and there. I go there every couple of months, and the gritty and spicy taste of the links still brings tears to my eyes.

LONG-AGO BARBECUE IN AUSTIN

It's hard to believe in these days of BBQ obsession and extended weeklong pilgrimages, when fans will routinely drive four or more hours each way or even fly in from other states to get a taste of places like Snow's in Lexington or Cooper's in Llano, that barbecue was once considered a normal local foodstuff that you ate and enjoyed but would never go way out of your way to get. That's the way it was during my college years. I routinely patronized a couple of places within the Austin city limits but never made the 45-minute trip by car to visit the more ancient barbecues like Kreuz Market and Black's in Lockhart, simply because I'd never heard of them. Nobody I knew had. Why would you sojourn when you had good barbecue in your vicinity? Also, back then I was not quite the food obsessive I am now. BBQ as it was in Austin was plenty good enough for me; I knew no better, since these places matched in quality those I'd known in Dallas (though they were sadly lacking in hot links).

Back then in Austin, there were black barbecues and white barbecues. If you wanted African-American, heavy on the sauce and centered on the plain pork sausage and pork ribs, you'd go to Sam's on Twelfth Street in East Austin, a neighborhood students were warned to avoid. Nowadays, East Austin is hipsterized and considered a prime location for upstart barbecues like John Mueller's and Micklethwait Craft Meats, often situated in trailers on vacant lots, the way Franklin Barbecue—now the most famous barbecue in Austin—started out.

Ensconced in a ramshackle white frame house, Sam's is still around. It was founded in the late 1940s by Sam Mays of Round Rock, Texas, a town just north of Austin. His cousin Dan Mays bought the place in 1978. Famously, it burned down in 1992, but was rebuilt. In 2011 it was plagued by a scandal that suggested the meat served in the establishment was routinely stolen from an H-E-B (a supermarket chain in Texas). Emblazoned across the façade at a crazy angle is the slogan "You Don't Need No Teeth to Eat My Beef," which is somewhat ironic, since generations have been going there for the pork ribs, which are big, meaty, and well glossed with sauce. (When it comes to Sam's ribs, I make an exception in my preference for no sauce. When in Rome . . .)

I remember going to Sam's with some friends on acid in 1971 and marveling at the furniture inside as it melted around us, paying scant attention to the barbecue. We later went to my friend Richard Maurer's house up on Duval Street and sat on the wide front porch and spent hours peering at a print of a Vermeer painting and trying to predict what the woman had in the pitcher she was about to pour from. Sam's Bar-B-Que was a longtime favorite of Stevie Ray Vaughan's, and in the late '80s, when his fame was at its height and he had many fans, the modest barbecue joint was the most common place for a sighting. And, as Texas food historian Robb Walsh noted of Sam's in his book *Legends of Texas Barbecue Cookbook* (2002), it was one of the few barbecue joints in the state open late at night: "Unlike the old meat markets out in the country, which often sell out at noon and close up before five, urban barbecue joints like Sam's are hopping at three o'clock in the morning."

What about the white barbecues? There was a long-running chain in the Austin area called the Pit, with a logo that showed a stack of flaming mesquite, but even then we knew the production-line barbecue 'tweren't too good there, though we patronized it when we were on our way to somewhere else, like the legendary

Lake Travis skinny-dipping spot, Hippie Hollow. If we wanted really good barbecue we'd go to a modern-seeming spot on Lake Austin Boulevard on the west end of town called Dale Baker Barbeque, not too far from the University of Texas married student housing.

It was apparently in business from 1952 to 1975, and the place is little remembered by anyone but my friends, who included Robbie Fox, a short skinny guy who grew up in the Westchester town of Irvington. He was the first New Yorker I ever met. Despite being a business major, he wore his hair to his waist and had a handlebar mustache, and was one of the few people at the time to ride a bicycle around town. He was usually to be seen wearing an olive-drab jumpsuit. It made me wonder what New York could possibly be like if this guy was so distinctive.

In researching this book, I discovered that Dale Baker's claim to fame was that he often catered barbecues at the LBJ ranch in Johnson City during the late '60s, serving people like Eddy Arnold, Walter Cronkite, and Mexican president Adolfo López Mateos. Baker's brisket was prodigal: smoky and well fatted, delivered generously on thick white-bread sandwiches or, as I recall, on rolls. I'd have to credit Baker with establishing the entire hegemony of brisket in my mind over all other forms of barbecue. There was undoubtedly pork ribs and sausage, too, and maybe even some chicken, but it was the brisket that even today dwells in my imagination. At the time, his barbecue restaurant, which was on the edge of the Hill Country, a semi-mountainous area that extends perhaps 80 miles west of Austin, seemed to be in the middle of nowhere. Now, the location is in the center of Austin's westward-tending urban sprawl.

I left Austin to attend grad school at the University of Wisconsin in 1972, but even before I went, a new generation of barbecues was already appearing, places I avidly sampled when I visited Austin during my residency in Madison, Wisconsin, where I studied English for five years, receiving a master's degree but never managing to finish my PhD. Perched in the Hill Country, County Line appeared in 1975 with gorgeous views to the east of the city skyline, the capitol dome, and the University of Texas tower gilded by the setting sun. Nothing like the smell of creosote and mesquite in your nostrils as you ate on the broad terrace, feasting on those huge beef ribs that were County Line's specialty. Talk about being prescient! No other place I knew of served them at that time. The establishment has since spread across the state and is now considered mediocre, but back then it seemed wonderful. Not only have our tastes in barbecue changed over the years, but I swear general barbecue quality has improved, too.

My brother David and his wife, Holly, had settled in the Austin area after going to college there and had a lovely rambling house that looked across a valley toward Dripping Springs. Willie Nelson lived not far away, in what was technically Fitzhugh but soon became gobbled up by the city of Austin, despite being probably 20 miles southwest of the capitol building. My parents eventually retired and moved to Georgetown, 20 miles north of Austin. In the 1980s, I visited the area often. I'd moved to New York City in 1977, but my heart was still in Texas.

It was during the late '80s and early '90s, after my daughter, Tracy, was born, that I became the barbecue obsessive I am today. Including my wife, Gretchen, our family threesome made frequent trips to the Lone Star State, for Tracy to visit her cousins and grandparents, but also to visit dude ranches in the Hill Country, where we delighted in seeing Tracy ride horses in full cowboy regalia. And the three of us, between excursions to Fitzhugh and Georgetown, would pay multiple visits to the great barbecue towns in the black-dirt farm country east of Austin, towns like Luling, Lockhart, Elgin, and Taylor, where country barbecues, all post oak and smoking pits, had been in place for a hundred years and more. Most were also originally meat markets and continued to be at least vestigially so, and the Texas style of barbecuing became supreme in my mind, even though during the '90s I also made targeted barbecue trips to Kentucky, North and South Carolina, Georgia, Memphis, Florida, and Kansas City to study the barbecues there. Nothing ever has or will ever beat Texas barbecue.

Indeed, it was institutions such as Kreuz Market—in the old location right on the square—with its smoke-blackened pits made of fire bricks half-sunk in the ground surmounted by hinged metal lids, presided over by soot-dusted figures like a scene from Dante's hell, its decorative rattlesnake skins and framed examples of barbed wire, its Mexican ladies selling cheese and avocados as a sideline in the dining room, and its overall-clad farmers who sat stolidly eating barbecue with soda crackers at nine in the morning, that permanently cemented my ideas of barbecue's culinary potential. And foremost in my mind was the fatty brisket, smoky as a prairie fire, so clearly the star of the show.

EARLY 'CUE IN NEW YORK

When I arrived in the East Village in 1977, escaping from the academic life contemplated in Madison, I had already developed a taste for barbecue, but nothing like the fanatic levels I would achieve in the 1980s as I ventured over and over again to Texas and other states to eat smoked meat. Of course, I looked for barbecues right in New York City. I found no shortage of places called barbecues, principally in Harlem, Clinton Hill, and Bedford-Stuyvesant, often proximate to the fried chicken places mentioned in a separate chapter. Like the fried chicken joints, they were based on Carolina models, but not the older type of Carolina barbecues that smoked whole hogs or shoulders over hardwood or charcoal. These places roasted rather than smoked their meats—smeared with barbecue sauce—in vertical, glass-fronted gas cookers. Typical were the pork and chicken at Singleton's, a place that once boasted two locations in Harlem. I favored the one just north of the Schomburg library at Lenox Avenue and 136th Street, even though the meat was low on smoke flavor.

Singleton's was a narrow space with a carry-out window on the street, a yellow Formica lunch counter seating five on swiveling stools, and a small dining room up a few steps with two or three tables. It was already an old wreck when I reviewed it in 1998 for the *Village Voice*, and by 2002, the place had closed down. The heart of the menu was pulled pork barbecue served with a smoky, sweet, and vinegary sauce already applied, very Carolina style. On a visit just before the place closed, my friend Philip Dray and I, fresh from doing research in the newspaper archives at the Schomburg Center, saw a rat ascending the stairs toward our table one midafternoon. We paid no attention and kept eating as he scampered past. Seeing a mouse or a roach in a restaurant in New York isn't all that uncommon. But seeing a rat—that's something you can tell your children about.

There were six or seven of those old Carolina barbecues in Manhattan and Brooklyn, and they could be good, but they emphatically weren't real barbecue. These places were evidence of something sometimes called "oven barbecue" in Brooklyn, whereby anyone with an oven and a bottle of barbecue sauce could be their own pit master and turn out chickens or ribs that would be widely recognized as barbecue among large segments of the population but weren't really barbecue as far as experts were concerned. Real barbecue involves wood, or at least charcoal, and doesn't depend on the sauce for flavor. Real barbecue flavor comes from the meat itself.

But you couldn't find more than traces of real barbecue in New York during the '80s, and little in the next decade, either. Those, like me, who loved it had to content ourselves with surrogates, foods dug up at local restaurants that tasted like real barbecue—at least partly. Let's call it the pursuit of smoke. One dish that provided that flavor was tandoori chicken. When tandoori hit the East Village in one of those myriad Bangladeshi places on Sixth Street in the '80s, more than a few BBQ aficionados started showing up regularly, mainly because of the smoky taste of the chicken. Pastrami at Katz's Delicatessen, which was smoked as part of the process, could almost satisfy a barbecue jones, and so could the tea-smoked duck that started appearing in some of the more sophisticated Sichuan places, first at the original Grand Sichuan on Canal Street and later at every Wu Liang Ye and Grand Sichuan in other parts of town. By 2000 you were never far from a spectacular tea-smoked duck, and if you squinted your eyes, the dark fragrant duck meat, once pulled from the bone, might almost be brisket.

As Uzbek and other Silk Road grills started appearing in the late '80s, my friends and I discovered the kebabs purchased at those places were invariably cooked over charcoal. The hyper-fatty lamb ribs absorbed plenty of smoke and were every bit as tasty as anything you could get in a barbecue in, say, Owensboro, Kentucky, where mutton barbecue is king. At Cheburechnaya in Rego Park, Queens, you could get a kebab made from lamb tail fat, which proved to be the smokiest of them all. We looked up the breed of sheep in a book and discovered they had fatty tails so large they had to pull a wheelbarrow behind to support the tail. At Cheburechnaya, the grilling was done over a charcoal fire in a little trough that ran along one side of the room, making us wonder how we all weren't getting asphyxiated. Note too that these kebabs acquire a smoky flavor through charcoal grilling, which is not the same thing as being smoked for hours at lower temperatures in an enclosed smoker. Surrogates have their limitations.

But there were harbingers of real barbecue that appeared in the city early on—though nothing like the quality of the places we would eventually have. Around 1980 a barbecue opened near the corner of 24th Street and Ninth Avenue in Chelsea, right across the intersection from the swanky London Terrace Gardens apartment complex, called Smokey's. It was run by a couple, native New Yorkers who had attended the University of Texas at Austin a few years previously. Being Gothamites, they paid a little too much attention to baby back ribs, but they did good pork spareribs, and a decent chopped brisket—but no sliced brisket. (When I lived in Texas, chopped brisket was considered lowbrow, though some barbecues served it.) Everything was washed down with green bottles of Rolling Rock beer. It was a rollicking place, causing Mimi Sheraton to proclaim enthusiastically in her *New York Times Guide to New York*

Restaurants (1982), "Smokey's . . . has an open-pit barbecue in each dining room and excellent spare ribs . . . and the city's best sauce, be it mild or hot."

Careless franchising on the part of the couple (sorry, I can't remember their names) led to a branch of Smokey's on the Upper West Side and an even larger spin-off on Third Avenue in the teens that often yawned empty. By mid-decade there were no more vestiges of Smokey's. Other previews of things to come included Tennessee Mountain, a long-running rib joint in Soho ensconced in a rambling frame house that seemed a total anomaly in that cast-iron-façade neighborhood, and Brother Jimmy's, another primarily rib spot, this one on the Upper East Side. Brother Jimmy's has hung on and created branches all over town. A retry of one of the newer outposts off of Union Square indicated that the Carolina-style pulled pork dressed with vinegar is pretty damn good—though it pains me to admit it, mainly because I consider Carolina barbecue to be inferior to that of Texas.

Another decent barbecue of ancient vintage and now defunct, this one trying to clone several different regional styles, was Brothers Barbecue, dating to the late '80s and originally situated in a narrow building that had once been a stable across from Film Forum on West Houston Street. Eventually it moved to the cursed southwest corner of Houston and Varick, a sprawling space that didn't take as well to the kitschy downmarket decor. Miraculously, though, Brothers persisted well into the next millennium, a 20-year run nearly unique among the city's barbecues.

I remember Brothers' barbecue being pretty good and plenty smoky, but when I looked back at a piece I wrote for the *Voice* in 1997 called "Manhattan's Barbecue Curse," I had nothing but bad things to say about the long-running institution.

This negativity was partly due to the arrival of Stick to Your Ribs, a real Texas-style barbecue in nearly all respects that opened in an obscure part of Long Island City, Queens, in 1992. It was a profound game changer.

PEARSON RIDES IN ON HIS WHITE HORSE

Originally from London but residing in Connecticut, Robert Pearson was a celebrity hairdresser, a tall amiable guy with a big shock of blond hair, an engaging English accent, and a hearty, almost back-slapping manner. His claim to fame was that he'd done mod hairstyles for the likes of Twiggy and Jean Shrimpton in the swinging '60s, becoming a tonsorial demigod. A chance trip to Austin, where he had been hired to teach a class in hairdressing, led him to pay visits to barbecues in central Texas, and Pearson suffered an almost-religious conversion where smoked meat was concerned. When he returned to the Northeast, he founded a barbecue in Stratford, Connecticut, in 1983 called Stick to Your Ribs. Lots of buzz eventually attracted the attention of the *Times*, which interviewed Pearson for pieces in 1988 and again in 1989. During the '89 conversation, he extoled the virtues of smoky meat and the secondary importance of barbecue sauce, a theme he was to touch on again and again:

> When you eat a steak do you want it swimming in bearnaise sauce?" asked Robert Pearson, who owns Stick to Your Ribs, a popular Texas-style barbecue restaurant in Stratford, Conn. Mr. Pearson is adamant that sauce should be optional, and that, in any case, should not be applied to meat while cooking, but served on the side.

Perhaps emboldened by the *Times*'s coverage, he opened a New York City branch three years later, located in an industrial area near the mouth of the Queens Midtown Tunnel, where he believed the smoke wouldn't bother the neighbors. The conventional wisdom at the time was that great barbecue was impossible in the city due to air-pollution regulations. As Eric Asimov, the *Times*'s "$25 and Under" restaurant reviewer, noted in 1993, "the inescapable fact is that pits produce smoke, which collides with another inescapable New York fact: neighbors." Pearson thought he'd prove all the skeptics wrong with a smoker from J & R Manufacturing—a distinguished outfit located in Mesquite, Texas. It set him back $13,000, a lot of money in those days, but the rig contained a "scrubber" that cleaned the contraption's exhaust of smoke smells, at least partly.

I went soon after the opening and was moved by the quality of the 'cue as I sat admiring the smoker in the rear yard, ringed with outdoor tables like some religious shrine. I remember being especially impressed by the brisket, and used it as an excuse to further disparage the other barbecues in town: "Forget Virgil's, forget Brothers, forget Zacki's—this is the best barbecue in town," I enthused in a Voice Choice in 1993. Then went on, "True to its Texas antecedents, brisket is the meat to order—sliced thick, and pink around the edges, with a flavor as smoky as a firefighter's helmet." In line with much modern barbecue thinking in Austin today, that brisket spent a whopping 18 hours in the backyard pit over a combination of oak, hickory, and mesquite, and the rich flavor of the fatty meat fully reflected it.

Pearson served a range of barbecue, not all of it quite as good as the sliced (also available chopped) brisket: chicken, sausage, pulled pork with a vinegary Carolina-style sauce already applied, long and short ribs of beef, and lamb ribs. (The last were quite an anomaly, though he may have gotten the idea from Cooper's in Llano, Texas, a barbecue aimed at hunters where goat and lamb are often available.) Pearson made other modest adjustments to his evocation of the Lone Star barbecue canon, reflecting a playful take on the New York terroir. Rather than serving sliced white bread or crackers, he deployed torpedo-shaped Portuguese rolls, sourced in Newark, New Jersey, brushing both sides of the split roll with a modest quantity of sauce. It worked magnificently and proved that where true barbecue is concerned, there's nothing wrong with innovation.

Pearson had also made adjustments in the sausage area. While Hill Country actually imports its loose-in-the-casings beef sausages from Lockhart, Texas, Pearson's dealt with the dilemma of what links to use in New York by deploying our own indigenous Polish sausages, which proved capable of absorbing lots of wood smoke and turning quite delicious. Other barbecues in town have since tried Italian sausage made locally, with less impressive results. Somehow, Italian flavors and barbecue don't go together. Finally, as I already mentioned, Mable's Smokehouse, an unpretentious place on the northern frontier of Williamsburg, imports hot links directly from Oklahoma, which is where proprietors Jeff Lutonsky and Meghan Love hail from. The barbecue traditions of northern Texas and southern Oklahoma are very similar, lucky for me and anyone else who loves hot links.

Though sauce was not the point of barbecuing, as Pearson frequently pointed out, his homemade sauces were so good, you wanted to use them. All tomato based, there was a choice of four: mild, medium, madness, and—hottest of all—mean. For a while, as a gimmick, he made you sign a legal release before he brushed "mean" on your sandwich. He also had a few other nutty ideas. For a brief period, he offered "houtnannies," burritos stuffed with chopped brisket, tomatoes, and parsley. Even now, many of his quirky ideas seem very contemporary, as chefs like Danny Bowien of Mission Cantina diddle with burritos and barbecue. Indeed, Bowien is now making a grilled brisket burrito. Too bad that the passage of time prevents us from comparing Pearson's and Bowien's.

The effect of Stick to Your Ribs (eventually known as Pearson's Texas Barbecue, and later, when it moved to Jackson Heights in 1998—as a result of smoke complaints from the neighbors—as Ranger Texas Barbecue) was incalculable. Many made pilgrimages to Long Island City and were wowed. Even old Texas hands. It seemed that once New Yorkers had a taste of great pit-smoked meats, they would never forget it. And every barbecuer who has come after has had to deal with Pearson's legacy in one way or another, and our own memory of how good, for the first time in the city, barbecue could be.

In the ensuing 23 years (Pearson's Barbecue opened in Long Island City in 1992), barbecue in New York has gradually grown from a flickering small flame to an inferno. Queens roadside shack Mississippi Barbecue caused a sensation in the mid-1990s, while restaurateur Danny Meyer's pit master Kenny Callaghan founded Blue Smoke on 27th Street in Manhattan in 2001. Grandson of a Lockhart mayor, Marc Glosserman established Hill Country in 2007, intentionally trying to get as close to the central Texas barbecue aesthetic as possible, and coming pretty damn close.

The walls of Hill Country are festooned with photos of Lockhart—still a center of the fading cotton-growing industry—and portraits of the town's notable pit masters. True to its roots, the meat is cut before you on rustic butcher blocks and deposited on butcher paper, sold by the pound. Sliced white bread and soda crackers are free. The only tip of the hat to modernity is "beer can chicken," which I've never tried, going instead for the brisket (sold lean or fatty), pork ribs, ginormous beef ribs, cooked-rare prime rib (also a quirk of Kreuz Market), and beef sausage imported directly from Lockhart, either plain or with cheese and jalapeños inside the natural sheep-intestine casing.

Much like the addition of beer can chicken to Hill Country's menu, New York pit masters who followed in Robert Pearson's footsteps felt they had the same license to indulge in similar experimentation. Hugh Mangum of Mighty Quinn's used an eggy and slightly sweet brioche roll to make his brisket sandwiches, and it worked just fine, giving a rural barbecue tradition city airs. At Fletcher's Brooklyn Barbecue near the Gowanus Canal, pit master Matt Fisher offers tiny potato rolls in lieu of bread, in line with the anticarb thinking that had grown to dominate the restaurant industry. (Even Hill Country only provides a paltry slice of white bread or two with each butcher-paper-wrapped barbecue order. People simply aren't eating carbs anymore.)

NEW YORK MEANS GREAT 'CUE!

Over the last two decades, inspired by the success of Stick to Your Ribs and the increasing popularity of Texas-style barbecue here in particular and barbecue across the country in general, New York has built an impressive collection of real pits, where once we just had oven barbecue. Nowadays, our brisket is as good and smoky as anything you'll find in Texas. Contemporary Austin barbecue god Aaron Franklin pays a visit once a year to Hill Country to show us his stuff. Wayne Mueller, third generation owner and pit master of Louie Mueller Barbecue in Taylor, Texas, has tutored Brooklyn native and former bodyguard Billy Durney, who went on to found Hometown Bar-B-Que in Red Hook, Brooklyn, capturing not only the cuisine but much of the ambiance of Texas barbecues.

Like Robert Pearson, New Jersey native Daniel Delaney went to Texas—and drove back dragging a smoker behind his van. First he used it to do barbecue pop-ups in unexpected places—I ran into him for the first time in the summer of 2012 selling smoked brisket in a centuries-old cemetery behind a Dutch Reformed Church in Flatbush, Brooklyn, and he went on to found BrisketTown in Brooklyn in the shadow of the Williamsburg Bridge. Barbecue breeds fanaticism, and here in New York we now have it in spades.

Which led me in a 2013 *Voice* cover story to proclaim our city, rather grandiosely, one of the barbecue capitals of the country. This ruffled a lot of feathers. R. L. Reeves, writing in the blog *Scrumptious Chef*, joked "Robert Sietsema had clown suit makers scrambling across the USA last week when [he] issued a broadside claiming that NYC barbecue is easily on par with traditional centers of smoked meat like Kansas City, Memphis and Central Texas."

Recently appointed *Texas Monthly* barbecue editor Daniel Vaughn—alongside Robb Walsh, one of the Lone Star State's great smoked meat champions—displayed somewhat more measured incredulity, detecting a bit of the tongue-in-cheek in my boast, under the headline "NYC Food Critic Moonlights as Satirical Publicist."

Vaughn, who has since become a friend, published that on March 20, 2013, and exactly two months later showed up in the Big Barbecued Apple to tout his new book, *The Prophets of Smoked Meat*. I had the chance to put my money where my mouth was as he and I—along with Vaughn's wife, Jennifer; Anthony Bourdain's professional tweeter, Helen Cho; *New York Times* restaurant critic, Pete Wells; and Vaughn's literary agent, David Hale Smith—went on a whirlwind barbecue tour of the city. Traveling only by subway, we hit Mighty Quinn's (East Village), Fletcher's Brooklyn Barbecue (Gowanus, Brooklyn), John Brown Smokehouse (Long Island City, Queens), and Delaney Barbecue (Williamsburg, Brooklyn), interspersed with a pie place (Four & Twenty Blackbirds, Gowanus) and a cocktail lounge (Dram, Williamsburg).

It's hard to imagine many other foods besides barbecue that could inspire such feasting: at Mighty Quinn's, the gargantuan beef rib, which weighed around one and a half pounds, was spectacular, coarse textured, and nicely marbled with fat, the exterior dark as midnight. Unexpectedly, Vaughn also liked some Chinese-leaning smoked chicken wings, glossed with soy, sesame seeds, and scallions. The brisket was great, too, but the pork ribs just so-so—low on smoke flavor. Unfortunately, Fletcher's couldn't quite compare. While we felt the burnt brisket ends were underdone, the lamb breast—an oddball offering—and the pork ribs were totally on the money, yet the tri-tip tacos, a little less than spectacular. At one point, Pavement bass player and trencherman Mark Ibold came dashing in to eat some barbecue with us. Our next stop, John Brown Smokehouse, was the biggest disappointment of the day; we tried a whopping eight items, and it all tasted like leftovers. "The barbecue here has been very good on several occasions," I lamented. We chalked it up to the pit master being involved in another project at the time. Luckily our spirits were lifted by the last barbecue stop, Delaney Barbecue, aka BrisketTown, where the brisket especially caused Vaughn to register his enthusiasm, later in print. It was fatty and spectacular, with just the right amount of "crust"—the rudimentary spice rub of black pepper and rock salt turned into pellicle by long smoking. As we agreed, there's nothing like a daylong barbecue run for satisfying your smoked-meat urge, and it also engenders a comparative approach to the subject matter.

I felt entirely exonerated that Vaughn pronounced the barbecue at both Mighty Quinn's and Delaney Barbecue up to his high Texas standards. And a great time was had by all as we scurried into the night, holding our stomachs and groaning as a result of extreme overeating. Plus I left the encounter with a new literary agent.

NINE GREAT (AND ALMOST GREAT)
NEW YORK CITY BARBECUES

Any place that can boast of nine great and almost great barbecues can be deemed a barbecue capital, it seems to me. We now have over two dozen within the city limits, and here are my favorites, each worth visiting.

1. DELANEY BARBECUE

359 BEDFORD AVENUE, BROOKLYN, 718-701-8909

Daniel Delaney is a barbecue experimentalist, though the bedrock of his Williamsburg menu remains his luscious brisket, which can be ordered fatty or lean. Lately, he's been tinkering with hot links sausage.

2. MIGHTY QUINN'S BARBEQUE

103 SECOND AVENUE, MANHATTAN, 212-677-3733; 75 GREENWICH AVENUE, MANHATTAN, 646-524-7889; OTHER LOCATIONS

Pit master and owner Hugh Mangum, who comes from a Houston family, has proven he can spin off multiple locations of his original East Village barbecue and keep the quality high. Though his focus remains on brisket and beef ribs, his wings are worth ordering—but skip the faddish edamame salad. The brisket sandwich is one of the city's best 'cue deals.

3. HILL COUNTRY BARBECUE MARKET

30 WEST 26th STREET, MANHATTAN, 212-255-4544;
345 ADAMS STREET, BROOKLYN, 718-885-4608

Founded in 2007, Hill Country is one of the city's most reliable barbecues, and the downtown Brooklyn branch is every bit as good, and a little more like the rural honky-tonk the first one sought to be. The beef sausage is a real taste of Texas; the sides good in their own way, and Blue Bell ice cream is available for dessert. Ask for a mixture of fatty and lean brisket.

4. MORGAN'S BROOKLYN BARBECUE

267 FLATBUSH AVENUE, BROOKLYN, 718-622-2224

Despite the unexpected location in Prospect Heights, this upstart barbecue proved much better than expected. The original pit master, John Avila, studied with Aaron Franklin in Austin, and the influence shows in the brisket, smoked 16 to 18 hours, and the pulled pork shoulder, which might have come from North Carolina's Piedmont. But the biggest surprise was the great Texas chili.

5. HOMETOWN BAR-B-QUE

454 VAN BRUNT STREET, BROOKLYN, 347-294-4644

This place started out in 2013 at a run and has only gotten better. A current obsession of pit master Billy Durney's is turkey breast, while the brisket and beef rib remain the focus. The maritime breezes of Red Hook only add extra savor to the true roadhouse ambiance.

6. MABLE'S SMOKEHOUSE

44 BERRY STREET, BROOKLYN, 718-218-6655

Started by a pair of Oklahoma natives, this place is friendly and informal. The 'cue is the closest in the city to the type I first ate in Dallas, including wonderful hot links sausages. One of the best eateries in Williamsburg.

7. BLUE SMOKE

255 VESEY STREET, MANHATTAN, 212-889-2005;
116 EAST 27th STREET, MANHATTAN, 212-447-7733

Restaurateur Danny Meyer established this pair of barbecues because he was nostalgic for the pork ribs of his native Saint Louis. Specializing in several regional 'cue styles, the old timer on 27th Street and its Battery Park City offshoot soldier on with generally decent and sometimes exemplary barbecue.

8. FETTE SAU

354 METROPOLITAN AVENUE, BROOKLYN, 718-963-3404

In barbecue years, this seven-year-old counts as an old timer, a walled stockade just off Williamsburg's Metropolitan Avenue with a constantly shifting menu that runs from doctrinaire to unusual, depending on the whim of the pit master. There's also an emphasis on craft beers and barrel-aged whiskies.

9. ARROGANT SWINE

173 MORGAN AVENUE, BROOKLYN, 347-328-5595

This notable newcomer is the first to present real Carolina barbecue in the grandiose fashion of the city's Texas barbecues, with a smoker out back and a big warehouse space where pork sausage and cubed pork shoulder (in the style of barbecues around Lexington, North Carolina) are king.

TEXAS-STYLE BARBECUE — GIANT BEEF RIBS

SERVES 2 TO 4

In Texas as well as New York City, beef ribs are the new brisket.

FOR THE RIBS:

1 cup kosher or other coarse salt (not rock salt)
1 cup black peppercorns, crushed roughly
$\frac{1}{4}$ cup paprika
1 rack of 4 beef short ribs, approximately 12 inches by 12 inches, left whole or cut into 4 large individual ribs (sometimes called a dino rib cut by butchers; smaller lengths will work, too)
Note: you can keep the rack whole for easier maneuvering around the smoker; or, if you want a more blackened crust, cut into individual ribs before applying the rub.

FOR THE SAUCE:

$1\frac{1}{2}$ cups ketchup
1 tablespoon molasses
1 tablespoon honey
1 tablespoon dry mustard powder
$\frac{1}{4}$ cup packed dark brown sugar
2 tablespoons Worcestershire sauce
$\frac{1}{3}$ cup cider vinegar
1 teaspoon red pepper flakes

1. Heat a smoker if you have one. Otherwise, heat a Weber or other enclosed barbecue grill for indirect cooking, placing an aluminum pan of water alongside the coals to catch drips, and soaking wood chips to add to the hot coals for smoke.

2. Put the salt, peppercorns, and paprika in a medium bowl and mix to combine. Coat the ribs (either the full rack or individual ribs) with the dry rub, pressing the spice mixture into all sides, corners, and crevasses. Smoke the ribs in the smoker or grill for 6 to 8 hours, adding more wood, wet wood chips, or charcoal as needed to maintain a low and slow cook. The ribs should reach an internal temperature of 160°F.

3. Combine all the sauce ingredients in a small saucepan. Bring to a simmer, whisking occasionally. Simmer the sauce for 5 to 8 minutes, until slightly reduced. Refrigerate the sauce until ready to use.

4. Once the ribs are ready, pull them from the smoker and let them rest for 30 minutes before serving. Serve with the sauce on the side.

CUY

Cuy will never be as popular as pizza. Heck, it will never be as popular as the alligator sausage you sometimes find in honky-tonk bars selling fake barbecue, or even the lamb-tail-fat kebabs that Uzbek restaurateurs save for their most loyal customers. Cuy is a dish that exists on the periphery of the city's mainstream food culture; it's a sort of fur-bearing unholy grail, and finding it and eating it is a mark of the most intrepid food explorers. The dish itself is rarely spoken of, even among the Ecuadorian immigrants who thronged to the city in the '80s and '90s, mainly from the port city of Guayaquil.

Cuy is the South American Spanish name (*quwi* in Quechua) for the common guinea pig, the same species as the furry pet-shop friend. (Note: this question provokes controversy; some say the livestock cuy is a slightly different species.) It belongs to a family known popularly as cavy, which refers to 14 species of rodents with short tails, big heads, beady eyes, stubby legs, and long fur, usually gray or light brown. The strangest of these is the mara, native to South America, which looks like a jackrabbit as it sits upright on its haunches, long ears pointed skyward. The Buenos Aires Zoo, which I visited in 2012, is overrun with them and also has an impressive pen of capybaras, the world's largest rodent, which looks something like a baby hippo as it swims. Indeed, you could fill a restaurant menu with nothing but cavies in their strange and possibly delicious diversity.

Ecuador, Peru, Bolivia, and, to a lesser extent, Colombia and Brazil, are the countries where cuy is most prized as food.

My original encounter with it in 1997 was striking. I was on my third reviewing visit to Salinas, an Ecuadorian restaurant on Brooklyn's Fifth Avenue in what has become the fringes of Park Slope but was then considered the northern end of Sunset Park. The restaurant had two huge dining rooms done in shades of industrial green, and the tables were covered with thick clear plastic sheets that allowed you to admire the flower-print tablecloths underneath.

I'd eaten my way through all the standard dishes associated with the Ecuadorian lowlands along the country's Pacific seaboard. I'd eaten excellent seco de chivo—big chunks of bony goat in a "dry" sauce, which meant it was delivered in gravy rather than soup; and the Chinese-influenced arroz con camarónes, essentially shrimp fried rice with scaldingly hot chiles carved into little green nuggets in lieu of the usual peas. Looking back over my notes after nearly 20 years, I was particularly taken with the llapingachos, griddle-warmed patties of potato and cheese, like something your mom might make from leftovers.

It being the weekend, the menu was extended with a panel of specials, local lowland favorites from back home in Ecuador. This part of the menu filled the immigrant café up with homesick extended families on Sunday afternoons. One dish in particular caught my eye, not only for its brief identification—only three letters—but also because of its cost—$20, more than triple the price of anything else on the menu.

Luckily, I'd read about cuy in an Ecuadorian travel guide. I kept a large collection of travel guides from all over the world on my bookshelves at the time, acquired in junk shops and secondhand bookstores. I was mainly interested in the four or five pages devoted to the food you might find in the countries described. Those guides, and a slew of cookbooks I'd bought at Kitchen Arts and Letters, the culinary bookstore founded by Nach Waxman on the Upper East Side, were my main source of intel when I traipsed into a restaurant of unfamiliar ethnicity. Before I went, I always boned up on the cuisine, long before the Internet made searches easy and immediate. Today you can Google even the most obscure cuisine—the scarf of a single Indonesian island or city deep in China—even as you sit in a restaurant, preparing to order.

I vaguely recalled that cuy was some kind of small furry animal, though I couldn't for the life of me remember anything else. I cast my eye warily at a pet shop across the street as I sat at the table with three fellow diners, and then ordered it. Having never seen anything like a cuy in any of the South American markets in Queens before, I immediately pondered the sourcing. The arrival of the dish was preceded by a pronounced sizzling sound from the direction of the kitchen, then the mineral smell of cooked meat.

Carried in ceremoniously on a tray, the animal looked something like a drowned rat, standing up on all fours with seeming alertness and glistening with grease on a bed of boiled potatoes. The waiter set the tray down before us with pride but also apprehension, then retreated a few steps, where, arms settled across his chest, he waited for us to respond. Our jaws must have dropped. The animal was devoid of the fur that made it look so big in the encyclopedia picture we later examined. The head in particular was small and outfitted with sharp teeth like tiny knives, with two pairs of long curved teeth protruding from the front of the jaw, like a beaver. The eyes were intact and glistening. The thing had been deep fried whole, but how had the innards been removed?

We worried aloud that we'd find intestines inside, but in whispers so the waiter wouldn't hear us. Turning the tray around, we discovered a giant gaping asshole, which explained how the creature had been cleaned of its organs—they had been pulled out through the rear end.

Hesitant, we tried one of the boiled potatoes, which lay under the animal like pale pebbles on a shoreline. It was good, but what potato isn't? Then we began the long process of dismantling the cuy, gingerly sawing at the haunches, then removing the limbs, leaving the carcass resting on the spuds like a stripped automobile. The thing was oddly delicious, tasting something like rabbit, though the flesh was a bit on the stringy and gamy side. There wasn't all that much meat, but what there was proved memorable.

That day my dining companions and I left the head on the plate, along with assorted other parts that we, in the ensuing years, learned to eat on the rare occasions that we encountered the cavy. The head, we later discovered, was a particular prize. Cuy is considered something of an aphrodisiac, and though the entire animal, which can weigh as much as two or three pounds, is enjoyed by the whole family, the head is reserved for Dad. In fact, as I later learned in Ecuador, acquiring a cuy and cooking it is intended as a sort of tribute to the patriarch of the family, done periodically, and most especially on Sundays.

Looking through my food library recently, I stumbled on this description of cuy from *Curiosities of Food* by Peter Lund Simmonds (1859): "The flesh of the guinea pig (*Cavia cobaya,* Desm.) is eaten in South America, and is said to be not unlike pork. When he is dressed for the table his skin is not taken off as in other animals, but the hair is scalded and scraped off in the same manner as it is in a hog."

A PIG IN A PARK

I was probably the first mainstream food writer in New York to describe eating cuy, in the 1997 review of Salinas in the *Village Voice.* As this was in the days before the web came to dominate the food dialog, feedback was slow to follow. But I did receive several responses in the ensuing weeks, in the form of cuy sightings around town at various small Ecuadorian cafés, most of which did not advertise the dish on their menus. This was probably, I reasoned, because the rodents, strictly speaking, were not a legal foodstuff.

How did the portly looking furbags get to the States? One informant told me they were smuggled in hand luggage, while another hinted at a clandestine cuy ranch somewhere in Westchester. I thrilled to think of gauchos on Shetland ponies, perhaps somewhere up near Katonah, herding and roping the tiny lethargic animals. As I mentioned, I'd never spotted a single cuy in any of the South American groceries that lined Greenpoint Avenue in Sunnyside, Queens (many are now closed), where you'd find canned potatoes in shades of purple and pink; the dozen types of beans used to make Lenten fanesca; and frozen fish such as corvina—unique to South American waters and especially prized in the uplands of Ecuador and Peru, delivery to which involved trucks laboring uphill for hours, jouncing over bumps and scooting around boulders.

On the other hand, I'd encountered what was known as bushmeat in West African groceries around town, especially that Korean-run African store, Sunny Grocery, that stood behind the Port Authority for 20 years, now defunct. So I knew that selling dodgy, uninspected meat in dried or frozen form was not unheard of among the ethnic food stores of the city. At the same store I once found a dried bat, certainly destined for some West African stewpot in America. More recently, the online edition of *Newsweek* was accused of racism for suggesting that bushmeat sold in African markets in the Bronx could be the vector for transmission of Ebola to the United States.

One persistent rumor involved outdoor cuy vendors. Two friends who'd visited the wonderful diorama of New York's five boroughs at the Queens Museum told me they'd seen a vendor hunkered furtively next to a hedge on the northern edge of Flushing Meadows Park, site of the 1964 World's Fair, selling something. On closer inspection, it proved to be small, spit-roasted animals in their entirety. But when I went there on three occasions in the years following my Salinas review, the vendor or vendors were nowhere to be found.

Queens ethnic food specialist Joe DiStefano, recounting his own experiences in 2005 in a Bronx Ecuadorian café with cuy, which he described as "dry, stringy, and devoid of flavor," claims actual sightings of the vendors in the sprawling park in his blog *Chopsticks and Marrow*: "I would see little old Ecuadorean ladies in Flushing-Meadows Corona Park slow spit roasting cuy over charcoal fires. It looked absolutely delicious, like a miniature suckling pig." He apparently wasn't moved to try it.

MY SOUTH AMERICAN QUEST FOR CUY

Having developed a taste for it in Sunset Park and unable to find the fabled spit-roasted cuy of Flushing Meadows, I decided to go to Ecuador and ferret out the dish on its home turf. The country is roughly divided into three culinary regions: the Andean highlands, the Amazonian jungle, and the Pacific seaboard—where many of New York's Ecuadorian immigrants hail from. As you might suspect from my experience in Sunset Park, deep fried is the way the critter is preferred on the coast, but folks like it stewed in the jungle and spit roasted in the Andes.

But I'd inadvertently made a fundamental error in my timing. Gretchen and I had planned our visit to coincide with our daughter's Easter vacation from PS3, not fully comprehending what Holy Week means in a Latin American country. Actually, apart from a few processions and the closed public offices, it was pretty much business as usual. But Holy Week includes avoiding meat, so a giant roadblock was up as far as our finding cuy was concerned.

Fortunately, Ecuador is also a country of bean, pea, and lentil enthusiasts. Though we were to fail in our early attempts to eat cuy, we were lucky enough to arrive in Quito—altitude pills firmly in hand—during the annual two-week run of fanesca, an amazing soup that contains just about every bean and grain imaginable. I had my first bowl at the Santa Clara Market in Quito, a poured-concrete structure that still manages to be charming. With a big "1951" stenciled on the façade, the market is only a couple blocks from the university on the north end of town. Shoe shines, workers for hire, and guys just passing the time congregate at its outside northwestern corner, and inside stalls sell meat, dry goods, and fruits and vegetables stacked in neat pyramids.

Within the market is a section of 20 *comedores*—mini lunch stalls, each consisting of a tile counter lined with stools facing a prep area alongside cauldrons bubbling over propane flames. Each stall has a very efficient and idiosyncratic system of storing and deploying ingredients and cooking utensils so that a multiplicity of dishes can be prepared and sold each day. Typically, the fare runs from hearty potato soups and thick stews called *secos* to simple fried and roasted meats. Some stalls exhibit winking pig heads perched on carefully arranged piles of fresh raw pork, prominently displaying every organ, fenced in like a Civil War stockade with stiff pork cracklings.

Others stalls display a few typical plates of food on cracked china, each entrée including a tossed salad, tons of rice, stewed fava beans, and a boiled potato or two. Llapingachos sizzle in pans of lard the shape of Chinese woks. At the end, a small shrine to the Virgin is flanked by trumpeting angels in blue and pink neon.

Following the advice of Calvin Trillin, who did a story for the *New Yorker* about it, and whom I later accompanied on a daylong search for it across the breadth of Queens, we asked around for fanesca, and hit a great version on the first try. We were to discover that nearly every restaurant, no matter how pretentious or humble, was hawking fanesca that fortnight. The wrinkled woman who ran the stall wore a tattered blue apron and ladled out a huge serving of the bean stew, which features a different bean for each of the apostles at the Last Supper. She sliced a boiled egg and carefully arranged it on top, then tossed on a few planks of fresh goat cheese resembling feta and a leathery piece of brownish salt cod.

The fanesca was creamy and bumpy and yellow green, supremely mellow, and one couldn't resist rooting around to identify as many agricultural products as possible: herbs, garlic, lentils, quinoa, pink beans, gandules, yellow split peas, lupine beans, potatoes, small kernels of fresh corn that contrasted nicely with the bigger lime-slaked kernels known as *mote* (hominy to us). There were various unidentifiable lumps. Like most soups in Ecuador, the flavor of leeks predominated. Leeks are sold on street corners in the commercial areas of town, and the high proportion of white to green would make a French person swoon. Flowering garlic chives are almost as ubiquitous.

Still desperate to locate cuy but finding only fanesca, we downed our second serving that evening at La Querencia, one of the few restaurants in Quito that serves the national cuisine in a plush setting. *Plush* in this case means a gracious colonial house elevated above street level, approached via a doorway in a stone wall that leads to a narrow stairway. A terrace offers views of the mountainside to the east, though automobile exhaust fumes render it almost unusable. As we entered, we inquired about cuy, but received only a polite shake of the head from the waiter.

From a central foyer radiated several high-ceilinged dining rooms, bare except for a few pieces of antique furniture, each holding two or three commodious tables. In an establishment of this caliber anywhere in the States, there would be certain unavoidable high-class flourishes to the food, like radicchio garnishes, infant lettuces, and colorful sauces squirted from bottles. Refreshingly, La Querencia served unadorned peasant fare fabricated with ingredients of high quality, each entrée sided with a plebian combo of rice, fried plantains, and a variety of vegetables and pulses.

First on the table was the de rigueur basket of fresh popcorn, which makes every Ecuadorian meal feel like a trip to the movie theater. Half the menu is seafood freshly transported from fishing villages and hatcheries around Esmeraldas and Pedernales, a drive of about six hours over bad roads. You should begin your meal with one of Ecuador's famous ceviches, which, in contrast to their Peruvian and Mexican counterparts, are more like cooling soups than seafood salads. Most exotic is ceviche de conchas, a marinade of black clams, purple onions, and bits of green chile and tomato inundated with limón. (As in Mexico, there's no demarcation between lemons and limes, only various sizes of limón, ranging from tiny fruits that resemble Key limes to whoppers with a mottled yellow-green skin and flesh that can be green or yellow.)

Other highlights of the meal included a vinegary seco de chivo made with lamb instead of goat, hunks of fried pork called *fritada*, a plate-sized empanada filled with white cheese and fried to an extravagant inflation (and oddly served with a bowl of white sugar), a stringy but flavorful steak served with stewed lentils called *menestra*, and, best of all, honeycomb tripe in a mild peanut sauce tinged yellow with achiote. I've eaten the same tripe soup perhaps a dozen times in Ecuadorian restaurants in New York, where it goes by the name of *guatita*. It was mellow, but still strongly enough flavored that you knew you were eating cow stomach—just a little skanky.

Seeing fanesca on a card clipped to the menu, we ordered it to pass around the table. A little more complex than the market version and more pureed, this slightly upscale version came with cornichons and baby pickled onions. As with the humbler market fanesca, the salt cod was tossed in just before serving, making it more of a chewy garnish than an integral part. Wonderful as it is, this soup always seems like some joker has cleaned out the grain and bean section of the health food store.

THE SEARCH TAKES US NORTHWARD

After a couple of days in the capital we embarked for Otavalo, desperately hoping to find cuy still being served in the funkier northern highlands section of the country. The Pan-American Highway twists through the northern suburbs of Quito till they halt abruptly as the landscape changes to desert. The road then tacks back and forth like a small boat sailing into the wind between furze-covered ridges, where there is no sign of habitation except an occasional dusty half-track, gas station, or rickety lean-to selling highway snacks, mainly pork tidbits and fritters that look like zeppole.

The road abounds with hitchhikers, and over half the traffic is smoke-spewing diesels wildly flying around curves, their wheels churning up clouds of dust as they try to make Colombia before sundown. Sometimes the road is wide and smooth, but often disintegrates into washboard ruts or dirt-filled craters. The perpetual presence of the sun directly overhead makes it impossible to tell what direction you're traveling, and if you hop out of the car, expect to be sunburned to a crisp inside of 10 minutes despite the cool air.

Things start looking up around Cayambe, where the road turns to the northwest and the plastic-wrapped greenhouses of the giant flower concerns begin to appear along the highway. Small farm plots dot the increasingly green hillsides, and gradually the margin of the thoroughfare turns into one continuous town. We've reached Ecuador's northern highlands, one of the world's lushest areas, with jungle-dense foliage reaching toward volcanic mountains that crest at an altitude of nearly three miles.

Thirty minutes later, Otavalo unfolds before us, backed by the twin peaks of Cotacachi and Imbabura. Every Saturday this hill town of 40,000 hosts South America's most famous market, which overflows the squares and market buildings to jam many of the town streets. It being Wednesday, we turn left off the highway up a black-cobbled road that seems hundreds of years old, toward the highland lakes of Mojanda, where we establish ourselves for the rest of the week at Casa Mojanda, an eco-resort that offers spectacular views of the surrounding foothills, where peasants in homburgs and colorful woven shawls drive cows, sheep, and llamas up narrow paths in search of fresh pasturage. Don't call them Incas, though, since these are Indians from the Cara tribe, who remained for centuries unconquered by the Incas, until a scant 50 years before the Spaniards arrived.

But Otavalo turned out to be more of a vegetarian friendly, backpacker-hippie type town teeming with cybercafes. We could find no cuy, only *hamburguesas* and toasted cheese sandwiches in its twisty streets, cradled in a teacup of mountains. Accordingly, we hired a driver to take us northward along the spine of the Andes on a fine sunny day when the temperature reached a near-scorching 68 degrees Fahrenheit.

The stretch of the Pan-American Highway that runs from San Antonio de Ibarra to Atuntaqui in Ecuador's northern highlands is sometimes called Cuy Alley because of its many roadside stands specializing in the spit-roasted animal. But instead of motoring Cuy Alley, our driver, who had been instructed to find us cuy at all costs, turned off in the direction of Chaltura, already knowing that the cuy stands along the main highway would be closed in observance of Holy Week. As the cobbled road zagged upward, juttering past cinder-block houses and fields lush with corn, the ragged clouds parted to reveal the raised bowl of the Cotacachi Volcano.

Eventually, we found ourselves in Chaltura's downtown cluster of colonial buildings. Surrounded by yapping dogs and wearing literal hopsack, a beggar was the only pedestrian—all the stores were shuttered for Maundy Thursday. Disappointingly, the town's cuy joints were also closed for the holiday. There are a half dozen sprinkled around Chaltura, each distinguished by a low stone wall, a sign shouting "Cuy," and a few picnic tables shaded from the equatorial sun by thatched umbrellas. And there we learned the unbendable rule of Holy Week: no Indian may butcher any creature that has red blood. Tuna is the sole exception.

We continued northward to Ibarra, one of the prettiest habitations in the highlands. It's often called *La Ciudad Blanca* due to its whitewashed houses, which settle among the foothills of the Imbabura Volcano, the name of which means "father" in the Quechua language. After passing a busy market near the railroad station on the south end, where a man was wrestling pigs into a truck and campesinos piled densely into pickups, we stopped for lunch at Delicias de Boris, a place enthusiastically recommended by our driver but not listed in any guidebook.

The mustachioed Boris presides over a clean white room, an unlit clay pipe dangling from his mouth. His shrimp ceviche was a wonder—soupy, red, and nearly overflowing from a large bowl, served with a big plate of fried plantain slices called *patacones*. We were lucky it was Thursday, the day the seafood truck arrives from the coast. The fried corvina was especially good, but even better were the camarónes a la plancha, a big pile of shrimp smeared with an oily red sauce and then grilled. The standard lunch plate also contained rice, salad, french fries, and a weird dish of cauliflower chopped very fine and dressed with mayonnaise that never got eaten, at least at our table.

Our return to Otavalo partly followed the old Pan-American Highway, a few kilometers east of the new, through the villages of Peguche and Iluman, the former noted for its exquisite weaving, the latter for the felt hats favored by the *indigenistas*. After visiting a workshop, we had a memorable drive along a rushing mountain torrent that flowed out of town flanked by rickety houses on stilts. "That's where the witches live," said our driver. "Water is sacred to them and they always live near water." In Peguche, a kid in front of the weaving workshop right on the dusty square sold gum, candy, and various warm sodas from a cart propped permanently against the building, while another kid rolled a hoop through the square with a stick. Not much happening at midday.

Back at the eco-resort, excitement mounted as market day approached. On Friday we made a reconnaissance visit to Otavalo, so as to distinguish the Saturday market from the daily ones. Even the Friday market was impressive, with food being sold at two expansive locations, one near the central square, another on the southwest side of town at a roofless market facing porticoed colonial buildings on two sides where vendors set up shop in the shade. Pancho Square is the derisive name the locals give to the tourist market further north, which has its own collection of fruit, vegetable, poultry, meat, and prepared-food hawkers, mainly for the vendors selling tourist crafts to the backpackers, who come principally from Germany and Australia. The tourist town radiates from Pancho Square, and I counted 11 cybercafes within a few blocks, patronized by tourists and locals alike. There were also a handful of pizza parlors, which turned out a surprisingly decent product.

Saturday arrives early in Otavalo, with a livestock market that begins at five in the morning and finishes up by nine, at which time the regular market is already in full swing. The routes connecting the regular markets are thronged with vendors and the intervening streets evenly divided between hawkers selling tourist crafts and those selling needful items like shoes, lingerie, housewares, and cattle. For snacks, men sell freshly squeezed juice from motorized carts with electric extractors (principally fruits like yellow-on-the-outside-green-on-the-inside naranjilla; mora, a berry something like a dark-red raspberry; and passion fruit), and, more prominently, women squat at the street corners with ceramic bowls filled with snail ceviche.

Returning exhausted to Casa Mojanda, we found the banquet table set for dinner. And in addition to enjoying vegetable pot pies, tamarillo (tree-tomato) juice, and vavaco—a fruit that looks just like a papaya, but, served cooked, bears a stunning resemblance to the pears in fruit cocktail—we finally sampled the local cuy. Our hostess had prevailed upon one of the cooks to raid her own stash of diminutive mammals.

It seems that indigenista women keep a herd of cuy in their home gardens, and these animals are so prolific that a pair of males and 10 females is enough to breed several new cuys each week. A small ledge around the garden prevents the cuys—which are incapable of scaling the smallest wall—from escaping. The animal arrived with a deeply burnished and glistening skin, like a pig skin only thinner, with a layer of fat separating the skin from the lush meat. This cuy, which had been spit roasted, tasted exactly like suckling pig, only tenderer, in contrast to the version sampled at Salinas in Brooklyn, which was meatier, drier, and more like rabbit. We collectively breathed a sigh of relief that, even during Holy Week, we'd managed to sample the local cuy from a garden right in town. My obsession satisfied, we could now proceed with our vacation.

QUESTING FOR CUY IN QUEENS

I hadn't eaten cuy since my visit to Ecuador over a decade ago, and I decided that, in preparation for this book, I should try it once again. Not only to renew my own enthusiasm for the critter, but to see if any apparent changes in recipe or source had occurred in the interim. There were nearly five times the number of Ecuadorian restaurants in town than there had been a decade before, and it seemed to me that cuy must have also become more common. But once again, finding it proved to be a challenge.

Tipsters reported they'd seen hand-lettered signs for it up and down Roosevelt Avenue, a thoroughfare that has gradually grown into a wonderland of Latin eats, from Jackson Heights to the eastern edge of Corona. But as I walked the length of it, popping into every Ecuadorian joint I could find, all I turned up were head-shaking "Nos!" Did they have it but simply refused to sell it to me? But now that we were in the midst of the web age, a resource that had barely existed when I first tried cuy, I put all my computer wiles to bear seeking out the rodent.

Not much had been written about eating cuy in New York since my piece on Salinas, which didn't particularly surprise me. Even foodies have their limits, and small furry rodents is apparently one of them. So I turned to MenuPages and clicked on the Find-a-Food search tab. I typed in *c-u-y*. Four listings immediately appeared. I went with a friend to the one in Ridgewood, but when we got there, the place was permanently closed. We ate guatita and the omnibus platter called bandera in a nearby Ecuadorian spot on Irving Avenue that didn't have cuy either. I called a restaurant on Junction Boulevard in East Elmhurst, but they claimed to no longer carry it.

I kept getting this nagging feeling that these restaurants really had cuy, but only if I said the magic word. Accordingly, I asked my friend Victoria Bekiempis, a former *Voice* colleague who once worked as a press correspondent in Bolivia, to call up the third and fourth places that claimed to have cuy. Not only was she a generally persuasive person, but she spoke perfect Andean Spanish. She called up a place in Corona a stone's throw from the Lemon Ice King. The owner bragged that he could obtain guinea pig, but only if we were willing to plunk down a $50 deposit, in cash.

Vic and the guy went back and forth over the phone, and he finally agreed to sell it to me if I'd agree to buy two at $50 apiece. Cuy had always been something of a luxury item, but that seemed steep, and the requirement to buy two, outrageous. The extreme price was one of the reasons it was getting harder to find cuy, I reasoned. Nevertheless, I consented and was on the 7 train with my daughter, Tracy, and an Italian friend once associated with Slow Food, Alida Borgna.

We arrived to find the restaurant on a quiet back street, the outside done up with lots of neon on the southern fringes of what had once been an Italian neighborhood. The place was pink and brightly lit inside, a handful of families chowing down on the usual fare, including stews served with mote, roast meats, and hearty soups swimming with pork parts or seafood.

The waitress seemed to know almost instinctively what we were there for. She served us Ecuadorian beers and then stood behind the bar nervously. A few minutes later, the door burst open and the mustachioed owner, with coal-black hair pushed back from a high forehead, appeared bearing a package, which he quickly removed to the kitchen through swinging doors. He then emerged to welcome us to his restaurant. He looked a bit like a cuy himself. He reiterated that we were on the hook for two, and then tried to sell us a third. We demurred, and after some rapid conversation in Alida's fluent but Italian-accented Spanish, we agreed that each of the women should get a half cuy apiece, while I'd receive a full one. Really, when you see the entire animal at once, it makes much more of an impact.

The creatures eventually arrived at our table, deep fried in the usual Guayaquil fashion, their bronze skins shining with grease, causing all heads to look up from their meals and gape. The animals were somewhat more gruesome than I'd remembered, their jaws frozen wide open to reveal rows of tiny teeth. I quickly tweeted a picture and an avalanche of replies ensued.

One guy replied in all caps as if shouting, "HOW RICH U GOTTA BE TO EAT A BABY DINOSAUR?" which was immediately retweeted by dozens of people. And indeed, the thing looking up out of its bed of mote and yellow potatoes, its jaws wide, appeared like a baby stegosaurus in a children's cartoon. Another wag tweeted, "Tastes like chicken?" A more thoughtful fellow retweeted an earlier request I'd made, asking if anyone knew a place to eat cuy, and replied I was better off buying it frozen in a store that he knew of in Sunnyside, Queens. Otherwise it would be way too expensive, even if I could find it. He was right.

The tweets continued as the three of us enjoyed the animals. Though the skin appeared damp, almost from perspiration, and tiny eyes seemed to gaze with malevolence—causing us to wonder whether we'd made a mistake ordering it—the mammal was quite tasty, in a greasy sort of way. In fact, the skin was superb. Crisp as a potato chip, it could be pulled away in nearly one piece and crunched on. The flesh was dark and stringy, like that of a game bird. And there really wasn't all that much of it. We finished up our meal, glad to have had the experience but not all that surprised that this dish was not in high demand.

For Ecuadorian immigrants, cuy represented an indigenous food that went back to prehistoric days. Back home, it was an animal easy to propagate and cook, and one shrouded in myth and long culinary practice. Once in this country, it was easy for the immigrants to forget cuy quickly, not only because it was expensive, but because the meal had lost its mountain magic. And did it ever catch on among foodies? The appearance of the cooked animal, with its sweaty, baby dinosaur looks, suggests probably not. New York only had a nodding acquaintance, at best, but one well worth considering and recounting.

But whether you eat cuy for its flavor or its uniqueness, or even for its supposed Viagra-like aphrodisiacal powers, the dish illustrates the trouble immigrants will go to in order to reproduce a recipe from their homelands, whether it be a bush-meat stew originating in West Africa, or a Chinese stir-fry of dried green sea snails. These are all dishes to be sought out and experienced—if not always savored. And the culinary terrain of New York is all the richer for it.

FIVE PLACES TO EAT ECUADORIAN
(IF NOT ALWAYS CUY)

1. ECUATORIANA

1685 AMSTERDAM AVENUE, MANHATTAN, 212-491-4626

The northwest corner of Harlem is maybe not the place you'd expect to find the city's largest Ecuadorian restaurant, sporting two huge dining rooms and a juice bar and serving humongous platters of fried corvine and guatita (tripe and turmeric stew) and big bowls of ceviche (my favorite featuring oodles of octopus).

2. HORNADO ECUATORIANO

76-18 ROOSEVELT AVENUE, QUEENS, 718-205-7357

Like the name says, this neon-festooned storefront in Elmhurst specializes in roast pig, and what roast pig it is: spice rubbed and unctuous, crisp skinned and bronze hued, and served with llapingachos and hominy. You've never had tenderer pork, and the place also mounts a complete Ecuadorian menu.

3. LA MORENITA

109-06 CORONA AVENUE, QUEENS, 718-699-2797

This is the restaurant where we enjoyed the cuy most recently. But make sure to call ahead. Not a bad place for Ecuadorian meal-sized soups, either. And make sure to get an ice at the Lemon Ice King of Corona—one block distant—afterward.

4. EL SOL DE QUITO

160 IRVING AVENUE, BROOKLYN, 718-417-4174

The hipster hordes have long since invaded this northern Bushwick neighborhood, but El Sol de Quito (The Sun of Quito) soldiers on. The omnibus platters—such as the bandera ("flag") or the montañero ("mountain climber")—are the perfect way to become rapidly familiar with Ecuadorian cuisine. There are also Chinese–South American offerings in abundance. And the portions are enough to feed two.

5. EL TESORO

4015 FIFTH AVENUE, BROOKLYN, 718-972-3756

This Sunset Park Ecuadorian spot ("The Treasure") specializes in ceviches (especially those featuring black clam), garlicky roast pork, and the kernel-studded sweet tamales called humitas. *And after dinner you'd be making a mistake if you didn't stroll over to the neighborhood's namesake park, plastered on the side of a steep hill with a spectacular view of New York's upper harbor.*

RABBIT IN THE STYLE OF CUY
SERVES 4 TO 6

Assuming that you don't have a source of edible guinea pig in your locale, a bunny will do almost as well. This recipe incorporates the animal in a stew, in the Ecuadorian jungle style.

FOR THE CUY:

1 tablespoon kosher salt

2 teaspoons ground cumin

$\frac{1}{2}$ teaspoon freshly ground black pepper

1 teaspoon ground achiote

2 rabbits or guinea pigs ($1\frac{1}{2}$ to 2 pounds each),
　cut into 6 to 8 pieces

3 tablespoons vegetable oil, for sautéing

FOR THE SAUCE:

6 garlic cloves

6 red aji peppers, seeds and veins removed, chopped
　(sometimes found in Andean groceries)

1 yellow bell pepper, seeds and veins removed, chopped

10 scallions, white and pale-green parts chopped, dark-green
　tops chopped and reserved

1 cup chicken stock or water

Salt

3 large Yukon gold potatoes, peeled, boiled, and sliced
　into rounds

1. First, marinate the meat. In a large bowl, combine the salt, cumin, black pepper, and achiote; toss with the rabbit pieces. Mix well to combine, then refrigerate overnight.

2. If you have access to an outdoor grill, grill the rabbit pieces until nicely charred on all sides; otherwise, sear them in the vegetable oil in a large sauté pan over medium-high heat, cooking on all sides until golden. Once the pieces are charred or golden, transfer them to a plate; set aside.

3. Make the sauce. In a food processor, combine the garlic, aji and bell peppers, and the white and pale-green parts of the scallions, and process until a rough paste forms. If you grilled the rabbit, get a large sauté pan and add the vegetable oil; if you seared the rabbit, use the same pan, adding more oil as necessary. Place the pan over medium-low heat.

4. When the oil is hot, add the garlic-pepper paste and cook, stirring frequently, until fragrant, just 1 to 2 minutes. Add in the stock or water, bring the mixture to a simmer, season with salt, and submerge the rabbit pieces into the pan, adding any accumulated juices. Simmer the rabbit over medium-low heat for 15 minutes or until tender (guinea pig will take longer). Serve the cuy in its sauce, poured over the boiled potatoes. Garnish with the reserved green onions.

PHO

First, let's dispense with the obligatory item that must be incorporated into every article, review, or blurb about Vietnamese food: *pho* is not pronounced *foe*!

Instead, it must be articulated *fa*, something like the musical note, only with a severely truncated and softened *a*, as in *fuh*. Or maybe like the sound of air escaping from a punctured pool toy. But this oft-repeated caution has done little to alter the popular pronunciation. To this day, despite 25 years of my harping in print, to say nothing of others' efforts, pho remains the most mispronounced dish name in the ethnic dining canon. (My own first correction came from Jonathan Gold, who has probably tried to promulgate the right way to say it more times than any other human being on earth.)

As the signature dish of Vietnamese cuisine, pho is a meal-sized soup said to have originated as a street food in the country's capital of Hanoi, or, alternately, a few miles southwest in one of three villages in Nam Dinh Province. It is based on what must be the most fussed-over beef broth in Asia, which can take days to prepare. Submerged in that broth, pale rice noodles of varying circumference—depending on where the soup was made—tangle around a catalog of add-ins, nearly all of them beef and beef byproducts. Beef instead of pork in Southeast Asia? Yes, indeed. In fact, the way you order pho in most cafés that sell it—there are around 150 in the New York City area that do, half of them mediocre "Asian fusion" restaurants, the other half Vietnamese cafés—is based on the beef cuts you want included in the bowl. The number of phos listed on a menu often corresponds to the number of combinations that can be formulated from the roster of meaty add-ins.

The variation called *xe lua* (perhaps a corruption of the word *deluxe*) typically includes raw eye of round steak, sliced thin; well-boiled lean brisket; navel—the fattier part of the brisket; gobs of gluey tendon; and omosa, which is cow tripe. But not just any cow tripe. While the most familiar variety comes from the second of the cow's four stomachs, with an appearance similar to honeycomb, omosa is from the third stomach. In its wobbly white opacity, with fine bumps providing traction, omosa might be made into bathmats. The taste recalls plastic, too: chewy in the extreme, but also reminiscent of a bleached-out aquatic plant. For most eaters of pho, this is the most challenging item, and much of it, I suspect, gets left in the bottom of the bowl. By tradition it is always included in deluxe editions of the dish; in fact the assortment of inclusions always seems arbitrary.

But pho is an exceedingly ingratiating soup, willing to transform itself in whatever way you want.

From the standpoint of most Western diners, the eye of round is the most desirable of the cuts used in pho. It is usually sliced thin and placed raw into your bowl of broth just before the soup is served, cooking as it floats atop the steaming liquid, thus allowing you to choose its level of doneness by picking it out of the bowl and eating it at just the right moment. Many diners prefer it nearly raw. On a more subtle level, the thin-sliced steak adds an extra valance of beefy savor to the broth, enhancing its bloody and mineral essence.

Fresh herbs and sprouts, served on a separate plate, provide further customization possibilities. In the sparer pho parlors, or in places where access to Southeast Asian herbs is limited, you're likely to get only so-called "holy" basil (smaller, darker green, and with a stronger flavor than the basil used in Italian cooking), and bean sprouts of an extremely plain sort. That's okay. Despite any trepidation you may have about using them (perhaps having encountered them before in a salad and having been slightly repulsed by their flavorlessness), sprouts enhance the texture of the soup without doing anything else except adding a slight sweetness. To use the holy basil: Pull the leaves off, leaving the stems behind, and add them one or two at a time as you slurp your way toward the bottom of the bowl. Before you add each one, crush it between your thumb and forefinger to release the leaf's essence. For larger leaves, tear them into three or four pieces before tossing them in.

In cities with large Vietnamese populations, such as Houston, San Jose, Atlantic City, and Falls Church, Virginia, a wider range of herbs is often available, and the side plate takes on a lusher, more junglelike appearance. (This is supposedly characteristic of pho made by immigrants from around Ho Chi Minh City in southern Vietnam. Northern Vietnamese pho is a far plainer soup.) Fresh spearmint or peppermint may be present, and also a variation on cilantro sometimes called sawtooth herb, the leaves of which are elongated and of even width, with a slight serration or perhaps a frill along both edges. The flavor is mild, and the herb provides a good chew. Occasionally I've spotted Vietnamese mint, which has one of the most intriguing flavors of any herb, only slightly minty with strong cinnamon overtones. In New York, one never finds it in Vietnamese restaurants, but it was popularized by Zak Pelaccio in a watermelon and pork belly salad at Fatty Crab, a Malaysian restaurant in the West Village. All the herbs that come with your pho are optional. Taste them before you toss them in the soup—they may vary wildly in potency.

As if this herbal barrage were not enough, a caddy of bottled sauces is also at the ready, placed alongside chopsticks, napkins, and spoons. Sriracha, certainly. But also hoisin, fish sauce, soy sauce, red wine vinegar, pickled peppers, and sometimes a homemade, coarse-textured red-chile paste with a vinegary kick. These are all to be spooned in and mixed in at your discretion. If it's heat you're after, the herb plate sometimes contains fresh jalapeños, and these are the most efficacious of all at conveying a burn without also adding notes of sweetness, soy, and vinegar, which are often present in the bottled hot sauces. The broth already contains onions, green onions, and cilantro. You are also welcome to not add anything to your pristine bowl of soup.

Made up your mind yet what you want to put in your pho? Any way you fix it up, it's delicious.

ME AND PHO

Despite the fact that I went to high school and college in Texas, where Vietnamese food has become more common than in New York, I never encountered it there, and couldn't have described its nature had I been asked. Vietnam was synonymous with an unjust war being waged by American oligarchs who'd chosen to ignore the French colonial experience, and few Vietnamese were to be found among the American populace.

No, the first pho I ever encountered was around 1978 in Manhattan's Chinatown, on Baxter Street. Right behind the city lockup called the Tombs was a line of three Vietnamese restaurants that specialized in snacks like spring rolls, over-rice dishes called *com dia*, and pho. I remember being perplexed by the number of soups listed with similar names, until I realized they were all basically the same soup. The best of the three restaurants was Pho Pasteur. The way we pronounced it back then, saying *pho* just like *faux*, the name of the boxy, modestly decorated café seemed to portend a sanitary disaster.

A little digging in my Vietnamese travel guide, prefatory to writing the place up in *Down the Hatch* a few years later, revealed that rue Pasteur was a street in colonial Saigon, one of many surnamed in Francophone fashion. Around 2000, the place changed its name to New Pasteur, which is not nearly as much fun to say, but by around 2005, the place wised up and returned to the original moniker.

But I'd abandoned Pho Pasteur by 1990 in favor of more far-flung and superior pho parlors. Eighty-Sixth Street in Brooklyn's Bensonhurst and Bath Beach was a hot spot. It took me a while to realize that not only were the Chinese who'd lived in Vietnam (our largest category of Vietnamese restaurant owners) moving to that corner of the Brooklyn seaboard along with other Chinese immigrants, but also more of our newly arrived Vietnamese ex-citizens. In addition, the Russians who were already living in the neighborhood craved good pho. After all, the USSR had been on the other side of the Vietnam War, and their larger cities and universities had long been filled with Vietnamese expatriates. In fact, the northern part of Vietnam experienced a techie brain drain due to this migration.

The best of these Vietnamese spots was Pho Tay Ho in Bath Beach, named after a district in Hanoi—pho's putative birth-place. In addition to wonderful pho from a northern perspective, Pho Tay Ho did the most with beef, a meat introduced to Vietnam by the French (but first brought to Southeast Asia by the Dutch), including an entire menu of cow-intensive recipes such as beef cubes sautéed in butter (sometimes called shaking beef); bánh mì bò kho (a rich ragout of beef and potatoes, served with a baguette); and bò nhúng dam (shaved beef you're supposed to swish in boiling vinegar as a flesh-based fondue).

Another standout spot, also in Brooklyn, was Pho Viet Huong, one of currently four Vietnamese cafés in Sunset Park's splendid Chinatown, which ran north (and now also south) from the N train stop at Eighth Avenue and 61st Street. This place also specialized in beef dishes, including an exemplary congee (Chinese rice soup) and beef charred inside of rolled grape leaves, which impart an astringency to the meat. Hmm, I wonder how that dish was invented, by French vintners? Indeed, the French tried to establish vineyards in the Gulf of Tonkin region in the north during the mid-19th century, but failed miserably due to mildew on the plants—though they subsequently made wine with fruits other than grapes. It wasn't until the 1990s that the Australians gave another go at producing grape-based wines in Vietnam.

But all in all, the pho in New York was a weak commodity in the 1990s. Not only the broth, which often tasted hastily thrown together, but the overall package. Even the best versions of pho available here were not transcendent. I never quite figured out why, but I had my theories. One was that many Vietnamese restaurants in town were owned by Chinese immigrants who may or may not have had experience in Southeast Asia. Chinese restaurateurs, in an effort to extend their customer base by capitalizing on current fads in Asian food, were often to be found opening Thai or Japanese restaurants in addition to Vietnamese.

Later, after writing an article for the *New York Times* on pho, I refined that theory to suggest that most of the pho in town made by actual Vietnamese immigrants originated in the Mekong Delta, to the southwest of Ho Chi Minh City, then called Saigon. That is where the American war effort found its staunchest supporters and where Vietnamese refugees to this country were most likely to come from. In the Mekong Delta, the population is influenced by Cambodian cooking and relatively indifferent to the national soup. In fact, they prefer pork-based soups like the rest of Southeast Asia and indeed China.

The theory might be verified by a study of where most Vietnamese refugees to the northeast United States came from, but the shortcut method is to study the names of Vietnamese restaurants in the New York metropolitan area, most of which name-check villages in (drumroll) the Mekong Delta. That said, one of my favorite phos in Manhattan's Chinatown has long been that of Pho Grand, named for the Lower East Side thoroughfare on which it lies. I'm also fond of Sao Mai in the East Village, where a particular passion for rubbery beef balls—another Mekong Delta thing—is in evidence.

More recently another star purveyor of pho appeared in Manhattan's Chinatown. Pho Vietnam 87 is a modest place located among the interstate bus depots around Canal and Chrystie. I brought a student from Bennington College, Mai Trang, who had grown up in Hanoi and had recently become my adviser where Vietnamese restaurants are concerned. As soon as we entered, she fell into a lively conversation in Vietnamese with the owners and discovered they were from the

Mekong Delta. The pho there was one of the better Chinatown versions I've tasted, heavily accented with star anise and charred onion, with all the usual beef additions, plus beef balls if you request them.

PHO FACTS

Over the years, I've accumulated lots of pho lore from sources as diverse as visitors who've returned from food tours of Vietnam, Vietnam vets, Vietnamese students, and, of course, the Internet.

Pho was originally sold in Hanoi as a street food by women who carted the pots of broth around and added the noodles and beef at the last minute. The broth and number of add-ins is much simpler in the soup's Hanoi rendition.

According to Time Life's *Pacific and Southeast Asian Cooking* (1970), "The cooking of pho involves such a long period on the stove that it is impractical for preparation at home," which explains why many Vietnamese cookbooks omit it.

In Hanoi, pho started out as a breakfast dish served by vendors in food markets but is now eaten at any meal.

This may be apocryphal, but I've heard that the best pho broths are made with bony cuts of beef that are boiled for five solid days, or until the bones completely dissolve into the broth. (An aside to CIA graduates—the culinary school, not the secret spy organization—is it even possible to boil bones until they dissolve?)

Pig bones are sometimes used in combination with beef bones to make pho broth.

Pho is more properly called *pho bo*, which means "pho with beef." In its most basic meaning, the word *pho* refers to rice noodles; but now it has become synonymous with the soup that contains them.

The best pho noodles are made with a special type of fragrant rice. One way many New York restaurants fall down in making pho is by featuring cheaper rice noodles that are too plain tasting.

Pho vendors in Hanoi traditionally have a special outfit that they wear. It features what is sometimes called a campaign hat—the one that soldiers wear that looks something like the paper hat worn in some fast-food chains. This stylish topper apparently originated in France, and it made the pho vendors look slightly military—and slightly French. I've seen the same hat worn by waitresses in an Atlantic City Vietnamese restaurant.

These days across Vietnam, pho is more often served in specialized shops or stalls than by street vendors.

Pho nuoc is the generic name for pho noodles incorporated into a soup, whether it be based on beef, chicken, or seafood. Thus pho bo—the most typical kind—is a species of pho nuoc.

Though every region of Vietnam has its own soup, most also have a version of pho. The one popular in Ho Chi Minh City is fussier and more complicated than the one in Hanoi, with more add-ins, more sauce options, and more diverse herbs, as I've already mentioned.

In the southern part of Vietnam, chicken pho (pho ga) outstrips beef pho in popularity. Never feel sheepish about ordering chicken pho in a Vietnamese restaurant—it's likely to be the version the proprietors prefer.

In mountainous northern areas of Vietnam, pho noodles are most often eaten, not in soups, but brothless and dressed with fish sauce, peanuts, and lemon juice in a preparation called *pho chua*.

FAUX PHO

How and when did I become dissatisfied with the pho in my city, and why do I still partly feel that way? Eleven years ago I found myself in Houston working on a story for *Gourmet* magazine. Pursuing an assignment from Editor in Chief Ruth Reichl to explore the spread of West African restaurants across the United States, I was chasing down Ghanaian and Nigerian eateries in the daytime, which served their main meal around 2:00 p.m. I naturally felt hungry again in the

evening and had exhausted most of the Tex-Mex and barbecue spots on my list.

I went to Houston's Chinatown and was surprised to find
the streets paved with Vietnamese cafés. It turns out that after
the Vietnam War, many refugees had settled in Houston,
Galveston, and New Orleans, where they'd joined the shrimp-
ing industry and worked their way up to owning their own
boats. I had a spectacular bowl of pho that evening, every bit as
elaborate and with a richer broth than anything I'd had in New
York, sowing deep seeds of dissatisfaction.

In subsequent years I had pho in several parts of the country that were all better than New York's. While visiting
Washington, DC, I was directed to the Eden mall in nearby
Falls Church, Virginia, easily attainable by subway. There I was
delighted to find two stores that specialized in Vietnamese tofu
(who knew?), offering such arcane flavors as bright-yellow screw
pine and a buff-colored, fermented type sometimes known as
Chinese cheese. I had a bowl of pho, too, in one of several small
Vietnamese cafés that spilled tables onto a sunny interior sidewalk. It, too, was memorably good.

When my daughter, Tracy, moved to Mountain View,
California, in the South Bay of San Francisco to work for
Google, I visited immediately. I was surprised to discover in the
downtown of this one-horse former agricultural town three pho
parlors that served the soup and almost nothing else. The pho
was spectacular, with a broth simpler and subtler than what I
was used to in New York, with the notes of star anise and cinnamon that sometimes dominate and defeat the soup here more
restrained. On subsequent visits, I explored the pho in San Jose,
which had an even larger Vietnamese expatriate community,
and in San Francisco itself. All were wonderful, with a variety of different-weight noodles and what seemed like a more
carefully selected choice of beef cuts. The tendon in California
versions, for example, was often excellent, offered in larger and
chewier chunks. The Californians making these phos were
clearly passionate about beef.

So I developed a broad idea of what pho could be like, but was not able to find a totally satisfying version back in New York. Frustrating! Still, on a damp winter day with the sniffles coming on, what better remedy to reach for besides a fragrant bowl of pho?

And then my friend and fellow University of Texas grad Andy Wang, a skilled semi-professional poker player and fellow journalist, told me that in Atlantic City he'd seen Vietnamese food being delivered to the gaming tables in the casinos from some outside location. And he'd actually stumbled on a Vietnamese restaurant not far from the boardwalk casinos. So, on my next trip to the New Jersey Pine Barrens—a very H. P. Lovecraft landscape of sand, stunted trees, and abandoned ghost towns in central southern Jersey—I dropped by Atlantic City for lunch.

There on the north end of the Atlantic Avenue of Monopoly fame, I spotted Com Tam Ninh Kieu, with a hot-pink façade that made the one-story stucco structure shine among the pawnshops, massage parlors, teetering frame houses, and beer-peddling bodegas that made this stretch an Atlantic City skid row. This was in September 2011, and on subsequent trips that year and next, I filled up my dance card with visits to small Vietnamese cafés, some of which catered to Asian gamblers and tourists, others to Vietnamese casino employees.

By 2013, I was ready to pitch a story to the *New York Times* about the six Vietnamese restaurants of Atlantic City, a municipality that had a permanent population of only 45,000, meaning that six restaurants constituted a very high proportion of the restaurants there. A little digging around revealed that the Vietnamese had arrived in Atlantic City in the decade following the Vietnam War. In some cases they had been recruited as croupiers—women, mainly—for their mathematical abilities, strong work ethic, and ability to hold a deadpan demeanor for hours, even when players became overly excited—this according to an employment director at Caesars Casino who asked not to be named. Others, men and women, were employed as housekeepers and food-service employees in low-paying, dead end jobs.

It wasn't long before Atlantic City had its own working-class Vietnamese refugee neighborhood, in the southwest corner of town centered on Arctic Avenue. There, small bodegas sold frozen freshwater fish, a fascinating range of green herbs, canned Southeast Asian products, juices, and imported snack foods. The first Vietnamese restaurant to appear was Little Saigon, founded in 1991 by Lien Pham, who'd worked as a dealer in the casinos since the mid-'80s. According to her account, she was goaded by her friends into opening the small café, which is decorated with photos of the patrons—many of them non-Vietnamese gamblers and tourists tired of the bland fare available in the casinos. In addition to six types of pho, she also served a rice-noodle soup Phnom Penh style, featuring shrimp and pork in the kind of Cambodian soup readily available in the Mekong Delta. She also did fancier dishes, like beef cubes sautéed in butter and paved with black peppercorns that were a legacy of French colonialism, as well as clay pot cookery with caramel that constituted a sort of Gallic-Vietnamese haute cuisine.

While Little Saigon is the oldest of the six cafés, the very best can be found across a bay on the mainland, concealed in the small food court of a shopping center called Asian Supermarket on Black Horse Pike in Pleasantville, New Jersey. The name of the place—decorated with heroic paintings of winged horses soaring over sunlit cliffs—is Hu Tieu Mien Tay, owned by Ha and Thomas Vu. The spectacular pho, one of the better versions available on the East Coast, is furnished with multiple herbs, simply bursting with beefy savor, and not dominated by its spices. But hu tieu constitutes the real specialty of the house, a pork-based soup preferred by the residents of Mien Tay, a town in the Mekong Delta where the owners originated.

Really, eating my way through multiple versions of pho in Atlantic City, haunting the boardwalk during the day—where a *Jersey Shore* mentality prevailed—and the casinos late into the evening, where I preferred gawking to gambling, was one of the best assignments I've ever had. And taking friends to Atlantic City to sample the pho has become a leitmotif of this decade for me.

Still, the pho in New York City has gradually improved as diners here become more sophisticated and more demanding. The rise of nontraditional Vietnamese cafés outside of Chinatown has helped—places such as Bún-Ker in Ridgewood, Queens (which serves only a chicken version); Sao Mai in the East Village; and An Choi on the Lower East Side, which is owned and staffed by second-generation Vietnamese hipsters who came to the city from Houston. Only in New York could such an evolved and ethnographically complex version of one of the world's best soups bubble on the stove!

And more great versions are certainly in our future.

TEN PLACES TO GET GOOD (OR EVEN GREAT) PHO IN NEW YORK

1. PHO GRAND

277 GRAND STREET, MANHATTAN, 212-965-5366

Based mainly on the high quality of its pho this place has doubled in size during the last few years. Expect a doctrinaire selection of beef (the tendon is particularly good), and few, but fresh, herbs.

2. PHO TAY HO

2351 86TH STREET, BROOKLYN, 718-449-0199

Overall, this is one of the best Vietnamese restaurants in town, located in a neighborhood with a demanding Russian and Chinese patronage clearly familiar with good pho. Haute-Vietnamese dishes such as bo luc lac ("shaking beef") and beef curry, served with a baguette, also excel.

3. SAO MAI

203 FIRST AVENUE, MANHATTAN, 212-358-8880

Comparative newcomer Sao Mai ("Morning Star") has a particularly good pho, not too dense or sweet, and sawtooth herb (Vietnamese cilantro) is often provided along with fresh holy basil, one of the few places in town where this is so.

4. AN CHOI

85 ORCHARD STREET, MANHATTAN, 212-226-3700

You may find it refreshing that only two forms of pho are offered here, a stripped-down version and one with all the bells and whistles, including beef balls. The ambiance is very modern bistro, and the food is great.

5. PHO MAC

1407 RICHMOND AVENUE, STATEN ISLAND, 718-982-9292

This Vietnamese in an unexpected location just off the Staten Island Expressway offers a deluxe upstairs dining room and better than average pho, which features rice noodles far more firm and fragrant than the usual. The dishes called bánh hoi (swatches of delicate rice stick noodles served with grilled meats and seafood and wrapped in lettuce leaves) are also highly recommended.

6. THANH DA

6008 SEVENTH AVENUE, BROOKLYN, 718-492-3253

There are now three Vietnamese restaurants in Sunset Park's Chinatown, and this is by far the best, also known for their over-rice dishes.

7. PHO PASTEUR

85 BAXTER STREET, MANHATTAN, 212-608-3656

The original place in Manhattan's Chinatown where I learned to love pho, right opposite the Tombs.

8. COM TAM NINH KIEU

2641 JEROME AVENUE, BRONX, 718-365-2680

Located in a Cambodian neighborhood in the Bronx not far from Edgar Allan Poe's cottage, this café has a staff that includes neighborhood Dominicans, and some interesting fusion on the menu.

9. BÚN-KER

46-63 METROPOLITAN AVENUE, QUEENS, 718-386-4282

This bistro-ized Vietnamese in an industrial wasteland of Ridgewood just north of Bushwick only does a chicken version of pho, but it's damn good.

10. PHO VIETNAM 87

87 CHRYSTIE STREET, MANHATTAN, 212-775-0999

A little off the beaten path on the Lower East Side, this restaurant, decorated with a miniature train and tracks around the ceiling, produces what is currently the city's best pho, with a long-boiled broth that dances with droplets of oil, and a tender selection of beef cuts. Beef balls optional.

FIVE PLACES TO GET GOOD (OR EVEN GREAT) PHO IN ATLANTIC CITY AND PLEASANTVILLE

1. HU TIEU MIEN TAY

700 BLACK HORSE PIKE, PLEASANTVILLE, NEW JERSEY, 609-646-8977

Hidden behind a Chinese supermarket in a faded food court on the Jersey mainland, this is the best of the Atlantic City and environs Vietnamese restaurants. The pho is based on a deeply amber beef broth; the first flavor to hit the tongue is star anise, followed by scallions, cilantro, garlic, onions, charred ginger, and perhaps a touch of pungent Chinese celery.

2. LITTLE SAIGON

2801 ARCTIC AVENUE, ATLANTIC CITY, NEW JERSEY, 609-347-9119

The oldest of Atlantic City's Vietnamese restaurants (founded 1991) is located in a residential Vietnamese neighborhood where small groceries abound. The caramel-laced dishes are particularly good, and so is the pho. Like dining in someone's living room.

3. PHO SYDNEY

2323 ATLANTIC AVENUE, ATLANTIC CITY, NEW JERSEY, 609-348-5946

Named Sydney because the proprietor used to live in Australia, this late-night spot is located right on the city's main drag and appears to once have been a Greek diner. The specialty of the house is bún bò hue, a lemongrass-laced beef soup that competes in popularity with pho among the café's patrons.

4. IPHO A.C.

3808 VENTNOR AVENUE, ATLANTIC CITY, NEW JERSEY, 609-340-0063

On the far south side of Atlantic City, iPho A.C. is an intimate spot with especially good my tho, a pork-based soup popular with refugees from the Mekong Delta.

5. COM TAM NINH KIEU

1124 ATLANTIC AVENUE, ATLANTIC CITY, NEW JERSEY, 609-572-9211

This bright-pink palace of pho offers the second-best version in Atlantic City and is the café closest to the boardwalk casinos. Over-broken-rice dishes are another specialty, as the name ("com tam") implies.

PHO

SERVES 4 TO 6

The legendary soup of Hanoi, here presented in a decidedly lush, Mekong Delta sort of version.

FOR THE BROTH:

4 star anise

1 cinnamon stick

$\frac{1}{2}$ teaspoon fennel seeds

4 cloves

$1\frac{1}{2}$ pounds beef bones or neck or shin

$1\frac{1}{2}$ pounds beef chuck

2 pounds oxtail

1 pound beef brisket

4 ounces beef tendon (available at Asian supermarkets, or ask your butcher)

2 large white onions, unpeeled

7-inch piece fresh ginger, unpeeled

$\frac{1}{4}$ cup fish sauce

2 tablespoons sugar

Salt

FOR THE SOUP:

4 to 6 servings pho noodles, about 1 pound total

1 small bunch basil, preferably Thai or opal (aka holy basil)

1 small bunch mint

2 cups bean sprouts

2 jalapeños, thinly sliced

2 limes, cut into wedges

8 ounces raw beef flank, sliced as thinly as possible

Sriracha

1. First make the broth. Make sure your sink is clean. Tie up all of the dried spices in a piece of cheesecloth and set aside. Place the beef bones, beef chuck, oxtail, brisket, and beef tendon into a stockpot. Cover with cold water and bring to a boil. Meanwhile, in a dry cast-iron skillet over medium heat, or directly over a gas flame, char the onions and ginger until blackened all over and softened. Boil the meat for 2 minutes, then drain by carefully pouring the entire contents of the pot, meat and all, into the sink. Rinse the pot of any scum and rinse each piece of meat, placing it back in the pot as you go.

2. Cover the meat with 4 quarts cold water, add the spice sachet, onions, and ginger, and bring to a simmer. Keep the broth at a bare simmer, skimming off any scum or froth from the top. Check the brisket after 2 hours; if tender, remove from the pot with tongs and refrigerate.

3. Continue simmering the broth for at least 2 more hours and up to 8 hours. Remove all of the pieces of meat and bones with tongs. Reserve all tender pieces of meat and tendon for the soup, picking any usable parts from the bones, tearing them into small pieces; refrigerate until ready to use. Carefully strain the broth through a fine-meshed sieve lined with cheesecloth into another pot or large bowl. Whisk in the fish sauce, sugar, and salt; taste (it should be aggressively seasoned—add more salt if necessary), and refrigerate until ready to use.

4. To assemble the soup, bring the broth to a simmer and keep it hot. Prepare the noodles in a separate pot according to the package instructions, rinsing and draining them when finished. Slice the brisket into pieces. Place the brisket and reserved meat in a small saucepan, add 1 cup of the broth, and keep warm over low heat. Assemble the herbs, bean sprouts, sliced jalapeños, and lime wedges on a plate.

5. To serve, place a portion of cooked noodles in each of 4 to 6 large bowls, then add pieces of brisket and boiled meat. Fill each of the bowls with some of the hot broth; add the flank slices. Serve immediately, allowing guests to customize their bowls with herbs, sprouts, chiles, lime, and Sriracha as they like.

SCRAMBLED BRAINS

While the ostensible theme of this chapter is veal brains and other offal, it's really more about the OMS—and my shifting relationship with that august and somewhat secretive body. Though Organ Meat Society, or OMS, is my coinage, we had plenty of other good names for this furtive dining club in the early days—the Offal Truth and the Innards Circle being two that stuck and are in occasional use even today. Our organ-izing e-mails still show a certain ambivalence about the official identity of the periodic—officially, monthly— conclave. I wasn't one of the founders but gradually got drawn in by the enthusiasm of its charter members. As it turned out, organs are not the worst theme for a dining society.

Like a rolling ball of goo, the dining club continues to pick up monikers and members as it tumbles merrily along. Over 17 years of existence, the membership has altered and expanded, with a core group of eight or so at all times and an extended membership of perhaps 60 who drop in only occasionally. We encourage new members, and receive perhaps 20 requests a year from those who want to join. We usually respond by inviting the prospective members to the next meeting, but in most cases when the actual day comes, they decline. Thinking about eating organs at some remote location is apparently more appealing than actually doing so.

We have no real bylaws and only a single principle: to eat as many organs and other variety meats as possible at each sitting. Why don't we limit ourselves just to organs? Early on, we decided that things like tendon and other connective tissue—anatomical details the butcher in, say, a Midwestern town might throw away or render unto the renderers—belonged in our canon. Our definition of organs and variety meats was necessarily intuitive rather than strictly technical. We loved them simply because they taste so damn good. There's nothing like finding a big gooey wad of tendon in your pho, is there?

Actually, accepting anything that might be rejected by the general dining public on whatever grounds made our job easier—because you'd really need an anatomy expert to tell you which parts are organs and which are not. Skin? Yes! Eyeball? Yes! Lips? No! Pancreas? Yes! Blood? Yes! Tendon? Maybe not. At this point our collective appetite craves such arcana as lungs, penis, "uteri" (as the packaging in Chinese supermarkets would have it), and brains. Though obviously, gizzards, sweetbreads, and tripe are far more common at our meetings.

It started back in 1998, when a pair of women contacted me out of the blue. Melissa Easton was an industrial designer who at least party specialized in jewelry and high-fashion Tupperware, while Marisa Bowe was an editor and writer. She ran a popular online magazine called *Word*, which published fiction and articles on hot topics of the day, way before careless blogging became the web prototype. Melissa, a slender brunette with a ready but subdued smile, something like the *Mona Lisa*'s, had been to boarding school and had lived her life partly in France. With curly blond hair, Marisa hailed from Minnesota and was a midwestern gal through and through—she might have just debarked from a hayride. Marisa had been recruited to New York as a girlfriend, in a romantic move that was then common, by another friend of mine, civil rights author Philip Dray. The two OMS founders, Melissa and Marisa, could not have been more different.

The women surprised me with their request: "Where can we find places that serve organs?" Such a question doesn't seem strange today, when ambitious chefs lard their menus with sweetbreads, bone marrow, and foie gras, but back then it was odd and a bit kinky. The contemporary focus on variety meats is partly the doing of chefs like Fergus Henderson, who advocated "nose to tail" eating at his restaurant St. John in London as a moral imperative; but it's also at least partly due to the OMS itself, which, from the very beginning, effortlessly garnered notoriety that would have made a publicist blush. Within its first few years it had engendered pieces in the *New Yorker*, *Gourmet*, and *Food & Wine*. Some of the onrush of articles were written by OMS members.

What made organs such a sexy topic? When Melissa and Marisa approached me, apart from liking sweetbreads and tendons and tolerating liver, I didn't really have much interest, other than eating them out of a sense of duty where they occurred on Chinese, Azerbaijani, and French menus. Organs have always been what's known as "critic porn": dishes easy to blab on about due to their exoticism to American middle-class tastes and due to a certain "yuck" factor, too. In France or China no one would have paid any attention.

In those days, an organ dish would occasionally seem a bit challenging to me, but scarfing unfamiliar things was the stock-in-trade of my profession. Eating Chilean anticuchos in Williamsburg's McCarren Park from a street vendor, I found these kebabs of beef heart a bit stringy and bouncy—though not repulsively so. I had the vague misapprehension that eating organs was a manly thing (I immediately thought of Leopold Bloom in *Ulysses*)—an idea that was quickly dispelled by Melissa's and Marisa's enthusiasm. And the love of offal turned out to be not only a dietary preference on their part, but a bona fide obsession. But while Melissa seemed to be a kidney and liver gal, Marisa was mainly into brains. As I described her in a *Gourmet* feature about the society published in 2006:

> She craved calves' brains, she explained somewhat shamefacedly, and consumed them on a regular basis. Did she suffer, I wondered aloud, from a vitamin deficiency? She admitted that even as a child being introduced to crab and lobster, she had nurtured a secret interest in

the green mushy parts—a desire that functioned on the deepest bio-logical levels.

And so it was that we sought out calves' brains at our initial meeting. The venue was a dark and serpentine cafe misspelled for branding purposes as La Lunchonette. Then, as now, it was located on the northern verge of the Meatpacking District at 10th Avenue and 18th Street. At the time this region was not the repulsive collection of effete hotels, nightclubs, and restaurants it is now but an actual neighborhood of meat purveyors to restaurants and hotels. Scary giant hooks hung over the cobbled thoroughfares of the district along rails to assist in sliding entire carcasses along the street over uneven pavement that started out slippery when the trucks first pulled in around 4:00 a.m.—displacing armies of transvestite prostitutes—and became virtual ice rinks of smeared tallow by the time the action had quieted down around two in the afternoon. No amount of steam or soap could dispel the smell.

At the head of this raffish district, La Lunchonette—which seemed as though it might have once been a scruffy seamen's bar—flaunted its meaty and organ-intensive menu. Two other charter members were present. Dan Okrent's claim to fame was the invention of Rotisserie League Baseball and the authorship of several nonfiction books. Later he was to cowrite an off-Broadway play, very popular with other members of the society, called *Old Jews Telling Jokes*. He often tried the jokes out on us. It later played in London, and then Chicago.

Midway through his tenure in the OMS, Okrent—a short guy with copious masses of straight white hair and a subversive sense of humor—would become the public editor of the *New York Times*. With him was his rail-thin wife, Becky, who at the time was working on a book for home cooks about locating hard-to-find ethnic ingredients in the city. They lived on the Upper West Side and have remained faithful and regular members throughout the organization's history. Melissa's husband, Chris Peacock, was there, too, even though he disliked organs, and so was my wife, Gretchen—no one wanted to miss the auspicious occasion of the organization's first meeting.

As I recall, we feasted on sweetbreads in a lemon-caper sauce that evening and a pâté studded with pistachios, washed down with a bottles of Côtes du Rhône. Entrées were two: a giant groaning platter of calves' livers in a red-wine sauce, perfectly cooked to a bright pink in the middle, and—the reason I'd picked this venue—veal brains in black butter. As I sat staring at my plate, with its rivulets of black vinegar running through the gray matter like a filthy river delta, I realized I'd never eaten brains before. Marisa dug in avidly, knife and fork flying. To me, they seemed utterly repulsive. What other organ besides perhaps kidney looks so much like its human counterpart as it sits upon the plate? I shivered involuntarily.

Not only was the appearance repulsive, so was the texture. The gray brains had the wobbliness of custard, to be strained between your teeth rather than chewed. Melissa complained about the lack of kidneys on what was basically a French bistro menu. More important, the OMS members discovered that we liked each other and the organization was duly launched. Nevertheless, for years I would claim not to be a member, but only an adviser. I figured it would be untoward for a restaurant critic to show such an enthusiasm for a single class of gastronomic raw materials. And there was something grotesque, wasn't there, about a group showing such an unhealthy preoccupation?

THE SECOND AND THIRD MEETINGS OF THE OMS

By the time of our second meeting, inquiries had started flowing in from prospective members. One such was Rob Boynton, a journalist who seemed on his way up. He had a bluff attitude and a shock of blond hair that threatened to conceal his magnificent towering forehead, which he swept away with his hand from time to time (the hair, not his forehead). We later discovered he was a stringer for the Talk of the Town section in the

New Yorker, but was he a dilettante or a true organ eater? Time would tell. While our first "meating" had been at a relatively safe locale—not that the meatpacking streets were entirely safe then, but that the restaurant was centrally located within Manhattan and easy for most of the members to find—our second venue was to be more obscurely situated.

It would be an outer borough romp. That was, after all, why the gals had sought me out, for my knowledge of far-flung, organ-rich cuisines and where to find them. Partly for its geographic shock value, I picked a restaurant located not far from the elevated F train in Kensington, a part of Brooklyn no one in the club besides me had ever set foot in. The restaurant went by the inscrutable name of Nostalgia. Nostalgia for what? Baku, Azerbaijan, as fate would have it, in the years of the oil boom, when immigrants from the Caucasus Mountains were living large—in Brooklyn, at least.

The room itself was not large, and in the gloaming we could barely make out walls hung with heavy Persian carpets in the manner of most post-Soviet restaurants of that era, with arches leading to the kitchen, bathrooms, and coat check that seemed to have been made of thick cardboard, crudely detailed with a Magic Marker with the intention of making them look something like marble. Amid a selection of 18 kebabs—many involving organs like liver and kidneys—and heaping platters of dill-dusted fried potatoes and mounds of pickled vegetables, the highlight of the evening was a skillet-fry that went by the suggestive name of *jiz-biz*. Was it a tribute to the fading porno film industry? We wondered facetiously. It turned out to be a delicious hash of heart, liver, kidneys, and other organs too denatured to identify (was lung, illegal in New York, among them?), along with crisp cubes of nicely browned potato and caramelized onions. It made us wish more of the spouses who eschewed variety meats were along with us, because the dish would have been palatable for everyone. A real culinary triumph!

After that fulsome meal was concluded, I led our party single file down darkened Ditmas Avenue, where only a few lights winked on in the stolid brick houses, toward Coney Island Avenue. There, at around 10:00 p.m., we further filled up at a 24-hour Pakistani cabbie hang called Bukhara, where the specialty was baby goat brains scrambled with eggs. We spotted the dish as soon as we entered the steamy premises on this cold evening in mid-March, a yellow flocculent mass traced with veins of red oil. Damn, it was spicy! If brains always tasted like this, I'd be more into them. The dish didn't really look like brains, but rather like scrambled eggs with little flecks of what might have been fat, with only the occasional glob of gray wrinkled tissue visible, which I pushed to the side of the plate, where Marisa scooped them up with a wink.

My idea was that these sequential meals in adjacent outer borough neighborhoods might become a prototype for further OMS meetings, but was not to be. A walk through unfamiliar darkened streets late in the evening turned out to be a scary notion not to everyone's taste, nor did all the others have quite the capacity for eating high volumes of fatty food that I apparently did. Anyway, that was to be our last duplex variety meat dinner; from then on we stuck to a single venue.

By the third meeting the weather had warmed considerably and we found ourselves in Corona, Queens. Our destination, El Gauchito, was situated in a crooked little Argentine and Uruguayan neighborhood at the intersection of Junction Boulevard and Corona Avenue, a locale still well worth visiting. El Gauchito was a combination meat market, restaurant, and grocery and was festooned with objects imported from the pampas. I noted in the Organ Meat Society minutes that I typed up at the time just for the fun of it, dated May 10, 1999:

A glass case near the ceiling held gaucho paraphernalia: silver belt buckles, a pair of steak knives in a leather holster, a stringed instrument the size of a small mandolin with a sound chamber made from an armadillo shell, etc. We were seated amid South American families in the cramped dining room, next to a ceramic tile frieze depicting Argentine heroes.

From my notes, we feasted on several of the regular parrillada (grilled meat) combinations, cooked over sputtering lump charcoal, including slippery chitterlings (veal small intestines), loamy blood sausage, and crisp sweetbreads, all done to a turn. The only complaint was that the blood sausage, somewhat loose in its casing, didn't contain the expected cumin found in the Spanish version of the sausage, which often gives it a flavor jolt.

Nearly 15 years later to the day we revisited the neighborhood. Among the crew were the Okrents, myself along with Gretchen and Tracy (who had returned from San Francisco to resume residence in New York), Melissa Easton, and Jeannette Seaver, who, along with her husband, Richard Seaver, had run the publishing company Arcade Books, which had issued the fourth edition of my restaurant guide, *The Food Lover's Guide to the Best Ethnic Eating in New York City* (2004), with a foreword by Calvin Trillin. Sadly, Richard had died unexpectedly the year before, thus depriving the organization of one of its staunchest advocates. Jeannette soldiered on.

That night we had dinner at La Esquina Criolla, a Uruguayan place that also doubled as a meat market, and cooked its chitterlings and other offal right in the front window. We sat at a long table, eight of us—which we had come to realize was the perfect number—and discussed Argentine wine and news of the day as we ate. The meeting was adjourned around 9:45 p.m., as half our number climbed into a car service limo to return to the Upper West Side, while the rest of us wended our way home via subway. Tracy, Gretchen, and I walked up Corona's Junction Boulevard under the Long Island Rail Road viaduct, a precinct that had turned into something like a small southern Mexican town. Tracy scooped up some tamales for her boyfriend, Aleks, along the way.

THE OMS: A BROAD SKETCH

These minutiae don't really begin to show the grandeur and sweep of the organization. Let me make a couple of further attempts. Over the years we've had a shifting roster of guests who appear occasionally. The list of attendees has included chefs like Sara Jenkins of the East Village restaurant Porsena, a regular but sporadic member who sometimes brought her young son along, and Nancy Harmon Jenkins, her cookbook-writing mom. Sara went to boarding school in New England with Melissa, and for one meeting she cooked a Tuscan organ meat dinner at Porsena for us. Her mother appeared at only one meeting, at the venerable Woodside Thai restaurant SriPraPhai, where we ate an Isaan bar snack of barbecued pig jowl and a Chiang Mai noodle soup thickened with pig blood, among other dishes, demonstrating, if nothing else, that blood is officially an organ, too. The blood imparted a muddy flavor to the soup. (Another prominent appearance of blood: sanguinaccio, an Eastertide blood pudding offered at the Sicilian bakery Villabate in Bensonhurst, Brooklyn, which we sampled after a Sichuan dinner nearby.)

Chef Cesare Casella—the creator of Tuscan cowboy cooking—joined us for one meeting, along with his wife, *Wall Street Journal* reporter Eileen Daspin. I don't remember the venue, but I do remember he offered to cook for the OMS, which we should have taken him up on. But we didn't. While Dan Okrent nearly won the Pulitzer Prize for his book on Rockefeller Center, we had an actual winner with us the day Jonathan Gold visited the Organ Meat Society for a lengthy meal at Kom Tang in 2005—at the time the only barbecue in Koreatown that still used charcoal, now closed. We dined on pork belly, tongue, and liver with a splendid view of 32nd Street from the picture window that our table faced. Altogether one of our more dramatic views.

While Casella never cooked for us, Mario Batali did. And his meal in 2006 formed the capper of my *Gourmet* piece about the OMS, which was nominated for a James Beard Award in 2007, but quite predictably lost. (It had gone up against another *Gourmet* piece by NPR's Scott Simon, who tearfully recounted feeding his sandwich to a Vietnamese orphan. How could anyone compete with that?) The meal Batali turned out was magnificent. We sat at a raised table with an L-shaped banquette at Babbo, just beyond the bar, with a superb view of the dining room. The rotund celebrity chef, in his signature white apron and orange clogs, his hair pulled back in a long ponytail, danced up to our table from time to time to see how we were doing.

Highlights of the meal included lardo-and-ramp bruschetta, a loose headcheese scented with nutmeg, beef cheek ravioli with squab liver and black truffle, and tripe bathed in vanilla and vinegar, served on pappardelle. Sommelier David Lynch poured the wine, and the cost of the meal topped out at just over $100 apiece. It was altogether the most memorable meal we'd had so far. That is, until we ate the penis.

It happened this way. About the same time as our Batali meal, I found myself dining extensively up and down Main Street in Flushing, Queens, where northern Chinese restaurants were appearing like welcome storm clouds in a sunny sky. The food these places served was downright confounding compared with the relatively bland Cantonese dishes the city had been used to. Sichuan peppercorns rolled like marbles, lamb appeared for the first time on Chinese menus, rice was generally eschewed in favor of steamed and baked breads, and dumplings ruled the roost, as the Taiwanese fare that had previously distinguished the neighborhood was forced to its outer edges along the Long Island Expressway.

On College Point Boulevard a few blocks downhill from Main Street and almost in the Flushing River, a quaint place called Dumpling House had appeared. It was difficult to identify its geographic origin, partly because the food—which consisted of dozens of dumpling types, plus a menu of unusual stews—was so damn strange. Certainly, some of the choices might have flown in southern China, but the majority seemed to be stuffed with powerful northern Chinese meats and seasonings, with none of the nuanced delicacy we normally associate with Cantonese food. Possibly the place was seeking to satisfy dumpling eaters from all across the vast expanse of

China, from southernmost Yunnan to the Dongbei region in the remote north.

The menu had rough translations of some of the fillings. There was lots of game, some of it on the stew menu, things like elk shoulder, goose intestine, and deer. Assuming the lead as she often does, Melissa took to pointing at untranslated things, and the waiter readily responded in broken English, about one-quarter of which we understood. When Melissa aimed her finger at something at the bottom of the stews list, the waiter blushed deeply and fell silent. Melissa persisted, and the waiter began a modest sort of charade, his hands weaving around his midsection. "He must mean cow penis!" Melissa chimed in. "Don't you mean bull penis," another of us replied with a nervous laugh.

The organ arrived in a bubbling broth, flayed like a party streamer, gelatinous in texture but still tough. One member refused categorically to eat it, till the others shamed her into tasting it, though I can't say she really enjoyed it. I'd eaten penis before—dog penis, in fact, unbeknownst to me, in a Korean joint in Murray Hill, Queens. Penis is not really worth eating. There's no meat at all, just gristle, pointing up the fact that an erection is a hydraulic phenomenon caused by the rush of blood, and the male organ merely an imperfect vessel to contain it. Still, as the centerpiece of our meal that day at the now-defunct Dumpling House, penis couldn't be beat.

BRAINS REAPPEAR

Seeking out organ dishes brought us across the five boroughs— we even once ventured to a restaurant out on Long Island, Southern Spice in New Hyde Park, where we were regaled with lamb trotter soup and goat brain masala, the latter said to be a bar snack in Chettinad in southern India and a bit soupy. This time I dug into the brains with resignation and perhaps a little relish. The impetus for that meal came from a couple who turned out to be the society's most avid members, now going on six years. Aparisim "Bobby" Ghosh is an Indian who grew up in West Bengal, a foreign correspondent for *Time* magazine who'd spent considerable time in Iraq during the war years. He was recruited by Dan Okrent to the OMS. We were told he was known as one of the few journalists who dared to leave the Green Zone in Baghdad. "I could easily pass for Arab," he told us one evening, "and by walking purposely and staring straight ahead with a fierce look on my face, I managed to not get shot or blown up."

His wife, Bipasha Ghosh, was a prominent educator who later went to work at NBC in a traveling capacity and henceforth missed the occasional meeting as a result of her international peregrinations. They were a power couple, par excellence. They'd been sweethearts in high school back in India. Bobby later assumed the International Desk at *Time*, and he recruited Howard Chua-Eoan, another prominent employee at the magazine, to our group. Chua-Eoan was of Chinese extraction and grew up in the Philippines, and his facility with Chinese was to hold us in good stead at future meetings in Flushing, where the expanding catalog of northern Chinese restaurants provided organs we'd never tasted before.

But we embraced upscale foodie destinations, too. One was M. Wells Dinette, a spinoff of the defunct M. Wells diner, where chef Hugue Dufour presided, a veteran of Montreal's pig-and-organ-centric Au Pied de Cochon. The restaurant—amusingly resembling a cafeteria in an elementary school—was located in PS1, an experimental art museum carved from an ancient public school. The museum had recently been taken over by MoMA, the Museum of Modern Art.

Our meal that evening featured a terrine of duck tongues and hearts, a veal heart ceviche with trumpet mushrooms and smoked gribiche relish, a very pleasant French onion soup with veal tongue in its depths (not a bad addition), and, among other offal dishes that left us gasping due to our full stomachs, a sweet conclusion: foie gras bread pudding with Québécois maple syrup. Yum!

Also in the course of the meal, we had a plate of veal brains grenobloise, sautéed into crisp nuggets with lemon, capers, and parsley—a treatment usually reserved for seafood. The dish was delicious, and I couldn't help reflecting to myself that I didn't mind eating brains so much after all. In fact, I even liked them.

SIX PLACES TO TRY BRAINS ENDORSED BY THE ORGAN MEAT SOCIETY

1. LA LUNCHONETTE

130 10TH AVENUE, MANHATTAN, 212-675-0342

Veal brains in black butter are still featured at this restaurant, where the Organ Meat Society had its inaugural meal.

2. SOUTHERN SPICE

1635 HILLSIDE AVENUE, NEW HYDE PARK, NEW YORK, 516-216-5448

Brains masala, the southern India bar snack, is not to be missed by organophiles who hope to extend the reach of their dining experiences.

3. M. WELLS DINETTE

MOMA PS1, 22-25 JACKSON AVENUE, QUEENS, 718-786-1800

Executive chef Hugue Dufour and his partner Sarah Obraitis preside over an offal-rich menu that often lists brains, foie gras, and liver among daily specials.

4. CHEBURECHNAYA

92-09 63RD DRIVE, QUEENS, 718-897-9080

Veal brains and lamb-tail-fat kebabs are among the many startling offerings of this Russian-Uzbek boîte.

5. BABBO

110 WAVERLY PLACE, MANHATTAN, 212-777-0303

Calf's Brain "Francobolli" with lemon and sage and vanilla-scented headcheese are on the current menu, but call ahead for organ specials at this Mario Batali flagship.

6. SHAMA

232 NEPTUNE AVENUE, BROOKLYN, 718-368-1721

This Pakistani cabbie hang in Coney Island features goat brain masala on the steam table.

Call ahead. Brains are not available at all times; you may find it necessary to special order them at these places.

SCRAMBLED BRAINS

SERVES 4

You know what's funny? I always think that the tofu scrambles eaten by holier-than-though vegans look quite like scrambled brains. Ha! If you're squeamish about brains—and I am—this recipe at least partly conceals the appearance.

4 lambs' brains, 1 to 2 pounds total (available at Middle Eastern markets, or call your butcher)

4 tablespoons butter

1 large white onion, thinly sliced

2 garlic cloves, minced

1-inch piece fresh ginger, peeled and minced

1 small hot green chile, thinly sliced

1 teaspoon ground cumin

1 teaspoon ground coriander

1 teaspoon ground turmeric

1 teaspoon salt

4 eggs, beaten

1. Bring a medium pot of water to a boil. Fill a bowl with ice water. Add the brains to the boiling water and blanch for 2 to 3 minutes. Transfer them to the ice water to cool for a minute and then drain. Slice each brain into 1-inch pieces, removing any extraneous membrane.

2. In a large sauté pan, melt the butter over medium heat. Add the onion and cook until softened and starting to brown, 8 to 10 minutes. Add the garlic, ginger, and chile and cook 1 to 2 minutes more. Add the cumin, coriander, turmeric, and salt and cook for another minute. Add the brains, stirring to incorporate. Cook for 2 minutes, then add the eggs. Reduce the heat to low and cook until the eggs are just set, 5 to 7 minutes. Taste and add more salt, if necessary. Serve immediately.

THE BLACK-AND-WHITE COOKIE

N ow that we've eaten our dozen New York dishes, it's time for some dessert. And what could be more apropos than the city's legendary black-and-white cookie, famous for at least a century already but made even more so by an episode of *Seinfeld*?

Some say the half-moon cookie came first. Many believe the half moon was invented a century ago at Hemstrought's Bakery on Oswego Street in Utica, New York, which is now defunct, though someone is still making the cookies under its name for mail-order distribution. Shaped like a stunted dome, the base is fine-textured chocolate cake, meaning that it's not really a cookie, but a "drop cake," as William Grimes points out in a 1998 *New York Times* article. The half moon is frosted with vanilla buttercream on one half and dark chocolate on the other; the two battle along a line that bisects the cookie, more or less. Sometimes the application of the frosting looks notably amateurish, with a wavering line and a sloughing of the fluffy frosting around the edges. One way to eat the thing involves licking off the frosting as a first step.

With the Utica half-moon cookie, the two frostings are of strikingly dissimilar thickness, with the chocolate side rising higher than the vanilla. Who doesn't like chocolate more than vanilla? As Lisa McNamara says of the pastry in her blog *Driving Inertia*, "One frosting should always be slightly taller than the other frosting. The chocolate frosting should be SO RICH that you have to take bites of the vanilla frosting for relief," suggesting another method of eating the cookie. As the years passed, Hemstrought's spun off many variations of the half moon, including cookies with all vanilla or all chocolate frosting, cookies with yellow rather than chocolate cake, and cookies with coconut in the frosting. In 2000 *Saveur* magazine published a recipe for Hemstrought's cookie that included margarine and cocoa powder in the dough—clearly, the chocolate cake recipe was considered the predominant one. The *Saveur* recipe yielded 30 large-circumference cookies, having been adapted from a recipe for 2,400!

As to when Hemstrought's invented the half moon, sources are vague, attributing it to "the early part of the 20th century." Conjectures place the date of its birth at 1902, when the bakery was founded, making it one of the shop's first offerings. Another possibility as to date would be 1909, when tremendous hoopla across the state attended the tricentenary of Henry Hudson's voyage of exploration up what would later be known as the Hudson River. There were parades and fireworks displays for two weeks, but perhaps the most dramatic event was a commemorative sail up the great river by a replica of the explorer's boat. And the name of Hudson's ship? The Halve Maen (Half Moon).

But proof that Hemstrought's actually invented the cookie—and its original iconographic meaning—is scant. The half-moon cookie's range currently covers central New York State, with pockets in New England, including a notable appearance at Bova's Bakery in Boston's largely Italian North End. But had it persisted there from an earlier era? Could the cookie, like the Old North Church, be of colonial antiquity? Significantly, there are no half-moon cookies to be found anywhere in New York City.

Instead, we have the similar-looking black and white. During the same time period, it flourished in the five boroughs. No dessert—except perhaps the cheesecake—is more closely associated with the city. The mesa of fine-textured white (not chocolate) cake, with a coating of chocolate and vanilla fondant bisected in the middle to keep the flavors apart, has an identical iconography to Utica's half-moon cookie. Signifying the mid-point of the lunar month to agrarian upstate peoples, to early and classically educated city dwellers the half moon more likely betokened the Greek goddess Artemis (the Roman Diana) and Mary, the mother of God, representing the virtues of knowledge and chastity. Don't ever give someone you want to sleep with a black-and-white cookie, because you're totally sending the wrong message!

But how did two cookies with parallel paths get invented and prosper in two different parts of the state of New York? And how are they related?

AMERICA'S EARLIEST COOKIES

The history of cookies as baked goods in the United States goes back to pre-Revolutionary times. The recipes were brought by Dutch and English housewives to New Amsterdam and New England beginning in the 17th century. The English word *cookie* is a direct rip from the Dutch *koekje*. The words are pronounced nearly the same, with the Dutch term representing a diminutive form of *koek*, which simply means cake. This suggests that the original American cookies might have been something that resembled little cakes, with a texture that was spongy rather than brittle or soft, as nearly all cookies are in the industrial age, when shelf life and durability have become paramount to cookie manufacturing. *The Oxford Companion to American Food and Drink* bears this out, listing as America's earliest cookies several things the modern cookie eater might see as more cake-like: gingerbread men, macaroons, and shortbread.

In New York City's earliest outdoor markets, dating to early colonial times, baked goods were often sold from stalls, and the type of spongy cake-cookie represented by the black and white was eagerly purchased by shoppers as a pick-me-up. Like the half moon, the form and iconography of our own black and white implies a rather ancient vintage. Elsewhere on the

Eastern Seaboard of the United States, similar types of early cookies continue to thrive. One such was brought to Baltimore by German immigrant Henry Berger, who arrived in 1835. He was a baker by trade, and the product he was to become famous for was a round cookie with a cake-like demeanor that came rather crudely frosted with dark chocolate. Berger cookies are still cherished by Baltimore residents today and are strikingly similar to the black-and-white cookie in shape and texture, though considerably smaller in size.

THE BLACK-AND-WHITE COOKIE REMAINS UBIQUITOUS IN NEW YORK CITY

Anyone who wanders the streets of the city will soon stumble upon the iconic black-and-white cookie. It looks out from the windows of bakeries, from the display cases of doughnut shops and bodegas, and from the rotating circular pastry cabinets of Greek diners. Often four inches or more in diameter, the frosting isn't fluffy (though there are exceptions), but a smooth and shiny fondant, as obdurate to the teeth as the crackling top of a crème brûlée. What a surprise to bite into it, then, and find that once past the frosting, the cake underneath is pleasantly soft.

Those who were born upstate often deplore the black and white for its subtle deviations from the half moon. You certainly can't lick the frosting off a black and white, but you can engineer your bites so you get any combination of chocolate and vanilla frosting you want. There is a uniformity to the black-and-white cookie that the half moon lacks—I've never seen one with a base of chocolate cake, for example, nor do any incorporate coconut in any form. Our black and whites are so uniform that they might be made at some central location in an underground bunker and floated throughout the city on little boats via the subterranean water supply pipelines.

Or are they? In preparation for this chapter, I did a massive search for examples of this signature cookie. What I found surprised me, representing a post-*Seinfeld* evolution. At a coffee shop with an ambitious pastry program on 23rd Street and Eighth Avenue, I found one with a wandering demarcation between chocolate and vanilla frostings. The cake was sweeter than usual, too. At a bagel shop in Battery Park City, you can get examples frosted all white or all black, but with the same underlying yellow cake base.

In Williamsburg, at a convenience store, I found miniature black and whites a scant two inches in diameter selling for 55 cents each, making it possible to dispatch them with one bite of the chocolate side and one bite of the vanilla. I sampled cookies with relatively dense cake and cookies where the texture verged on angel food. I tasted cookies where the fondant was strongly flavored with vanilla and cocoa powder, and examples where the frostings tasted identical—the "chocolate" a purely visual element. I found one on the Upper East Side shaped like a heart rather than a circle, but the cookie was an actual cookie, hard as rock.

Perhaps the best black and white I tried was at Glaser's Bake Shop, a Yorkville institution that dates to the time when the neighborhood was mainly German. It opened in 1902, and according to Herb Glaser, current baker and direct descendent of the founder, the recipe for the cookie originated with the bakery, which has been making them for over a century—meaning that the vintage is about the same as Hemstrought's half moon. Take that, upstate! But one aspect of Glaser's and Hemstrought's is strikingly similar: Glaser's cookie is paved with real frosting rather than fondant, a characteristic that pertains to several of today's bakery black and whites. Presumably this is because bakery cookies are often sold right on the premises and don't need the kind of shelf life conferred by fondant.

Grimes's *Times* piece also makes some savvy observations about the nature of the black-and-white cookie and how it got to be the way it is. He notes that the batter is like cupcake batter, only thickened with a little extra flour so it doesn't keep spreading as it bakes. Just how much flour is quintessential. As quoted by Grimes, Glaser says, "The trick is to add enough flour so the batter holds a shape, but not so much that the cookie becomes dry, which is a common problem with the black-and-white." Note that the fondant also preserves the moisture of the cookie, topside at least, better than frosting, which can itself become dry, while the fact that the cookie usually rests on the metal tray it was baked on might also help to prevent it from desiccating.

So maybe the cake-type cookie has been a feature of New York baking since colonial times, and the black and white evolved partly isolated from the half moon, though both trace their antecedents to Germany or perhaps the Netherlands. In Germany, a similar cookie is available today, but it's called an *Amerikaner*. Certainly, you can see the black and white as a savvy urban variation on some prior ur-cookie, one in which the cake can stay moist longer in the doughnut-shop window, and in which the more precise application of fondant over frosting lends a more streamlined curb appeal, making the half moon look rustic by comparison. Slicker cookies for more sophisticated city dwellers. Or maybe for people who are less likely to visit an actual bakery for their cookies and pastries, more prone to pick them up on the run at random places where the cookies have sat out for who knows how long. And the distribution of black-and-whites purveyors across the modern face of the metropolis is about as eclectic as it gets.

A strange thought occurred to me as I ate my way through the piles of black-and-white cookies that I had collected. In altered form, the elements of the black and white—chocolate and vanilla, frosting and cake—somewhat resemble the Oreo cookie, which was invented by Nabisco in Manhattan at its Chelsea factory (the building that now houses the Chelsea Market) in 1912. In fact, the ritual of eating the Oreo by taking off one of the chocolate wafers, licking off the vanilla frosting, and then separately eating the wafers is strikingly similar to the rituals that arose around eating the black-and-white cookie. Perhaps the Oreo can be seen as a modification of the black and white to suit post-industrial manufacture and boxed distribution, just as the fondant may be an adaptation of fluffy frostings to permit a longer shelf life and diverse points of sale around the city.

LOOK TO THE COOKIE

The moon symbology of both black and whites and half moons was blown out of the sky by *Seinfeld* in a 1994 episode entitled "The Dinner Party." Set in a bakery, it shows Jerry rethinking the cookie as an antiracist icon: "Look, Elaine, the black-and-white cookie. I love the black and white—two races of flavor living side by side in harmony," which remotely echoes the Stevie Wonder and Paul McCartney duet "Ebony and Ivory." Jerry later instructs Elaine on how to properly eat one: "See, the key to eating a black-and-white cookie, Elaine, is that you want to get some black and some white in each bite . . . yet still somehow racial harmony eludes us. If people would only look to the cookie, all our problems would be solved!"

EIGHT PLACES TO FIND BLACK-AND-WHITE COOKIES

These days, black and whites remain widely available in many parts of town, averaging four inches in diameter and retailing at around $3 each. But many have been oddly transformed. Here are my tasting notes, listing the sources in alphabetical order.

1. AMY'S BREAD
CHELSEA MARKET, 75 NINTH AVENUE, MANHATTAN, 212-462-4338

The black-and-white cookies at the Chelsea Market branch are notably fresher and more cake-like than average. As with most bakery versions (see Glaser's, below), the frosting tends to be fluffier than the fondants found on cookies not sold in bakeries.

2. BAGELSMITH
566 LORIMER STREET, BROOKLYN, 347-294-0046

Interesting that one of the most popular bastions of the black and white seems to be bagel shops, though the cookies are usually not made on the premises. Williamsburg's Bagelsmith sells miniature versions, a scant two inches in diameter, for 55 cents each.

3. CHELSEA DELI & BAKERY
254 EIGHTH AVENUE, MANHATTAN, 212-243-8444

The adamantine fondant school of black and whites is here demonstrated by this corner deli specializing in overly sweet baked goods. The cake is unexpectedly moist and flavorful and not as stale as you might expect.

4. THE DONUT PUB
203 WEST 14TH STREET, MANHATTAN, 212-929-0126

Though most black-and-white cookies sold in independent doughnut shops (notably, Dunkin' Donuts doesn't carry them) are trucked in, Chelsea's Donut Pub insists on making its own. Not really a cookie, the result is a flattish, custard-filled donut.

5. GLASER'S BAKE SHOP
1670 FIRST AVENUE, MANHATTAN, 212-289-2562

The version here—which is closer to Utica's half moon than we may care to acknowledge—is coated with very fluffy frosting, and the chocolate is more profuse than the vanilla. The cake is plain, suggesting that the frosting is the cookie's raison d'être. And the result ($2.25) is very, very good.

6. LE GOURMET
1267 FIRST AVENUE, MANHATTAN, 212-772-8811

This carry-out and catering concern, like Bagelsmith, makes a miniature black and white, in this case shaped like a heart. The pastry is more sugar cookie than cake, topped with a very firm fondant. Does it still qualify as a black-and-white cookie if it's not round?

7. PICK A BAGEL
102 NORTH END AVENUE, MANHATTAN, 212-786-9200

At this Battery Park institution, open 24 hours, not only are decent black and whites available, but you can also get the same cake base topped exclusively with either chocolate or vanilla fondant. Are those versions racist by their very nature?

8. RUTHY'S BAKERY & CAFÉ
CHELSEA MARKET, 75 NINTH AVENUE, MANHATTAN, 212-463-8800

The cookie may come wrapped in plastic, but Ruthy's are pretty good anyway, a little on the sweet side and a little firmer than most. It's one of two versions available at Chelsea Market.

BLACK-AND-WHITE COOKIES
MAKES 8 FOUR-INCH COOKIES

No one is quite sure of the origin of this historic New York cookie, which is really more like a cake. This one is frosted, bakery style, rather than using fondant, which is a tricky business if you're not a professional baker.

FOR THE COOKIES:

1 stick unsalted butter, at room temperature,
   plus more for greasing
1 cup all-purpose flour
$\frac{1}{2}$ cup cake flour
$\frac{1}{2}$ teaspoon baking powder
$\frac{1}{2}$ teaspoon salt
$\frac{2}{3}$ cup granulated sugar
1 egg
$\frac{1}{2}$ vanilla bean, slit lengthwise, seeds scraped from the pod,
   or 1 teaspoon vanilla extract
$\frac{1}{2}$ cup milk

FOR THE ICING:

2 cups confectioners' sugar
1 tablespoon light corn syrup
1 teaspoon vanilla extract
2 to 3 tablespoons water
$\frac{1}{3}$ cup unsweetened cocoa powder

1. Preheat the oven to 375°F. Grease a baking sheet with butter. Sift the flours, baking powder, and salt into a medium bowl; whisk to combine.

2. In a stand mixer on medium speed, cream together the butter and sugar until light and fluffy, about 3 minutes. Scrape down the sides of the bowl, add in the egg and scraped vanilla seeds or the extract, and mix well to combine. Reduce the speed to low, add half of the flour mixture, then the milk, then the rest of the flour mixture, mixing to just combine after each addition. Scrape down the sides and bottom of the bowl one last time.

3. Spoon ⅓-cup mounds of dough onto the greased baking sheet, 1½ inches apart (8 should fit on a standard baking sheet, but use a second sheet if necessary). With wet hands press down gently on each mound to flatten slightly. Bake until the edges of the cookies are set and light golden brown, 16 to 18 minutes. Allow the cookies to cool on the sheet slightly before removing them to a wire rack to cool completely before icing.

4. To make the icing, stir together the confectioners' sugar, corn syrup, vanilla extract, and 2 tablespoons water until smooth, adding more water a teaspoon at a time to make a smooth, spreadable icing. Transfer half of the icing to another bowl and whisk in the cocoa, adding more water, ½ teaspoon at a time, to achieve a similar consistency as the white icing.

5. To frost, spread the vanilla icing over half of the flat surface of each cookie, letting the excess drip off. Let the vanilla icing set for 15 minutes, then spread chocolate icing onto the other half of the cookie. Let the icing set for an hour before eating. Store the cookies in an airtight container for up to 3 days.

ACKNOWLEDGMENTS

Thanks to all my editors over the years, who changed my idea of how to write: Robert Christgau, Nanette Maxim, Laurie Ochoa, Amanda Kludt, Adam Kowit, Peter Meehan, Rachel Khong, Brian Parks, Greg Morabito, Sonia Chopra, and Patrick Farrell. Thanks to those writers who went before me and served as literary models: A. J. Liebling, Calvin Trillin, Jonathan Gold, Ruth Reichl, Seymour Britchky, and Mimi Sheraton. Thanks to my literary agent, David Hale Smith. Thanks to Scarlett Lindeman for developing the recipes that appear in this book. Thanks to my wife, Gretchen Van Dyk, and my daughter, Tracy Van Dyk, and to my parents, Jacob and Marilyn Sietsema. Thanks to Houghton Mifflin Harcourt and thanks to the book's illustrator, James Gulliver Hancock, and designer, Alex Camlin. And especially, thanks to all those who accompanied me on far-flung dining expeditions with no more recompense than a good meal.